Art as Religious Studies

ART AS
RELIGIOUS
STUDIES

Edited by Doug Adams
and
Diane Apostolos-Cappadona

Wipf and Stock Publishers
EUGENE, OREGON

Wipf and Stock Publishers
150 West Broadway
Eugene, Oregon 97401

Art As Religious Studies
By Adams, Doug
Copyright©1987 Adams, Doug & Apostolos-Cappadona, Diane
ISBN: 1-57910-635-8
Publication Date: April, 2001
Previously published by Crossroad Publishing Company, 1987.

For Laurence Pereira Leite
and William H. Poteat

Contents

vii

INTRODUCTION

1

Art as Religious Studies:
Insights into the Judeo-Christian
Traditions

In September 1957 during a stay in Florence, the historian of religions Mircea Eliade made the following entry in his journal:

> Of the frescoes that decorate the monks' cells I remember—for reasons other than artistic—the *Transfiguration* and the *Two Marys at the Tomb*. . . . In these two compositions the Christ is shown to us in his glory, as though in an immense egg of dazzling whiteness. I feel a limitless admiration for the metaphysical and theological genius of Angelico. In this image of the Divine Glory, similar to the Cosmogonic Egg, he says more than could be said in a whole book.[1]

This is an amazing statement about the power of the visual image from someone who spent his life expressing himself through the written word. The suggestion that Fra Angelico says more in this one image than could be said in a whole book indicates not only the power of this particular image but the importance of the visual modality for the communication of religious ideas. In recent years, art historians and critics, and a few theologians, have argued for a contemporary recognition of the visual modality as a means of theological, philosophical, and cultural reflection, not just as a mirror for aesthetic values and tastes.

Perhaps the most persuasively argued and controversial of those presentations has been Leo Steinberg's *The Sexuality of Christ in Renaissance Art and in Modern Oblivion*.[2] In this profusely illustrated and competently argued text, Steinberg not only calls attention to the works of art he is studying and to the coalition of art and theology in the Renaissance but also demonstrates conclusively that no matter how much one has *looked* at works of art, especially the same works of art, there is still something more to *see*. It is this something more that offers the theological interpreter an entry into art or allows for the work of art to be labeled "a classic."

What is most important, however, is that Steinberg shows his readers that no viewer has scrutinized a painting fully no matter how carefully he or she has looked. The image's power constantly to engage and transform the viewer and admit new interpretations suggests another important facet of the work of art. For Steinberg, works of art are *primary documents* in their own right. Just as a written text is a world in itself and simultaneously reflective of the world from which it comes, so too is the work of art.

In this way, works of art are not illustrations nor evidence that validate a particular interpretation of a theological or cultural argument. Rather, works of art are in their own right a mode of human expression that generates theological interpretation and reflection, and that reveals its cultural and theological milieu. In order for an interpreter of works of art to be able to understand and to operate in this way, he or she must be carefully trained in the discipline of seeing.

The primacy of the visual modality has been denied and deprecated in Western culture since the Reformation. With the Reformation, the aural modality was retrieved as primary. The power of the scriptural word, which was primary and transformative for Luther and Calvin, has been re-formed in the mid-twentieth century by the power of the press. The classic distinction and choice of word over image has reigned in the development of modern Western culture. Nevertheless, the visual modality has continued to exist and even to flourish.

It is this visual modality that is developed and nurtured by the discipline of *seeing*. The problem of course with the discipline of seeing is that it makes demands and challenges the viewer. One is no longer able quickly to pass through a museum corridor or a cathedral aisle. One is almost driven to careful attention to the images, and to their purpose and to their meaning. Learning to see is a difficult task involving its own hermeneutic.

In 1 Corinthians, Paul describes the process of the discipline of seeing when he tells us:

For now we see through a glass darkly; but then face to face: now
I know in part; but then shall I know even as also I am known.
(13:12)

To be trained in the discipline of seeing involves the total engagement of the viewer, and the viewer in turn is transformed. This is a
central part of the hermeneutic of the discipline of seeing.

Once a student has learned to see not merely to look, the visual
arts take on a new and central place in human experience. Art
becomes a primary document in its own right. Examined in this
light, the work of art can open up a whole world for a student
whether the work of art is contemporary and abstract, or traditional and representational. For example, if one were to compare
such distinctly different works of art through the lens of religious
studies, the distinctions and similarities between the religious
worldviews and the cultural milieus would become just as apparent as the differing styles of art.

For example, consider such diverse works of art as the *Pantocrator* (11th century; Monastery at Daphni, Greece; fig. 1) and Barnett
Newman's *Stations of the Cross: Station #12* (1965; National Gallery of Art, Washington; Robert and Jane Meyerhoff Collection; fig.
2). In its own way, each of these works of art reflects the historical
period from which it comes: the *Pantocrator* images the theocracy
of the Byzantine Empire while Newman's *Station #12* suggests the
openness of the 1960s. Both works have religious subject matter
and an aura of spiritual authenticity to them. Both are primary *visual* documents which can offer to those engaged in religious studies some cultural or theological perspective on the individual artists and their respective cultures, but they also share a common
attribute in human experience.

Both the *Pantocrator* and Newman's *Station #12* emphasize
frontality, not merely in terms of the work of art itself but outside
its proper boundaries in terms of its engagement with the viewer.
Traditionally, Byzantine icons are frontal, that is to say, they emphasize the one-dimensionality of the central figure represented
and its straightforward encounter with the believer. The image
of the Pantocrator is placed in the central dome of a Byzantine
church representing his central role both as risen savior and as
ruler of the universe. He is a larger-than-life figure who dwarfs and

1. *Pantocrator* (11th century; Monastery at Daphni, Greece).

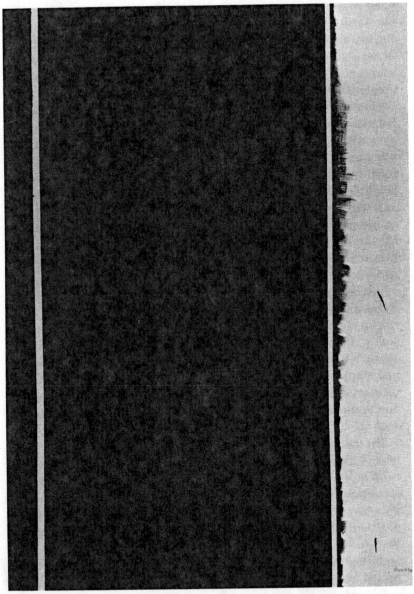

2. Barnett Newman, *Station #12* (1965; The National Gallery of Art,
Washington, D.C.).

overwhelms Christian believers both in his size and in his symbolic significance. The frontality of the Pantocrator combines with his stature to dictate to the viewer. The visual saving grace of the Pantocrators is that they are placed within the curve of the central dome giving them a sense of illusion and depth which acts as a visual relief. The heavenly ruler, the Pantocrator, is thus imaged as greater than the earthly ruler, the Byzantine emperor.

Through its open fields of black and white, and through its two balanced vertical zips down the canvas, Newman's *Station #12* also offers the viewer the experience of frontality. The size and placement of the work of art are again significant. Newman's painting is approximately life-size when it is hung at the proper height from the floor. Thus the viewer is engaged in a conversation as if with another human being. The work of art and the viewer are transformed into conversation partners. Even Newman's intention of painting "flat" evokes the flatness of the Daphni *Pantocrator* as in both instances the initial visual response is to a one-dimensional surface.

Just as the *Pantocrator* evokes the hierarchical structure of the Byzantine world, so Newman's *Station #12* makes present the pluralism of the 1960s in New York City. In the former the human person is dictated to, in the latter conversed with. Through an encounter with either or both works of art, the viewer is engaged and transformed. In that engagement with another presence, the viewer experiences transcendence. The discipline of seeing allows one to understand how and why this happens, and what the reasons are for the different responses to these two works of art.

The common attribute of these two works of art is the characteristic of frontality. How that frontality is utilized and expressed results in the viewer's reactions to the works of art. It is not the abstractness of Newman's *Station #12* that demands and challenges its viewer but its openness to conversation. It is much easier to deal with the hierarchical dictation of the Byzantine Pantocrator than to be held responsible for oneself. Yet both the *Pantocrator* and Newman's *Station #12* are visual documents that can be interpreted and reflected upon through reference to the earlier quoted passage from 1 Corinthians, for each creates in its own way a "face to face" encounter with its audience which results in their transformation: "but then shall I know even as I am known."

Art as Religious Studies was designed to investigate the integration of the discipline of seeing into religious studies. A breadth of methodological approaches has been encouraged in the contributions to this collection. The only requirements made of each contributor were, first, that art be interpreted as a primary document for religious studies and, second, that the discipline of seeing be central to the investigations.

This volume, then, suggests the creative and multiple ways that scholars in religious studies have chosen to consider the visual arts in their teaching and research. *Art as Religious Studies* is focused on the Judeo-Christian traditions, and, as such, the volume is divided into three major sections: the history of Judaism, the history of Christianity, and the practical aspects of the Judeo-Christian traditions.

Each essay is a sample lecture from a religious studies course that integrates the visual arts. The essays begin with a brief description of the course's content and then go on to show how the arts illuminate the study of the Judeo-Christian traditions. In this way, *Art as Religious Studies* is a practical book which offers its readers insights into the development of religious studies courses, lectures, and programs that integrate the visual arts as primary texts for the Judeo-Christian traditions.

With this goal in mind, we invited Jane Dillenberger to reflect on the history and development of the field of religion and art. In her essay, she indicates how she has developed a wealth of courses based on her commitment to the visual arts as primary texts. She concludes her essay with an autobiographical sketch of her own academic training and a brief analysis of how she views the field of religion and art today.

Part 1: Visual Arts in Judaism is an overview of the creative ways that contemporary religious studies scholars have studied Jewish art to broaden and illumine Judaic studies. This section begins with Jacob Neusner's analysis of E. R. Goodenough's classic contribution to the history of Judaism and to Jewish art history. Neusner raises the central and pertinent questions dealing with the fundamental issue of the restrictions in Judaism on the visual modality.

Jo Milgrom suggests how Jewish artifacts can in fact add to our knowledge of Jewish ritual traditions. Stephen Breck Reid turns the reader's attention to the contemporary paintings of Marc Chagall and his reinterpretation of the Hebrew scriptures. Diane Apostolos-Cappadona traces the visual image of the Jewish heroine Judith in Christian art for its suggestions about the role of the Jewish woman living in a Western Christian culture.

Part 2: Visual Arts in Christianity is composed of essays reflecting the thesis that the visual arts offer the possibility of new understandings of well-known historical and theological materials. Margaret R. Miles's essay suggests a new way of interpreting the role of Mary and thus of women in the Italian Renaissance period. Nicholas Piediscalzi shows how Michelangelo's art can be seen both as artistic classics and as visualizations of human and faith development. John W. Cook's study of the paintings of El Greco reminds us not only of their theological relevance but also of their relationship to liturgical settings and architectural designs. William Hendricks raises the "forbidden" questions about how and why art is evaluated as good religious art.

Part 3: Visual Arts in Religious Praxis indicates the innovative ways of integrating the visual arts as primary texts into the more "practical" dimensions of religious studies: social justice, pastoral counseling, religious education, and religious communication. James L. Empereur calls to our attention the fact that the visual portrays not only the beautiful but the painful and the unjust as well. Archie Smith, Jr., reveals a new way of interpreting the action within a painting and shows how that offers a helpful parallel for learning the methods of pastoral counseling. Doug Adams suggests a creative new way of interpreting works of art through the tacit knowing of the human body. Finally, Gregor Goethals introduces the reader into the contemporary visual arts with her analysis of the religious and sociological dimensions of commercial television.

A most pragmatic ending to a practical volume is a bibliography. This one contains two fine bibliographic surveys. The first by Joseph Gutmann reviews the books available on Judaism and the arts; the second by John W. Cook lists the books available on Christianity and the arts. These are complemented by Special Topic Bibliographies.

Art as Religious Studies has had a long gestation period since we first discussed the need for a volume of methodological essays on religion and the arts. We are grateful to all of those individuals who offered their counsel and criticisms of this project. We wish to thank the individual contributors for their cooperation during the editorial process. Most especially, we are grateful to Werner Mark Linz at the Crossroad Publishing Company who supported this idea from the beginning, and to Frank Oveis who has overseen its final presentation.

No one of us has embarked upon the study of religion and art without the presence of a guiding spirit. In most cases, that person was a teacher or mentor whose style of presentation and method of analysis captured more than a student's imagination. Rather, that person showed us how to *see* and by so doing helped to determine our scholarly selves. In this light, the editors would like to dedicate *Art as Religious Studies* to Laurence Pereira Leite and William H. Poteat who taught us to see the visual arts as primary texts.

Doug Adams and
Diane Apostolos-Cappadona

NOTES

1. Mircea Eliade, *No Souvenirs* (New York: Harper and Row, 1977), p. 23.
2. Leo Steinberg, *The Sexuality of Christ in Renaissance Art and in Modern Oblivion* (New York: Viking/Pantheon, 1984).

2

Reflections on the Field of Religion and the Visual Arts

JANE DILLENBERGER

"From the Catacombs to *Guernica*" was the title of the first art history course which I taught at Drew Theological Seminary in 1950. It was my initial experience teaching in a seminary and one of the first such courses given in any American seminary. When I proposed teaching art history classes, I was asked by Dean Clarence T. Craig to write a statement on why art history should be taught in a theological seminary. He wanted to take it to the faculty who were pondering the appointment. The reasons I gave then still seem valid to me now.

Church history can hardly be taught without some knowledge of art history. For example: Is medieval church history meaningful without some knowledge of the Gothic cathedral? the division between the Eastern and Western church without knowledge of Byzantine mosaics and icons? the Reformation and Counter-Reformation without Baroque art? With regard to scriptural studies, the choices of artistic subjects at successive historic periods, and how the scriptural themes are interpreted and reinterpreted giving a visual gloss on the scriptural verses, bring a new perception to Scripture itself. In perceiving how the verses were understood then, we experience a dual knowing: a historical understanding and a fresh seeing for our own day.

In terms of theological studies, the great works of religious art are visual affirmations of the historic doctrines of the church: Creation, Incarnation, and Redemption. Michelangelo Buonarroti's (1475–1564) *Creation of Adam* (1508–12; Sistine Chapel, Vatican City) is as much visual theology as Mathias Grünewald's (ca. 1470/

80–1528) *Crucifixion* from the Isenheim Altarpiece (1515; Musée d'Unterlinden, Colmar).[1] Paul Tillich's four levels of relationship between religion and modern art were a theological analysis of modern art.[2] Though the four levels were completely unacceptable to art historians, Tillich's basic premise that art reveals ultimate reality brought the discussion of modern art into the theological world.

On the pragmatic level, most seminary graduates who have a church or synagogue will eventually be involved in the building or decoration of a church or synagogue; or additions to, or refurbishing of, an existing building. They need some knowledge of the history of church architecture, including those distinctive Western architectural styles which evolved as styles of Christian church architecture such as Byzantine, Romanesque, and Gothic. Furthermore, they need to learn the procedures for commissioning good, or one may hope, distinguished, artists and architects, and how to work with those artists and architects. An art history course should develop a sense of discrimination, some humility regarding one's own limited taste, and the good sense and valor to seek out the finest architects and artists for church and synagogue.

These are convincing reasons why art history should be part of every seminary curriculum. More significantly, such a course will provide the occasion, at least once, for that transfixing moment when a work of art is experienced, not as something outside of one's self, but as something within one's own being. For a precious moment, we stand within the work of art, see with the artist's eyes, and feel with the artist's pulse beat. In that instant all of our accustomed and limited ways of thinking and feeling are transcended. As the moment fades we are like travelers returning from a strange and wondrous country to our own. But that new seeing remains with us and hallows even the most familiar and mundane details of everyday living.

My first course at Drew Theological Seminary, "From the Catacombs to *Guernica,*" was a slide-lecture class covering over sixteen hundred years. This was not taught in the usual introductory course method of presenting a little information about a vast number of works of art. Instead, a select number of paintings and sculptures were studied intensively and interpreted as embodying the artistic and religious focus of their own time. Thus Giotto's (1276–

1337) frescoes for the Arena Chapel (ca. 1306–13; Padua) were seen as reflecting both the artistic temper of the late medieval and the nascent Renaissance worlds, and the spiritual impact of the life and thought of St. Francis of Assisi (1182–1226). And Pablo Picasso's (1881–1973) *Guernica* (1937; Prado, Madrid; fig. 22), painted before World War II and Hiroshima, is seen as one of the greatest expressions of the horrors of war in our own century.

The Giotto frescoes and *Guernica*, along with other selected works of art, were studied first on the level of identification of subject matter; for example, using the scriptural sources and the *Little Flowers of St. Francis* for the Giotto paintings, and Picasso's preparatory studies for *Guernica* and the newspaper reports on the bombing of the Basque town of Guernica which inspired Picasso's great mural. Second, a careful stylistic description of the work of art was undertaken. Finally, its content or meaning was explored. It is at this level that the work of art speaks for its own epoch. This exploration of the works of art should be done in discussion with the class as class members often have specialized knowledge that contributes to the mosaic of information and insight in the work of art. My first book, *Style and Content in Christian Art*, developed from, and is an example of, this pedagogical method for teaching art history to seminarians.[3]

A practical but significant excursus: the use of two projectors and two screens for the showing of slides is essential to my teaching. The screens should be large in size. Small works of art seldom suffer by enlargement, but the reduction of the grand vision of Michelangelo to a parlor-sized screen is disastrous. With two screens the entire span of the Sistine Ceiling can be projected on the one screen while the individual frescoes of the Creation and the Noah cycles can be shown on the other. In viewing Chartres Cathedral (twelfth and thirteenth centuries), a ground plan can be shown on the left screen and interior shots on the right screen, allowing the class to locate the site of the details on the plan. The facade of Chartres Cathedral (fig. 3) can be shown on the left screen and held there, while details of the central tympanum (fig. 4) and rose window are shown on the right screen. By showing the entire work on the left screen and component parts on the right screen, art is always seen in context. This is an advantage the classroom has over the museum, where altarpieces formerly enframed in the apse

3. Facade of Chartres Cathedral (12th and 13th centuries).

4. *Majestas Domini*, central tympanum of Chartres Cathedral.

of a church and the ambience of worship, now hang in a neutral setting.

In the classroom, a good slide of an altarpiece can be shown on one screen, while on the other screen a slide can be projected to show this altarpiece enframed over the altar in the apse of a church. Thus, imaginatively we can return the work of art to its appropriate setting and sense the great spaces about it, the candles and the flowers on the altar, and the shifting light from the high stained-glass windows which move across the altarpiece.

The museum is also an essential matrix and adjunct for teaching art history. Seminary courses in the arts should be centered as much as possible around paintings and sculptures the class can see and experience at first hand. Although dramatic contrasts and comparisons of two works of art can be made in the classroom with the use of double screens, even such thoughtfully prepared pairs cannot give the experience that the painting in its physical actuality and radiance gives. Thus good teaching incorporates both approaches: classroom study and comparison of slides, and museum trips to see the original paintings and sculptures. Some of the most interesting papers from students are those dealing with a single painting or sculpture studied at first hand in the museum. The power of the work of art to convey profound meanings, even to those making an initial visit to a museum, has been attested to again and again by the thoughtful and substanceful papers received from students.

During the first two weeks of any of my classes, students are given an assignment to look carefully and at length at a single work of art in a museum, or to make comparisons between two works of art which have similar subject matter. They are given a selected list of works of art in the museum from which they may choose. Then they write a brief paper of two to four pages on the work of art without footnotes or bibliography. This is a *seeing* assignment. Once these papers have been written, the atmosphere and attention in the class changes dramatically. From being passive listeners, the students become actively engaged in viewing slides, in discussion, and in inquiry. They gain a self-assurance in articulating what they see and feel and know. They begin to draw upon their own latent knowledge and their information from other courses and sources. And they begin to realize that all of life and all of history are related to these works of art. At this point, teaching becomes exhilarating.

I have always taken my classes to a museum and lectured there in the presence of works of art. At Drew Theological Seminary, the administration hired a bus each semester, and my class, spouses, faculty wives, and occasionally even other faculty members embarked on a day-long journey.[4] We started at the Cloisters Collection of the Metropolitan Museum of Art in Fort Tryon Park with its famed collection of medieval art and architecture. I shall never forget the singular experience of leading my group into the Cuxa Cloister where row upon row of violet-blue irises were radiant in the morning sunlight; just as I was about to discourse on the early Romanesque chapter-house structure and vaulting, the noble chords of a Bach fugue filled the Cloister, seeming almost to issue from the ancient stones themselves. We all fell silent, caught up in the glory of the moment. But our voices returned while scrutinizing the famed, and once again contested, Chalice of Antioch (ca. 550) in the Treasury. The group then went to the Metropolitan Museum of Art to view the Renaissance and Rembrandt galleries; and finally, to the Museum of Modern Art. Can people who are not specifically trained in the visual arts sustain their interest and physical energy over a day-long museum marathon? Indeed, they can! They become exhausted but the exhilaration carries them along, and their élan never wanes.

An effective adjunct to my teaching at Drew Theological Seminary was a well-placed bulletin board in an area where students and faculty gathered for informal meetings. I used it for eye-catching color plates that related to the week's lectures, or those that were of general interest, such as the beautiful photo essays on art then appearing in *Life* magazine, or topical clippings from newspapers. In the latter category was a brief review in the *New York Times* of an art exhibition held at Union Theological Seminary in December 1952. The reviewer reported that the exhibition had been undertaken with the guidance of Professor Paul Tillich. At once I went to New York City to see the exhibition. I was greatly excited to find a fascinating selection of contemporary works, many of them abstract, and most by acknowledged masters of modern art: Ad Reinhardt (1913–67), Max Weber (1881–1961), Mark Tobey (1890–1976), and Graham Sutherland (b. 1903) among them.

I soon found that my colleagues and students were intrigued by the clipping. They told me that Professor Tillich was to talk at Drew in a few months. I queried my colleagues, couldn't Professor Tillich speak on the "four levels of the relationship between religion and art" which he had outlined in connection with this exhibition? They vaguely said something in the nature of "why not?" So I went to the phone, and soon was putting my query to this unknown, deep-voiced, German-accented professor. He liked the idea very much, and asked if I could provide him with slides for his talk. Thus began what later became his well-known essay "Existentialist Aspects of Modern Art."[5] Only later, when I saw that my colleagues were astonished that I had so directly and unceremoniously telephoned Paul Tillich did I realize their esteem for him. I clearly had been short on protocol, and unaware of who he was in the theological world.

For me, then as now, his importance lay in his sensitivity to and love of works of art, and in his incorporation of art into his theological thinking, teaching, and preaching. He seemed to me an ally in my efforts to draw the study of art into the center of theological thinking, rather than keeping it at the periphery as a mere matter of personal edification and individual gratification. When he returned to Drew at a later date to speak, I was again able to persuade the faculty to have him talk on art. I asked him if he would talk from his own perspective on my dissertation topic, "The Demonic in Art," which he did.[6]

The above digression seems to me justified since it offers an example of how discussions of art can be drawn into the theological curriculum. Today as a result of Tillich's example, more theologians are seriously interested in and conversant with art. They need to be encouraged to speak, to write, to teach, and to enter into dialogue with art historians. Similarly, professional artists who are articulate and thoughtful should be brought into the classroom and engaged in dialogue about their own work, the creative process, and how the artist views commissions from the church or synagogue.

An easily accessible resource in theological seminaries is the faculty. Difficult questions such as identification of details in a scriptural painting mean a conversation with the Hebrew and Christian Scripture professors. Doctrinal questions go to both church history and theology professors. In these forays, I always found I was teaching as well as learning. Furthermore, these conversations led to some bridge building. As time went on I gave a series of lectures in Franz Hildebrandt's church history course; and lectured on the Creation in art for Bernhard Anderson's Old Testament course; and on mysticism in art for Carl Michalson's seminar on mysticism. My most challenging experience was a team-taught course conceived by Stanley Romaine Hopper entitled "Man's Self-Interpretation in Art and Poetry of the 20th Century."[7] We alternately presented a research paper, he on a poet and I on an artist. The juxtaposition of the two became the source for new information and freshly minted insights.

Something of the content of my courses and of my attempt to integrate my own teaching with those of my colleagues has been suggested in the foregoing. For my own teaching and for my students' research projects, there are two basic approaches I have used. First is the chronological study of one theme such as Abraham and Isaac. I begin by searching out its first use in a Christian context, and then studying representative examples by great artists from the successive historic periods unto the present day.[8]

A second way of organizing an art history course is around the intensive study of a coherent body of work. Though the body of work may be overtly secular, the religious dimensions of the work can be explored. In this category, I have done a whole course dealing with Picasso, and a seminar in which a study of Vincent van Gogh's (1853–90) paintings was synchronized with the reading of his letters.[9] During the Vietnam War, I taught a course titled "War and Peace in Art." I began with the Olympian Apollo presiding over the Battle of the Centaurs and the Lapiths, then went on to the medieval theme Death on a Pale Horse (and Benjamin West's reinterpretation in 1817), Jacques Callot's seventeenth-century *Disasters of War* and Francisco Goya's eighteenth-century etchings of the same title, Georges Rouault's *Miserere et Guerre* (1948), done after World War I, and Picasso's etchings *Dream and Lie of Franco* (1937).

In the category of intensive studies of a circumscribed body of work was a seminar on the "Art of William Blake" which culminated with a study of his drawings for the Book of Job. This course was given additional perspectives by my colleagues: David Noel Freedman discussed the Book of Job as Scripture and literature, and Ted Stein considered the text from the psychological viewpoint.[10]

A course with a format which could be easily adapted to a variety of different needs was one team taught with Durwood Foster at Pacific School of Religion, called "Art, Theology, and the Contemporary World." The two of us addressed the class in the initial sessions, laying out how we saw our own field today. Then followed a two-hour session with a sculptor, a painter, an architect, a theologian, and an art critic, all of them eminent in their own fields. The guest speakers were asked to talk about how they viewed their own work: past, present, and future. As the course progressed, with the probing of students and the team of speakers, the convergence and disparities, both enlightening, between our speakers and their fields became increasingly fascinating.

Another flexible format is basing a course on the works of art in a nearby museum. "Religious Dimensions of Modern Art" was the title of a course I taught for the San Francisco Museum of Modern Art, using its own paintings as the touchstone for a mini-history of modern art. Thus the class was able to see and know *Sarah Stein* (1916) through the haunting portrait by Henri Matisse (1869–1954) of this woman who was his student, friend, and patron. This firsthand contact with the artist's work made the class's study of works of art they could not study at firsthand, such as Matisse's Chapel of the Rosary (1948–51; Vence), more meaningful.

Similarly, I used the works of art in the traveling exhibition, "The Vatican Collections: The Papacy and Art," as the basis for a mini-history of Western art from the Apollo Belvedere (ca. 130–40) to Matisse's designs for the Chapel of the Rosary. In the classroom I provided the missing links. For example, since there was nothing by Michelangelo in the exhibition, I showed his sculptures which had influenced and been influenced by works of art they could see. There was but one Leonardo da Vinci (1452–1519), the unfinished but moving *Saint Jerome* (ca. 1482). Therefore I showed paintings by Leonardo. The textbook for this course was the exhibition catalogue which reproduced all the works of art in full color. The assignment was a paper of four to six pages comparing and contrasting two works of art in the exhibition.

"Worship and the Arts" was a course masterminded by Wayne Rood at Pacific School of Religion and team taught by him (worship and drama), Harland Hogue (worship and church history), John Burke (music), and myself. Rood's objective was to present a synthesis of these four fields to give a general cultural profile of the various historic periods we portrayed, and to feature each of the four fields to be seen and experienced in its own right. For example, for the medieval era, we all converged in presenting a multimedia "event" with medieval music, drama, and mural-sized slide projections of Chartres Cathedral (figs. 3 and 4). Subsequently, each professor had a two-hour period to enlarge on his own contribution. For instance, I was able to lay out the scheme for the iconography of the portals and windows of the cathedral, showing individual details and how each of these was a part of the vast symphonic totality: this totality is so astonishing in its beauty and interrelatedness that continued study and viewing make the cathedral more awesome, rather than less, as one's knowledge of it deepens. So the four of us, each in our own discipline, dealt in detail with selected historic periods such as the classical world, the medieval world, the Reformation world, and the modern world. I was sorry that I continually lost my argument for sessions on the Renaissance world. With Leo Steinberg's recent book, *The Sexuality of Christ in Renaissance Art and Modern Oblivion,*[11] the provocative but substantively presented subject matter may awaken some theologians to a new interest in Renaissance art and theology.

A good slide collection and a sound selection of art books are essential teaching and learning resources. Those who can use the slide collection of a museum or of an art history department are fortunate. Others should ideally have a budget item for the purchase of slides for the seminary. Some may prefer to build their own personal collections, which can be done not only by purchases from art slide dealers and museums but also through photocopying plates from the fine color-plate books abundantly available today.[12]

It must be apparent from the foregoing that more than a selection of art books is necessary for this kind of teaching. Each new course demands a new syllabus. Both the library and the bookstore must have a range of materials that urges the reader on from one book to another. In regard to art books for a seminary library, Joseph Gutmann's "Sources for the Study of Judaism and the Arts" and John W. Cook's "Sources for the Study of Christianity and the Arts" are excellent recent bibliographical essays in the range of their choices and the availability of the books noted.[13]

In my own training at the University of Chicago and at the Fogg Art Museum at Harvard University, I was never assigned a textbook. We were given a list of artists' names, turned loose in a magnificent library, and directed to bins and bins of mounted photographs. We read and read, and looked and looked and looked. Consequently, I have little confidence in textbooks which circumscribe reading and limit investigations into other authors and other viewpoints. In fact, I have used only two: Ernst Gombrich's *The Story of Art*[14] and Joshua C. Taylor's *The Fine Arts in America*,[15] both estimable and satisfying volumes. I should add, however, that I have always taught in an urban area where seminary holdings were supplemented by good art libraries in nearby museums, public libraries, universities, and colleges.

I was once asked by a religion department professor how he could start teaching art and religion at Phillips University in Enid, Oklahoma, where the relatively modest collection of the school library is the prime intellectual tool of a vast geographic area. My off-the-cuff reply was to rent a bus and take the class to the Art Institute of Chicago, have them read all night in the Art Institute's Ryerson Library, and sit before the paintings all day. Should any reader be teaching in Enid, Oklahoma, do not despair. Cajole the librarian into buying vast numbers of art books, and hire students to mount color photos from periodicals to form a collection of material which can be used on bulletin boards, and as study material for your class.

The Training of This Professor of Art and Theology

I had come to Drew Theological Seminary with an A.B. from the University of Chicago and an M.A. from Harvard University, both in art history. As an undergraduate I had also had studio courses, including a year's study with Grant Wood at the University of

Iowa. Though the studio courses, particularly life-drawing, and classes in mural painting with Wood were immensely absorbing, I never viewed myself as a budding artist.

Consequently, I was easily persuaded by Ulrich Middeldorf, the head of the art department at the University of Chicago, to cross over into art history. He predicted, quite accurately, that I would never regret the change. I remain today grateful for his wisdom. Not long after at the Art Institute of Chicago as I held in my hands a drawing by Rembrandt van Rijn (1606–69) for the first time, all desire to continue drawing myself vanished as I beheld the miracle of his spontaneously penned sketch. Though I gave up my own creative work in art, ever since my apprenticeship with Grant Wood I have had many artists as friends, and have greatly valued their contribution to my life and teaching.

My first employment in art history was at the Art Institute of Chicago as assistant to the eminent Curator of Prints and Drawings, Carl Schniewind. There began the intimate physical acquaintance with works of art which is the privilege of museum curators: the day-to-day living with masterworks, reverently handling (not touching!) prints by Albrecht Dürer (1471–1528), drawings by Raphael Sanzio (1483–1520) and Rembrandt, and lithographs by Odilon Redon (1840–1916). It was a feast for this newly born art historian.

From Chicago, I went to Harvard University for my M.A. studies at the Fogg Art Museum with Wilhelm Koehler in medieval art, Jacob Rosenberg, the great Rembrandt scholar, and Kenneth John Conant, under whose tutelage I reconstructed one of the earlier phases of the work on St. Peter's Basilica in Vatican City. Harvard did not then require an M.A. thesis, but my studies focused on Rembrandt's scriptural drawings and prints. It was, however, Koehler, the Carolingian scholar who was a mentor in subsequent years when I began teaching, and who helped me to acquire classroom skills as opposed to the connoisseurship methods I had absorbed at Harvard.

Before going to Drew, I worked at two other museum collections at the Boston Atheneum where for a year I was in charge of the art library and their American Collection; and at the Newark Museum where I got to know their varied collections. What preparations had this art historian for teaching in a theological seminary? Precious little, I fear. Consequently, a great deal of hard work went into those first seminary classes at Drew. However, I did become fascinated by my colleagues' fields, persistently attended their lectures, and took my problems to them.

As I became deeply involved with my teaching, the inevitable question of proper credentials arose, not from my colleagues or the administration, but on my own part. Certainly a Ph.D. in art and theology was the solution. Drew Theological Seminary agreed to work with another institution on a hybrid degree. Consequently, I enrolled, passed the German reading exam, and began theological studies. I registered for doctoral seminars, formulated a dissertation topic, "The Demonic in Art," and persuaded both Paul Tillich and Erwin Panofsky, who was then at the Institute of Advanced Studies at Princeton University, to serve on my doctoral committee. I recall Professor Panofsky's bemused smile as, with a twinkle in his eye, he queried, "Why is evil a subject of such interest to women?"

In the meantime conversations with faculty at New York University and Columbia University both proved to be disappointing. Both would grant a degree in art history, but were unwilling to work with another institution. I would have had to get two separate Ph.D.s in two different fields at two different institutions. The complications logistically and in terms of time were too great for a young mother of two children. I withdrew from the doctoral program at Drew, and started to work on my first book, *Style and Content in Christian Art.*

The current situation is quite different. A doctoral program in theology and the arts is available at the Graduate Theological Union in Berkeley. Yale Divinity School and Pacific School of Religion have fine training programs for seminarians at the M.A. and M.Div. levels. A more accurate and detailed picture of this situation will be available with the publication of Wilson Yates's detailed study, *The State of the Arts in Theological Education.*[16] I rejoice in the vitality, range, and variety of teaching today in this hybrid area, art and religion, and in the creative new generation of teachers now at work, many of whom are contributors to this volume.

NOTES

1. The distinctions and similarities between the artistic and theological sensibilities present in Grünewald and Michelangelo were carefully discussed in my lecture, "Michelangelo and Grünewald: Northern and Italian Religious Sensibilities on the Eve of the Reformation," given at the Pacific School of Religion in February 1981.

2. Paul Tillich, "Existentialist Aspects of Modern Art," in *Christianity and the Existentialists*, ed. Carl Michalson (New York: Charles Scribner's Sons, 1956), pp. 128–47. This essay is included in the collection of Paul Tillich's writings titled *On Art and Architecture*, ed. Jane and John Dillenberger (New York: Crossroad Publishing Co., 1987).

3. *Style and Content in Christian Art* was originally published by Abingdon Press in 1965. It was reissued by the Crossroad Publishing Company in 1986.

4. Nicolas Zernov, the Russian Orthodox theologian, went on one of these junkets and luminously discoursed on the Byzantine *Deisis* at the Metropolitan Museum of Art in New York.

5. See n. 2 above.

6. This previously unpublished essay is included in Paul Tillich, *On Art and Architecture*.

7. This course was offered in 1959 and again in 1961.

8. For example, see my essay, "George Segal's *Abraham and Isaac:* Some Iconographic Reflections," in *Art, Creativity, and the Sacred*, ed. Diane Apostolos-Cappadona (New York: Crossroad Publishing Co., 1984), pp. 105–24.

9. In this case, I used W. H. Auden's selection, *Van Gogh: A Self Portrait/Letters revealing his life as a painter*, selected by W. H. Auden (New York: E. P. Dutton, 1963). This combination of van Gogh and Auden led to some memorable discussions on creativity and insanity.

10. The latter speaker was included as Blake's imagery has been explored and expounded rather extensively by Jungian thinkers.

11. Leo Steinberg, *The Sexuality of Christ in Renaissance Art and in Modern Oblivion* (New York: Viking/Pantheon, 1984).

12. A discussion of the care and purchase of art slides as well as an index of the names and addresses of art slide dealers is available in *The Slide Buyer's Guide* which can be ordered from the College Art Association.

13. Both of these bibliographic essays can be found in Part V: Bibliographies of this collection.

14. Ernst Gombrich, *The Story of Art* (London: Phaidon Press, Ltd., 1950).

15. Joshua C. Taylor, *The Fine Arts in America* (Chicago: University of Chicago Press, 1976).

16. This fine study sponsored by the Lilly Foundation is scheduled for a 1987 publication date through Scholars Press.

PART I

VISUAL ARTS
IN JUDAISM

3

Studying Ancient Judaism through the Art of the Synagogue

JACOB NEUSNER

What we learn about Judaism from the art of the ancient syngogues has been debated for most of the twentieth century. When we follow those debates, we shall understand how the visual arts—with stress on the problem of interpreting the meaning of art and symbolism—affect our understanding of the religious life of people we know, otherwise, only from holy books. The particular case at hand brings us to the critical issue in the study of ancient Judaism, from the first to the seventh centuries. The literary evidence overall portrays that Judaism in one way; the artistic evidence, in a quite different way. That is why synagogue art presents a problem in the study of ancient Judaism.

The visual materials we shall consider contribute in three ways to the study of Judaism as a religion. First, any introduction to Judaism, from its beginnings to the present, will raise questions about modes and media of religious expression, and, among these, art in iconic and other graphic form will take pride of place. The intense interest in the art and architecture of synagogues, ancient, medieval, and modern, finds full justification. For these speak vividly and concretely about the world view and way of life of the Judaism for which those synagogues were constructed. Second, a study of ancient Judaism will require attention to the varieties of the Judaic systems of late antiquity. As I shall emphasize, critical to such a study—hence to all courses on ancient Judaism—will be the interpretation of synagogue art, with special attention to its symbolism. Finally, a course on art in religion will derive from Judaism a most interesting case study of a religious tradition that, at one and the same time, prohibits the representation of God and also makes ample use of representational art (not merely abstraction) for religious expression. These three types of courses only begin the list of the important ways in which we learn about religion from the study of the art of Judaism—not to mention of the complex relationships between Judaism and the arts.

Most ancient synagogues, both in the land of Israel and abroad, reveal important decorations on their walls. The decorations turn up fairly consistently. Some symbols recur nearly everywhere. Other symbols never made an appearance at all. A *shofar*, a *lulab* and *ethrog*, a menorah, all of them Jewish in origin, but also such pagan symbols as a Zodiac, with symbols difficult to find in Judaic written sources—all of these form part of the absolutely fixed symbolic vocabulary of the synagogues of late antiquity. By contrast, symbols of other elements of the calendar year, at least as important as those that we do find, turn out never to make an appearance. And, obviously, a vast number of pagan symbols proved useless to Judaic synagogue artists. It follows that the artists of the synagogues spoke through a certain set of symbols and ignored other available ones. That simple fact makes it highly likely that the symbols they did use meant something to them, represented a set of choices, delivered a message important to the people who worshipped in those synagogues.

Because the second commandment forbids the making of graven images of God, however, people have long taken for granted that Judaism should not produce an artistic tradition. Or, if it does, it should be essentially abstract and nonrepresentational, much like the rich decorative tradition of Islam. But from the beginning of the twentieth century, archaeologists began to uncover in the Middle East, North Africa, the Balkans, and the Italian peninsula, synagogues of late antiquity richly decorated in representational art. For a long time historians of Judaism did not find it possible to accommodate the newly discovered evidence of an on-going artistic tradition. They did not explain that art; they explained it away. One favorite explanation was that "the people" produced the art, but "the rabbis," that is, the religious authorities, did not approve it or at best merely tolerated it. That explanation rested on two premises. First, because talmudic literature—the writings of the ancient rabbis over the first seven centuries of the common era—made no provision for representational art, therefore representational art was subterranean and "unofficial." Second, rabbis are supposed to have ruled everywhere, so the presence of iconic art had to indicate the absence of rabbinic authority.

Aware of the existence of sources which did not quite fit into the picture that emerged from talmudic literature as it was understood in those years or which did not serve the partly apologetic purposes of their studies, scholars such as George Foot Moore[1] posited the existence of "normative Judaism," which is to be described by reference to talmudic literature and distinguished from "heretical" or "sectarian" or simply "nonnormative" Judaism of "fringe sects." Normative Judaism, exposited so systematically and with such certainty in Moore's *Judaism*, found no place in its structure for art, with its overtones of mysticism (except "normal mysticism"), let alone magic, salvific or eschatological themes except within a rigidly reasonable and mainly ethical framework; nor did Judaism as these scholars understood it make use of the religious symbolism or ideas of the Hellenistic world in which it existed essentially apart and at variance.

Today no informed student of Judaism in late antiquity works within the framework of such a synthesis, for this old way is no longer open. The testimony of archaeology, especially of the art of the synagogues of antiquity, now finds a full and ample hearing. In understanding the way in which art contributes to the study of this history of a religion, we find in Judaism in late antiquity a fine example of the problems of interpretation and how they are accommodated and solved. Let us trace the steps by which people began to accept the importance of art—symbolic, representational, abstract, iconic—and survey the more important figures in the labor, now completed, of absorbing art as evidence of religious belief.

Erwin R. Goodenough and the Symbolism of Judaism

In teaching about ancient Judaism through reference to the art of the synagogue, we deal with one towering figure. Erwin Ramsdell Goodenough was the greatest historian of religion America ever produced, and his *Jewish Symbols in the Greco-Roman Period* is his major work.[2] Goodenough provided for the artistic remains of the synagogue a complete and encompassing interpretation, and, to the present time, his view remains the principal theory by which the art of the synagogue is approached.

Along with Moore's *Judaism* and Goodenough's *Jewish Symbols* no other single work has so decisively defined the problem of how to study religion in general, and, by way of example, Judaism in particular. Goodenough worked on archaeological and artistic evidence, so took as his task the description of Judaism as a systematic theological structure. Between the two of them they placed the systematic study of Judaism in the forefront of the academic study of religion and dictated the future of the history of religion in the West. It would encompass not only the religions of nonliterate and unfamiliar peoples but also of literate and very familiar ones. In all, Moore and Goodenough have left a legacy of remarkable power and intellectual weight. Through the study of Judaism they showed how to describe, analyze, and interpret religious systems, contexts and contents alike.

The importance of reading Judaism's art with Goodenough cannot be overstated. Goodenough frames issues as they should be addressed in teaching religious studies, because he treats the study of religion as a generalizing science; and he examines a particular case because it serves to exemplify matters of wider interest. Through the specific case of the symbolism of ancient Judaism and problems in its interpretation, Goodenough raises a pressing general question. It is how to make sense of the ways in which people use art to express their deepest yearnings, and how we are to make sense of that art in the study of the people who speak, without resort to words, through it. The importance of Goodenough's work lies in his power to make the particular into something exemplary and suggestive, to show that, in detail, we confront the whole of human experience in some critical aspect. Goodenough asks when a symbol is symbolic. He wants to know how visual symbols speak beyond words and despite words. Goodenough studied ancient Jewish symbols because he wanted to explain how that happens and what we learn about the human imagination from the power of symbols to express things words cannot or do not convey. It is difficult to point to a more engaging and critical problem in the study of humanity than the one Goodenough took for himself. That is why, twenty years after the conclusion of his research, a new generation will find fresh and important the research and reflection of this extraordinary man.

Goodenough's Review of the Archaeological Evidence for Jewish Art in the Synagogue

The first three volumes of Goodenough's *Jewish Symbols* collect the Jewish realia uncovered in the past by archaeologists working in various parts of the Mediterranean basin. Goodenough's interest in these artifacts began, he reports, with the question of how it was possible, within so brief a span as fifty years, that the teachings of Jesus could have been accommodated so completely to the Hellenistic world. Not only central ideas, but even widespread symbols of early Christianity appear in retrospect to have been appropriated from an environment alien to Jewish Palestine. "For Judaism and Christianity to keep their integrity, any appropriations from paganism had to be very gradual" (1:4). Yet within half a century of Jesus's death, Christian churches were well established in Hellenistic cities, and Christian teachings were within the realm of discourse of their citizens. If the "fusion" with Hellenistic culture occurred as quickly as it did, then it seems best explained by reference to an antecedent and concurrent form of Hellenistic Judaism that had successfully and naturally achieved a comfortable accommodation with Hellenism. Why so? Goodenough maintains that the Judaism known from the writings of the ancient rabbis, hence, "rabbinical Judaism," could not accommodate itself to Hellenism. Goodenough's main point follows: "While rabbinical Judaism can adjust itself to mystic rites . . . it would never have originated them."

That is to say, we would look vainly in the circles among whom talmudic literature developed for the origins of various symbols and ideas of Hellenistic Judaism. It follows that evidences of the use of the pagan inheritance of ancient civilization for specifically Jewish purposes derives from Jews whose legacy is not recorded in the pages of the Talmud. So Goodenough's first question is: If the rabbis whose writings we possess did not lead people to see the symbols at hand, then who did? If, as Goodenough contends, not all Jews (perhaps, not even many Jews) were under the hegemony of the rabbis of the Talmud, who did not lead the way in the utilization of pagan symbols in synagogue decoration, than what should we think if we discover that forms we should expect to uncover not in a Jewish but rather in a pagan setting have been put to substantial, identifiably Jewish purposes?

One conclusion would render these finds insignificant. If illegal, symbolic representations of lions, eagles, masks, victory wreaths, not to mention the Zodiac and other astral symbols were made for merely ornamental purposes, "the rabbis" may not have approved of them, but had to "reckon with reality" and "accepted" them. That view was commonly expressed but never demonstrated. For his part Goodenough repeats litanously, symbol by symbol and volume by volume (see 1:108), that it is difficult to agree that the handful of symbolic objects so carefully chosen from a great variety of available symbols, so frequently repeated at Dura (fig. 6), Randanini, Beth Alpha (fig. 5), Hammam Lif, and elsewhere, used to the exclusion of many other symbols, and so sloppily drawn that no ornamental artist could have done them, constituted mere decoration. Furthermore, it begs the question to say that these symbols were "merely" ornamental: Why specifically these symbols and *no others*? Why in these settings?

Goodenough attempts to uncover the meaning of various symbols discovered in substantial quantities throughout the Jewish world of antiquity. His procedure is, first, to present the finds *in situ*, second (and quite briefly), to expound a method capable of making sense out of them, and, third, to study each extant symbol with the guidance of this method. Goodenough presents a majestic array of photographs and discussion, for the first time presenting in one place a portrait of Jewish art in antiquity, one as magnificent as will ever appear. The Bollingen Foundation deserves credit for making possible Goodenough's remarkable edition of the art. Nothing like it has been done in the thirty years since the first three volumes made their appearance.

In his survey Goodenough begins with the art of Jewish tombs in Palestine and of their contents, studying the remains by chronological periods, and thus indicating the great changes in funerary art that developed after A.D. 70. Goodenough proceeds (1, chap. 5)

5. *Sacrifice of Isaac, Beth Alpha Synagogue.*

to the synagogues of Palestine, their inscriptions and contents, describing (sometimes briefly) more than four dozen sites. He concludes (1:264):

> In these synagogues certainly was a type of ornament, using animals, human figures, and even pagan deities, in the round, in deep relief, or in mosaic, which was in sharp distinction to what was considered proper for Judaism. . . . The ornament we are studying is an interim ornament, used only after the fall of Jerusalem, and before the completion, or reception, of the Talmud. The return to the old standards, apparently a return to the halachic Judaism that the rabbis advocated, is dramatically attested by the destruction, obviously by Jews themselves, of the decorative abominations, and only of the abominations, in these synagogues. Only when a synagogue was abandoned as at Dura . . . are the original effects preserved, or the devastations indiscriminate.

The decoration in these synagogues must have seemed more than merely decorative to those who destroyed them so discriminatingly.

Goodenough argues that distinction between fetishistic magic and religion is generally subjective, and imposed from without by the embarrassed investigator. He points out (2:156) that magical characteristics, such as the effort to achieve material benefits by fundamentally compulsive devices are common (whether we recognize them as such or not) in the "higher" religions. It is certainly difficult to point to any religious group before the present time that did not quite openly expect religion to produce some beneficial consequence; and if that consequence was to take place after death, it was no less real. Hence Goodenough concludes that "magic is a term of judgement," and thus the relevance of charms and amulets is secured. Goodenough summarizes the consequences of his evidence as follows (2:295):

> The picture we have got of this Judaism is that of a group still intensely loyal to Iao Sabaoth, a group which buried its dead and built its synagogues with a marked sense that it was a peculiar people in the eyes of God, but which accepted the best of paganism (including its most potent charms) as focusing in, finding its meaning in, the supreme Iao Sabaoth. In contrast to this, the Judaism of the rabbis was a Judaism which rejected all of the pagan religious world (all that it could). . . . Theirs was the method of exclusion, not inclusion.

The problem is then how to establish a methodology by which material amassed in the first three volumes may be studied and interpreted.

Goodenough's Interpretation of Symbols: The Method

Goodenough argues that the written documents, particularly the talmudic ones, do not suffice to interpret symbols so utterly alien to their spirit, and in any case, so rarely discussed in them. Even where some of the same symbols inscribed on graves or synagogues are mentioned in the Bible or Talmud, it is not always obvious that those textual references engage the mind of the artist. Why not? Because the artists follow the conventions of Hellenistic art, and not only Hellenistic art, but the conventions of the artists who decorated cultic objects and places in the same locale in which, in the Jewish settings, the symbols have turned up. Goodenough asks for a general theory to make sense of all the evidence, something no one else gives, and asks (4:10):

> Where are we to find the moving cause in the taking over of images, and with what objective were they taken over? . . . It seems to me that the motive for borrowing pagan art and integrating it into Judaism throughout the Roman world can be discovered only by analyzing the art itself.

An interpretive method needs to be devised. Goodenough succinctly defines this method:

> The first step . . . must be to assemble . . . the great body of evidence available . . . which, when viewed as a whole, demands interpretation as a whole, since it is so amazingly homogeneous for all parts of the Empire. The second step is to recognize that we must first determine what this art means in itself, before we begin to apply to it as proof texts any possible unrelated statements of the Bible or the Talmud. That these artifacts are unrelated to proof texts is a statement which one can no more make at the outset than one begin with the assumption of most of my predecessors, that if the symbols had meaning for Jews, that meaning must be found by correlating them with talmudic and biblical phrases. . . . The art has rarely, and then only in details, been studied for its possible meaning in itself: this is the task of these volumes.

If the succeeding volumes exhibit a monotonous quality, as one
symbol after another comes under discussion and produces an interpretation very close to the ones already given, it is because of
his tenacious use of a method clearly articulated and clearly applied throughout. What is this method? The problem here is to explain how Goodenough determines what this art means in itself.
Goodenough begins by asking (4:27):

> Admitting that the Jews would not have remained Jews ... if they
> had used these images in pagan ways and with pagan explana-
> tions, do the remains indicate a symbolic adaptation of pagan fig-
> ures to Judaism or merely an urge to decoration?

Goodenough defines a symbol as "an image or design with a significance, to the one who uses it, quite beyond its manifest content ...
an object or a pattern which, whatever the reason may be, operates
upon men, and causes effect in them beyond mere recognition of
what is literally presented in the given form." Goodenough emphasizes that most important thought is in "this world of the suggestive connotative meaning of words, objects, sounds, and forms."
He adds (4:33) that in religion a symbol conveys not only meaning
but also "power or value." Further, some symbols move from religion to religion, preserving the same "value" while acquiring
a new explanation. In the long history of Judaism religious
"symbols" in the form of actions or prohibitions certainly endure
through many, varied settings, all the while acquiring new explanations and discarding old ones, and perpetually retaining religious "force" or value or (in more modern terms) "meaning." Hence
Goodenough writes (4:36):

> Indeed, when the religious symbols borrowed by Jews in those
> years are put together, it becomes clear that the ensemble is not
> merely a "picture book without text," but reflects a lingua franca
> that had been taken into most of the religions of the day, for the
> same symbols were used in association with Dionysus, Mithra,
> Osiris, the Etruscan gods, Sabazius, Attis, and a host of others, as
> well as by Christianity later. It was a symbolic language, a direct
> language of values, however, not a language of denotation.

Goodenough is far from suggesting the presence of a pervasive syncretism. Rather, he points to what he regards as pervasive reli-

gious values applied quite parochially by various groups, including some Jews to the worship of their particular "Most High God." These values, while connotative and not denotative, may, nonetheless, be recovered and articulated in some measure by the historian who makes use of the insights of recent students of psychology and symbolism:

> The hypothesis on which I am working . . . is that in taking over the symbols, while discarding the myths and explanations of the pagans, Jews and Christians admitted, indeed confirmed, a continuity of religious experience which it is most important to be able to identify . . . for an understanding of man, the phenomenon of a continuity of religious experience or values would have much more significance than that of discontinuous explanations. (4:42)

At this point Goodenough argues that the symbols under consideration were more than merely space-fillers. Since this matter is crucial to his argument, let me give his reasons with appropriate emphasis. These are:

First, they were all *living* symbols in surrounding culture.

Second, the vocabulary of symbols is extremely limited, on all the artifacts not more than a score of designs appearing in sum, and thus highly selected.

Third, the symbols were frequently not the work of an ornamental artist at all.

Fourth, the Jewish and "pagan" symbols are mixed on the same graves, so that if the menorah is accepted as "having value" then the peacock or wreath of victory ought also to have "had value."

Fifth, the symbols are found in highly public places, such as synagogues and cemeteries, and not merely on the private and personal possessions of individuals, such as amulets or charms.

Goodenough therefore must state carefully where and how each symbol occurs, thus establishing its commonplace quality; he must then show the meaning that the symbol may have had *universally*, indicating its specific denotative value in the respective cultures which used it. He considers its broader connotative value, as it recurs in each culture, because a symbol evokes in man, not only among specific groups of men, a broader, psychologically oriented meaning. Goodenough notes that the formal state religions of Athens, Rome, and Jerusalem had quite different bases, and little (if any) use for the symbols at hand. These symbols, he holds, were of use "only in religions that engendered deep emotion, ecstasy— religions directly and consciously centered in the renewing of life and the granting of immortality, in the giving to the devotee of a portion of the divine spirit or life substance" (4:59-60).

> At the end . . . these symbols appear to indicate a type of Judaism in which, as in Philonic Judaism, the basic elements of "mystery" were superimposed upon Jewish legalism. The Judaism of the rabbis has always offered essentially a path through this present life, the Father's code of instructions as to how we may please him while we are alive. To this, the symbols seem to say, was now added from the mystery religions, or from Gnosticism, the burning desire to leave this life altogether, to renounce the flesh and go up into the richness of divine existence, to appropriate God's life to oneself. . . .
>
> These ideas have as little place in normative, rabbinic Judaism as do the pictures and symbols and gods that Jews borrowed to suggest them. That such ideas were borrowed by Jews was no surprise to me after years of studying Philo. (4:60-61)

What is perplexing is the problem of how Jews fitted such conceptions into, or harmonized them with, the teachings of the Bible.

The Meaning of Artistic Symbols

In volumes four to eight Goodenough turns back to the symbols whose existence he traced in volumes one to three. Now he attempts a systematic interpretation according to the method outlined in volume four, part one. In his discussion of symbols from the Jewish cult, Goodenough attempts to explain what these symbols may have meant when reproduced in the noncultic settings of synagogue and grave, specifically, the menorah, the Torah shrine, *lulab* and *ethrog*, *shofar*, and incense shovel. These symbols are, of course, definitely Jewish. But they seem to have been transformed into symbols (4:67) which, when "used in devotion, . . . have taken on personal, direct value," to mean not simply that the deceased was a Jew but to express a "meaning in connection with the death and life for those buried behind them" (4:68). It would be simple to assign the meaning of these symbols to their biblical and cultic origins, except for the fact that they were often represented with less obviously Jewish, or biblical symbols, such as birds eating grapes and the like.

Rather, Goodenough holds that these devices may be of some direct help in achieving immortality for the deceased, specifically "the menorah seems to have become a symbol of God, of his streaming Light and Law . . . the astral path to God. . . . The lulab and ethrog carried on the association with Tabernacles as a festival of rain and light, but took on mystical overtones, to become a eucharist of escape from evil and of the passing into justice as the immaterial Light comes to man" (4:210). He concludes (4:212):

> They could take a host of pagan symbols which appeared to them to have in paganism the values they wanted from their Judaism, and blend them with Jewish symbols as freely as Philo blended the language of Greek metaphysics with the language of the Bible.

In *Fish, Bread, and Wine*, volumes 5 and 6 of *Jewish Symbolism*, Goodenough begins by discussing the Jewish and pagan representations of creatures of the sea, in the latter section reviewing these usages in Egypt, Mesopotamia, Syria, Greece, and Rome (a recurrent inquiry), then turns to the symbolic value of the fish in Judaism, finally, to bread. The representations of "bread" often look merely like "round objects," however; and if it were not for the occasional representation of baskets of bread, one would scarcely be convinced that these "round objects" signify anything in particular. The section on wine is the high point of these volumes, both for its daring and for its comprehensive treatment of the "divine fluid" and all sorts of effulgences from the godhead, from Babylonia and Assyria, Egypt (in various periods), Greece, Dionysiac cults in Syria and Egypt, as well as in the late syncretistic religions. Goodenough finds considerable evidence in Jewish cult and observance, but insists that fish, bread, and wine rites came into Jewish practice during and not before the Hellenistic period, and hence must be explained by contemporary ideas. Wine, in particular, was widely regarded as a source of fertility, but its mystic value was an expression of the "craving for sacramental access to Life."

Pagan symbols used in Jewish contexts include the bull, lion, tree, crown, various rosettes and other wheels (demonstrably not used in paganism for purely decorative purposes), masks, the gorgoneum, cupids, birds, sheep, hares, shells, cornucopias, centaurs, psychopomps, and astronomical symbols. Goodenough treats this body of symbol last because while some may have had biblical referents, the symbolic value of all these forms seem to him to be discovered in the later period. Of the collection, Goodenough writes (8:220).

> They have all turned into life symbols, and could have been, as I believe they were, interpreted in a great many ways. For those who believed in immortality they could point to immortality, to give man specific hopes. To those who found the larger life in a mysticism that looked, through death, to a final dissolution of the individual into the All . . . these symbols could have been given great power and a vivid sense of appropriation. . . . The invasion of pagan symbols into either Judaism or Christianity . . . involved a modification of the original faith but by no means its abandonment. Symbolism is itself a language, and affected the original faith much as does the adopting of a new language in which to express its tenets. Both Christians and Jews in these years read their Scriptures, and prayed in words that had been consecrated to pagan deities. The very idea of a God, discussion of the values of the Christian or Jewish God, could be conveyed only by using the old pagan *theos;* salvation, by the word *sōtēria;* immortality, by *athanasia.* The eagle, the crown, the zodiac, and the like spoke just as direct, just as complicated, a language. The Christian or Jew had by no means the same conception of heaven or immortality as the pagan, but all had enough in common to make the same symbols, as well as the same words, expressive and meaningful. Yet the words and the symbols borrowed did bring in something new.

Goodenough continues (8:224): "When Jews adopted the same lingua franca of symbols they must . . . have taken over the constant values in the symbols."

Finally, Goodenough reviews the lessons of the evidence. From the cultic objects we learn that the Jews used images of their cultic objects in a new way, in the pagan manner, for just as the pagans were putting the mythological and cultic emblems of their religions on their tombs to show their hope in the world to come, so too did the Jews. From fish, bread, and wine, we learn that the Jews were thus partaking of immortal nature. In reference to the symbols that had no cultic origins (vols. 7 and 8) and, on the face of it, slight Jewish origins (apart from the bull, tree, lion, and possibly crown, which served in biblical times), Goodenough proposes that the value of these objects, though not their verbal explanations, were borrowed because some Jews found in them "new depths for [their] ideas of . . . [their] own Jewish deity, and [their] hope of salvation or immortality."

The Debate on the Art of the Synagogue at Dura-Europos: Goodenough and Kraeling

When the painted walls of the synagogue at Dura-Europos (fig. 6) emerged into the light of day in November 1932, the modern perspective on the character of Judaism in Greco-Roman times had to be radically refocused. Until that time, it was possible to ignore the growing evidence, turned up for decades by archaeologists, of a kind of Judaism substantially different from that described in Jewish literary remains of the period. It is true that archaeological discoveries had long before revealed in the synagogues and graves of Jews in the Hellenistic worlds substantial evidences of religious syncretism, and of the use of pagan symbols in identifiable Jewish settings. But before the Dura synagogue these evidences remained discrete and made slight impact. They were not explained; they were explained away.

After the preliminary report, the Dura synagogue was widely discussed, and a considerable literature, mostly on specific problems of art but partly on the interpretation of the art, developed; in the main, the Dura synagogue was studied by art historians, and not, with notable exceptions, by historians of religion or Judaism. But, as I said, from 1932 to 1956 Goodenough was prevented by colleagues from discussing the finds at Dura since the final report on the excavation was still in preparation. In 1956 Carl H. Kraeling published *The Synagogue*.[3] Then the issue could be fairly joined. In no way can Goodenough's volumes nine to eleven be considered in isolation from the other and quite opposite approach to the same problem. So as we take up Goodenough on the Dura synagogue, we deal with Goodenough only in the context of the debate with Kraeling.

Let me state the issue in a general way. Under debate is how we make use of literary evidence in interpreting the use of symbols, and, further, which evidence we consider. Goodenough looks at the symbols in their artistic context, hence in other settings besides the Jewish one, and he invokes literary evidence only as a second step in interpretation. Kraeling starts with literary evidence and emphasizes the Jewish meanings imputed in literary sources to symbols found in Jewish settings. This he does to the near exclusion of the use and meaning of those same symbols in non-Jewish settings in the same town, indeed on the same street. Goodenough reads Hellenistic Jewish writings at his second stage; Kraeling reads rabbinic and related writings at his first stage. Now to make the matter concrete.

Kraeling opened the Talmud and Midrash and related writings and then looked at the walls of the synagogue. Kraeling argued that the paintings must be interpreted for the most part by reference to the so-called rabbinic literature of the period, and used the talmudic, midrashic, and targumic writings for that purpose. He writes (pp. 353, 354):

> The Haggadic tradition embodied in the Dura Synagogue paintings was, broadly speaking, distinct from the one that was normative for Philo and for that part of the ancient Jewish world that he presents. . . . This particular cycle [of paintings] as it is known to us at Dura moves within a defineable orbit of the Haggadic tradition, . . . this orbit has Palestinian-Babylonian rather than Egyptian relations.

Goodenough took the opposite position. Characteristically, he starts with systematic statement of method, only then proceeding to the artifacts demanding interpretation.

Kraeling argues that the biblical references of the Dura paintings are so obvious that one may begin by reading the Bible, and proceed by reading the paintings in the light of the Bible and its midrashic interpretation in the talmudic period. He says:

> Any community decorating its House of Assembly with material so chosen and so oriented cannot be said to have regarded itself . . . remote from religious life and observance of the Judaism that we know from the Bible and the Mishnah. . . . It would appear that there is a considerable number of instances in which Targum and Midrash have influenced the pictures. (pp. 351, 352)

Kraeling provides numerous examples of such influence. He qualifies his argument, however, by saying that the use of midrashic and targumic material is "illustrative rather than definitive." While he makes reference, from time to time, to comparative materials, Kraeling does not in the main feel it necessary to examine the broad iconographic traditions operating in Dura in general, and most manifestly in the synagogue art. Whatever conventions of pagan art may appear, the meaning of the synagogue art is wholly separated from such conventions and can best, probably only, be understood within the context of the Judaism known to us from literary sources.

Goodenough's argument, repeated in the later volumes from the earlier ones, is that literary traditions would not have led us to expect any such art as this. We may find statements in talmudic literature which are relevant to the art, but we must in any case after assembling the material determine:

> what this art means in itself, before we begin to apply to it as proof texts any possibly quite unrelated statements of the Bible or the Talmud. That these artifacts are unrelated to proof texts is a statement which one can no more make at the outset than one can begin with the assumption of most of my predecessors, that if the symbols had meaning for Jews, that meaning must be found by correlating them with talmudic and biblical phrases. (4:10)

Even though the art of the Dura synagogue may at first glance seem to be *related* to midrashic ideas, even found in a few cases to reflect midrashic accounts of biblical events, nonetheless one is still not freed from the obligation to consider what that art meant to a contemporary Jew, pagan, or Christian who was familiar with other art of the age. Since both the architectural and the artistic conventions of the Dura synagogue are demonstrably those of the place and age, and not in any way borrowed from preexistent "rabbinic" artistic conventions—because there weren't any!—one must give serious thought to the meaning and value, or the content, of those conventions elsewhere and assess, so far as one can, how nearly that value and meaning were preserved in the Jewish setting.

Both Kraeling and Goodenough agree that there was a plan to the art of the synagogue. All concur that biblical scenes are portrayed not only as mere ornament or decoration but as a means of conveying important religious ideas, so that the walls of the sanctuary might, in truth, yield sermons. So we may now turn away

from the argument that, anyhow, symbols are not always symbolic. *These* symbols were symbolic. One may continually say that
the use of pagan art is wholly conventional, just as the critics of
Goodenough's earlier interpretations repeat that the symbols from
graves and synagogues were "mere ornament" and imply nothing
more than a desire to decorate (none surely can say this of Dura,
and no one has, for the meaningful character of Dura synagogue
art is self-evident). But having asserted that pagan art lost its value
and became, in a Jewish setting, wholly conventional, we have
hardly solved many problems. For by saying that the "art has lost
its value," we hardly have explained *why* pagan conventions were
useful for decoration.

Let the scholars speak for themselves, first, on the general meaning which emerges from the paintings as a whole and, second, on
the nature of Judaism at Dura. While both scholars interpret the
pictures in detail, each provides a summary of the meaning of the
art as a whole. Kraeling's is as follows (pp. 350–51):

> A closer examination of the treatment of Israel's sacred history
> as presented in the Synagogue painting leads to a number of in-
> ferences that will help to appraise the community's religious out-
> look. . . . These include the following:
> a. There is a very real sense in which the paintings testify to an
> interest in the actual continuity of the historical process to which
> the sacred record testifies. This is evidenced by the fact that they
> do not illustrate interest in the Covenant relationship by a combi-
> nation of scenes chosen from some one segment of sacred history,
> but provide instead a well-organized progression of scenes from
> the period of the Patriarchs and Moses and Aaron, from the early
> days of the monarchy, through the prophetic period, the exile, the
> post-exile, to the expected Messianic age as visualized by proph-
> ecy. . . .
> b. There is a very real sense in which the history portrayed
> in the paintings involves not only certain individuals, but con-
> cretely the nation as a whole, and in which the course of events in
> time and space are for the individuals and the nation a full and
> completely satisfactory expression of their religious aspirations
> and ideals. . . .
> c. There is a very real sense in which the piety exhibited in, and
> inculcated by, the paintings finds a full expression in the literal
> observance of the Law. This comes to light in the effort to provide
> the historical documentation for the origin of the religious festi-

vals . . . in the attention paid to the cult and its *sacra,* including the sacrifices: and in the opposition to idolatry.

d. Because they have this interest in the historical process, in the people of Israel, and in the literal observance of the Law, the paintings can and do properly include scenes showing how those nations and individuals that oppose God's purposes and His people are set at naught or destroyed. . . .

In other words, the religious problem which the Synagogue paintings reflect is not that of the individual's search for participation in true being by the escape of the rational soul from the irrational desires to a higher level of mystical experience, but rather that of faithful participation in the nation's inherited Covenant responsibilities as a means of meriting the fulfillment of the divine promises and of making explicit in history its divinely determined purpose.

Since the west wall contains the bulk of the surviving frescoes, we turn to Goodenough's interpretation of that wall:

> The west wall of the synagogue as a whole is indeed coming to express a profoundly consistent Judaism. On the left side a miraculous baby is given by Elijah, but he ties in with the temporal hopes of Israel, exemplified when Persian rulership was humiliated by Esther and Mordecai. Divine intervention brings this about, but, here, brought only this. Above is the cosmic interpretation of the temple sacrifice of Aaron, and Moses making the twelve tribes into the zodiac itself. . . .
>
> On the right, just as consistently, the immaterial, metaphysical, values of Judaism are presented. Moses is the divine baby here, with the three Nymphs and Anahita-Aphrodite. Kingship, as shown in the anointing of David by Samuel, is not temporal royalty, but initiation into the hieratic seven. Above these, the gods of local paganism collapse before the Ark of the Covenant, the symbol of metaphysical reality in Judaism, which the three men beside the Ark also represented, while that reality is presented in a temple with seven walls and closed inner sanctuary, and with symbols from the creation myth of Iran. At the top, Moses leads the people out to true spiritual Victory.
>
> In the four portraits, an incident from the life of Moses is made the culmination of each of these progressions. He goes out as the cosmic leader to the heavenly bodies alongside the cosmic worship of Aaron, the menorah, and the zodiac. He reads the mystic law like the priest of Isis alongside the Closed Temple and the all-conquering Ark. He receives the Law from God on Sinai beside a Solomon scene which we cannot reconstruct; but he stands at the

Burning Bush, receiving the supreme revelation of God as Being, beside the migrating Israelites, who move , . . to a comparable, if not the same, goal. (10:137–38)

The reader must be struck by the obvious fact that, in the main, both scholars agree on the substance of the paintings, but they disagree on both their interpretation and their implications for the kind of religion characteristic of this particular synagogue.

Concerning Dura Judaism, Kraeling argues that the Jews of Dura had fallen back "visibly" upon the biblical sources of religious life (p. 351). Kraeling says throughout that the Jews in Dura were, for the most part, good, "normative," rabbinic Jews:

> If our understanding of the pictures is correct, they reveal on the part of those who commissioned them an intense, well-informed devotion to the established traditions of Judaism, close contact with both the Palestinian and the Babylonian centers of Jewish religious thought, and a very real understanding of the peculiar problems and needs of a community living in a strongly competitive religious environment, and in an exposed political position. [p. 353]

Goodenough, in his description of Judaism at Dura (10:196–209), holds that these were not participants in the "established traditions of Judaism," and that they did not have close contact with Babylonian or Palestinian Judaism. The walls of the synagogue are not, he argues, representations of biblical scenes, but *allegorizations* of them (as in the specific instances cited above). The biblical scenes show an acceptance of mystic ideas which the symbolic vocabulary of Jews elsewhere in the Greco-Roman world, studied in the first eight volumes, suggested. He says:

> While the theme of the synagogue as a whole might be called the celebration of the glory and power of Judaism and its God, and was conceived and planned by men intensely loyal to the Torah, those people who designed it did not understand the Torah as did the rabbis in general. Scraps stand here which also appear in rabbinic haggadah, to be sure. . . . But in general the artist seems to have chosen biblical scenes not to represent them, but, by allegorizing them, to make them say much not remotely implicit in the texts. . . . On the other hand, the paintings can by no means be spelled out from the pages of Philo's allegories, for espe-

6. Copy of the wall painting from the Dura-Europos Synagogue: *The Temple of Jerusalem* by Herbert Gute.

cially in glorifying temporal Israel they often depart from him al-
together. Kraeling astutely indicated . . . that we have no trace of
the creation stories, or indeed of any biblical passages before the
sacrifice of Isaac, sections of the Bible to which Philo paid almost
major attention. This must not blind us, however, to the fact that
the artist, like Philo, presumed that the Old Testament text is
to be understood not only through its Greek translation, but
through its reevaluation in terms of Greek philosophy and religion. Again, unlike Philo in detail but like him in spirit, the artists
have interpreted biblical tradition by using Iranian costumes and
such scenes as the duel between the white and black horsemen.
. . . The Jews here, while utterly devoted to their traditions and
Torah, had to express what this meant to them in a building designed to copy the inner shrine of a pagan temple, filled with
images of human beings and Greek and Iranian divinities, and
carefully designed to interpret the Torah in a way profoundly
mystical. (10:206)

Goodenough takes account of the high probability that, under
such circumstances, Jews learned from their neighbors and com-
mented, in a way they found appropriate, on their neighbors' religions. Kraeling's approach rests on the premise of a group of Jews
quite separate from the diverse world around them. Yet so far as
we know, there was no ghetto in Dura, and neither physical nor
cultural isolation characterized the Jews' community there. They
assuredly spoke the same language as others, and they knew what
was going on.

The notion, moreover, of an "Orthodoxy," surely applies to the
third century a conception invented in the nineteenth (a point students of religion will find particularly suggestive), and that anach-
ronism has confused many, not only Kraeling, in reading the artistic and literary sources at hand. There was no single Judaism,
there was never an Orthodoxy, any more than today there is a single Judaism, Orthodox or otherwise. That conception is a conceit
of Orthodoxy. Indeed, throughout Babylonia (present-day Iraq)
Jews lived in the same many-splendored world, in which diverse
languages and groups worshipped different gods. And Jews themselves prove diverse: there were many Judaisms. And the art, properly interpreted, forms the principal testimony to the most widespread of the Judaisms of late antiquity. That is why the study of
the art is essential for the study of ancient Judaism.

The Debate on Goodenough's Interpretation:
Nock and Smith

Students will gain a clear picture of the difficulty of interpreting the religious life by reviewing the debate Goodenough precipitated. That will show them how to differentiate the main point from matters of detail. Anyone with an interest in symbolism will follow that debate with intense interest. A mark of the success of scholarship, particularly in a massive exercise of interpretation such as the one at hand, derives from how a scholar has defined issues. Did Goodenough succeed in framing the program of inquiry? Indeed he did. Nearly all critics concede the premise of his work, which, when he began, provoked intense controversy. Goodenough demanded that the Jewish symbols be taken seriously, not dismissed as mere decoration. That view formed the foundation of his work, and he completely succeeded in making that point stick. Few today propose to ignore what, when Goodenough began to work, many preferred to explain away. So Goodenough's greatness begins in his power to reframe the issues of his chosen field. In his day in his area few scholars enjoyed equivalent influence, and, in ours, none in the field at hand.

But that fact should not obscure differences of opinion, both in detail and in general conclusions. Goodenough would not have wanted matters any other way. Teachers of ancient Judaism through art will find useful an account of two interesting approaches—those of Morton Smith and Arthur Darby Nock—to the criticism of Goodenough's *Jewish Symbols*.

Arthur Darby Nock (1902–63)

Nock presented a systematic critique of Goodenough's first eight volumes, under the title "Religious Symbols and Symbolism."[4] Nock first summarizes the main lines of Goodenough's approach to the interpretation of symbols. He then expresses his agreement with what I regard as the principal result of Goodenough's work for the study of Judaism (pp. 880–82, passim):

> G[oodenough] has made a good case against any strong central control of Judaism: it was a congregational religion and the local group or, in a large city such as Rome, any given local group seems to have been largely free to follow its own preferences.

Again, in art as in other things, Judaism seems to have been now more and now less sensitive on questions of what was permissible. From time to time there was a stiffening and then a relaxing: down into modern times mysticism and enthusiasm have been recurrent phenomena; so has the "vertical path" as distinct from the "horizontal path." To speak even more generally, from the earliest times known to us there has been a persistent quality of religious lyricism breaking out now here, now there among the Jews.

The point conceded by Nock is central to Goodenough's thesis: that Judaism yielded diversity and not uniformity. Again, since Goodenough repeatedly turns to Philo for explanation of symbols, it is important to see that Nock concedes how Philo may represent a world beyond himself:

So again, in all probability, Philo's attitude was not unique and, deeply personal as was the warmth of his piety and his sense of religious experience, we need not credit him with much original thinking. The ideas which he used did not disappear from Judaism after 70 or even after 135. Typological and allegorical interpretation of the Old Testament continued to be common. G.'s discussion of the sacrifice of Isaac is particularly instructive; so are his remarks on the fixity and ubiquity of some of the Jewish symbols and (4.145ff.) on lulab and ethrog in relation to the feast of Tabernacles, "the culminating festival of the year" with all that it suggested to religious imagination.

Menorah, lulab, ethrog, Ark and incense-shovel were associated with the Temple and as such could remain emblems of religious and national devotion after its destruction; the details of the old observances were discussed with passionate zeal for centuries after their disuse. G. has indeed made a strong case for the view that, as presented in art, they refer to the contemporary worship of the synagogue (as he has produced serious arguments for some use of incense in this). It may well be that they suggested both Temple and synagogue.

But Nock provided extensive and important criticism of Goodenough's ideas. He expresses his reservations in detail (pp. 882–83).

The improbability of many of G.'s suggestions on points of detail does not affect his main theses, but those theses do not themselves call for very substantial reservations. Thus the analogy between Isis and Sophia is more superficial than real, and so is that between allegorical explanations of the two types of religious vestments used by Egyptians and the two used by the High Priest. No these are not minor matters; the first is one of the foundations of what is said about the "saving female principle" and the second is made to support the supposition of Lesser and Greater Mysteries of Judaism.

The crucial question is: was there a widespread and long continuing Judaism such as G. infers, with something in the nature of a mystery worship? Before we attack this we may consider (a) certain iconographic features regarded by G. as Hellenistic symbols—in particular Victories with crowns, Seasons, the Sun, and the zodiac; (b) the cup, the vine and other motifs which G. thinks Dionysiac; (c) the architectural features which he interprets as consecratory.

The important point to observe is how Nock calls into question not only detail but the general approach: the main results. That is how scholarly debate should go forward. But Nock concludes (p. 918):

> Once more such points do not destroy the essential value of the work. I have tried to indicate . . . what seem to be the major gains for knowledge which it brings and naturally there are also valuable details.

In the balance, Nock's systematic critique confirms Goodenough's standing as the scholar to insist that the symbols matter. More than that Goodenough could not have asked. More than that Nock did not concede.

Morton Smith (b. 1915)

Morton Smith provides a list of reviews of Goodenough's work, which he compiled from *L'anee philologique*, as well as a systematic reconsideration of the work as a whole.[5] As a statement of an experience of the history of Judaism and Christianity in the formative age, Smith's essay stands as the definitive account of his own viewpoint on Goodenough's work. Smith first calls attention to the insistence on distinguishing the value of a symbol from its verbal explanation (p. 55):

> The fundamental point in Goodenough's argument is his concept of the "value" of a symbol as distinct from the "interpretation."

He defined the "value" as "simply emotional impact." But he also equated "value" with "meaning" and discovered as the "meaning" of his symbols a complex mystical theology. Now certain shapes may be subconsciously associated with certain objects or, like certain colors, may appeal particularly to persons of certain temperaments. This sort of symbolism may be rooted in human physiology and almost unchanging. But such "values" as these do not carry the theological implications Goodenough discovered.

The premise of a psychic unity of humanity, on which Goodenough's insistence on the distinction at hand must rest, certainly awaits more adequate demonstration. Smith proceeds (pp. 55–56):

> After this definition of "value," the next step in Goodenough's argument is the claim that each symbol always has one and the same "value."
>
> Goodenough's position can be defended only by making the one constant value something so deep in the subconscious and so ambivalent as to be compatible with contradictory "interpretations." In that event it will also be compatible with both mystical and legalistic religion. In that event the essential argument, that the use of these symbols necessarily indicates a mystical religion, is not valid.

So much for the basic theory of symbolism. Smith proceeds (p. 57) to the specific symbolism at hand:

> The lingua franca of Greco-Roman symbolism, predominantly Dionysiac, expressed hope for salvation by participation in the life of a deity which gave itself to be eaten in a sacramental meal. This oversimplifies Goodenough's interpretations of pagan symbolism; he recognized variety which cannot be discussed here for lack of space. But his thesis was his main concern, and drew objections from several reviewers, notably from Nock, who was the one most familiar with the classical material.
>
> It must be admitted that Goodenough's support of this contention was utterly inadequate. What had to be established was a probability that the symbols, as *commonly* used in the Roman empire, expressed this hope of salvation by communion. If they did not *commonly* do so *at this time*, then one cannot conclude that the Jews, who at this time took them over, had a similar hope. But Goodenough only picked out a scattering of examples in which the symbols could plausibly be given the significance his

thesis required; he passed over the bulk of the Greco-Roman material and barely mentioned a few of the examples in which the same symbols were said, by those who used them, to have other significance. These latter examples, he declared, represented superficial "interpretations" of the symbols, while the uses which agreed with his theory expressed the symbols' permanent "values." The facts of the matter, however, were stated by Nock: "Sacramental sacrifice is attested only for Dionysius and even in his cult this hardly remained a living conception"; there is no substantial evidence that the worshipers of Dionysus commonly thought they received "his divine nature in the cup." So much for the significance of the "lingua franca" of Greco-Roman Dionysiac symbolism.

Smith then points out that Goodenough "ruled out the inscriptional and literary evidence which did not agree with his theories." He maintains that Goodenough substituted his own intuition, quoting the following: "The study of these symbols has brought out their value for my own psyche." By contrast, Smith concurs with Goodenough's insistence on the hope for the future life as a principal theme of the symbols. Still, Smith maintains that Goodenough failed "to demonstrate the prevalence of a belief in sacramental salvation" (p. 58). In Smith's view, therefore, "the main structure of his argument was ruined."

In reviewing the Goodenough debate, students will learn from examples of how not to pursue an argument. Smith provides a fine instance of a mode of discourse students will recognize as inappropriate. For, as is his way in general, Smith makes a long sequence of *ad hominem* points about Goodenough's background, upbringing, religious beliefs, and the like, for example, "He is the rebellious son of G. F. Moore" (p. 65). In this way he personalizes and trivializes scholarship. He lays down such judgments as "enormous exaggerations," "his pandemic sacramental paganism was a fantasy," and on and on. Smith underscores his views with lavish use of italics. He declares Goodenough's view nothing less than "incredible." He leaves in the form of questions a series of, to him "self-evident," claims against Goodenough's views. These claims in their form as rhetorical questions Smith regards as unanswerable and beyond all argument. For example: "But the difficulties in the supposition of a *widespread, uniform* mystical Judaism are formidable [italics his]. How did it happen that such a system and practice disappeared without leaving a trace in either Jewish or Christian polemics? We may therefore turn from the main argument to incidental questions" (p. 59). Those three sentences constitute Smith's stated reason for dismissing Goodenough's principal positions and turning to minor matters. Personalizing, then trivializing issues of scholarly interpretation form a common mode of debate, and students will benefit from a direct encounter with this debate, since, after all, the evidence—the art itself—is there for them to interpret as well. Goodenough, for his part, had worked out answers to these questions, which he recognized on his own, and, had he lived, had every capacity of dealing with them to (at least) his own satisfaction.

Still Smith's criticism cannot be dismissed as that of a mere self-important crank. Nor should we wish to ignore positive assessment (p. 61):

> Goodenough's supposition that the Jews gave their own interpretations to the symbols they borrowed is plausible and has been commonly accepted. His reconstruction of their interpretations, however, being based on Philo, drew objections that Philo was an upper-class intellectual whose interpretations were undreamt of by the average Jew. These, however, missed Goodenough's claim: Philo was merely one example of mystical Judaism, of which other examples, from other social and intellectual classes, were attested by monuments. For this reason also, objections that Goodenough misinterpreted Philo on particular points did not seriously damage his argument; it was sufficient for him to show that Philo used expressions suggestive of a mystical and sacramental interpretation of Jewish stories and ceremonies. The monuments could then show analogous developments independent of Philo. Some did, but most did not.

The single most important comments of Smith is as follows (p. 65):

> Goodenough's theory falsifies the situation by substituting a single, anti-rabbinic, mystical Judaism for the enormous variety of personal, doctrinal, political, and cultural divergences which the rabbinic and other evidence reveals, and by supposing a sharp division between rabbinic and anti-rabbinic Judaism, whereas actually there seems to have been a confused gradation.

Declaring Goodenough to have failed, Smith concludes (p. 66): "Columbus failed too. But his failure revealed a new world, and so did Goodenough's." For more than that no scholar can hope. For learning is a progressive, an on-going process, an active verb in the continuing present tense. In teaching about ancient Judaism through the study of art, that is the principal lesson of all education.

NOTES

1. George Foot Moore, *Judaism: The Age of the Tannaim* (Cambridge: Harvard University Press, 1927).

2. Erwin R. Goodenough, *Jewish Symbols in the Greco-Roman Period*, 13 vols. (Princeton: Princeton University Press, 1953–68). The complete bibliography of his writings by A. Thomas Kraabel appears in Jacob Neusner, ed., *Religions in Antiquity: Essays in Memory of Erwin Ramsdell Goodenough* (Leiden: E. J. Brill, 1968), pp. 621–32. My abridged edition of his *Symbols* will be published shortly by Princeton University Press. In what follows I have drawn on parts of my introduction to that book, as well as my introduction to the literature on Goodenough's work, printed in the appendix of the same book.

3. A. R. Bellinger, F. E. Brown, A. Perkins, and C. B. Welles, ed., *The Excavations at Dura Europos Conducted by Yale University and the French Academy of Inscriptions and Letters. Final Report*, vol. 8, no. 1, *The Synagogue*, by Carl Kraeling, with contributions by C. C. Torrey, C. B. Welles, and B. Geirger (New Haven: Yale University Press, 1956).

4. *Gnomon* 27 (1955), 29(1957), and 32(1960); now reprinted in Zeph Stewart, ed., *Arthur Darby Nock: Essays on Religion and the Ancient World* (Oxford: Clarendon Press, 1972), 2:877–918.

5. Morton Smith, "Goodenough's Jewish Symbols in Retrospect," *Journal of Biblical Literature* 86 (1967): 53–68.

4

The Tree of Light Springs from the Threshold

JO MILGROM

My course, "Roots and Art of Jewish Spirituality," combines and integrates liturgy and art of the biological life cycle with the liturgy and art of the holy days. For example, sacred nonchronological time of the Sabbath encourages higher consciousness of ordinary time engendering greater control and pleasure. Although biology demands the cycle of birth-reproduction-death, religion denies, interprets, and mediates the inexorable journey of human life. This methodology allows for a deeper understanding of the Jewish roots of Christianity which enables contemporary Christianity to be nourished from its primary sources; the open flourishing of Christian-Jewish dialogue; and a sense of the human condition through examination of critical issues transcending doctrinal differences.

The following lecture is typical of my methodology. A well-known visual artifact, the menorah or temple lampstand, is traced in its form as a stylized Tree of Light or Tree of Life back to the cylinder seals of the third millennium B.C.E. This is followed by an analysis of light symbolism from its hoary beginnings and linguistic roots to its current metamorphoses and psychological reverberations in contemporary art forms and in religious texts such as the Book of Psalms, Midrash, and Zohar. In this way, the work of art is studied on three levels: its physical form; its conventional use and meaning (iconography); and its deeper symbolic meaning (iconology). Word and image work together, and alternately illumine the other. Each is a primary text.

It is late Yom Kippur afternoon. The fast has gone on for twenty-four hours. The shadows lengthen. The congregation gathers up new energies for the final hour. The doors of the Ark open once again to the sight of the regal Torah scrolls dressed in their embroidered mantles, bedecked in silver crowns and pointers, like monarchs at a summit meeting. At attention in the viewing stand, they return the gaze of their loyal subjects. We open the High Holiday Maḥzor to page 464.[1]

The medieval *piyyut* is laconic and staccato; almost all the words are monosyllables, as though the poet is too weary and impatient for language to reach the ears of the Almighty. It is *Ne'ilah*, the concluding service. *Ne'ilah* means more than concluding, for it really says "the locking" (of the gates).

פְּתַח לָנוּ שַׁעַר· בְּעֵת נְעִילַת שַׁעַר· כִּי פָנָה יוֹם:
הַיּוֹם יִפְנֶה· הַשֶּׁמֶשׁ יָבֹא וְיִפְנֶה· נָבוֹאָה שְׁעָרֶיךָ:
אָנָּא אֵל נָא· שָׂא נָא· סְלַח נָא· מְחַל נָא· חֲמָל
נָא· רַחֵם נָא· כַּפֶּר נָא· כְּבוֹשׁ חֵטְא וְעָוֹן:

Open the gate for us, at the time of the locking of the gate, because
    the day is turning.
The day will turn; the sun will set and turn; let us come into your
    gates.
O God, please forgive; please excuse; please pardon; please pity;
    please commiserate; please grant at-one-ment; please subdue sin
    and wrongdoing.

This is the liturgical setting for the *Ne'ilah* service which is accompanied by the prayer that the gates not be closed and which is recited during the gate-locking service. At the twelfth hour, we are still doing *teshuva*; we are repenting.

Two weeks later on the last day of the Sukkot festival, we discover from a ninth-century midrashic text that there is still time to do *teshuvah*. Somehow the gate is still open. With authorized midrashic *ḥutzpah*, 2 Chronicles 7:14 is drafted to serve as a proof text outside of its original context:

If my people, upon whom my name is called, shall humble themselves and pray and seek My face, and turn from their evil ways
[there is still time for *teshuva*] then I will hear from heaven and
forgive their sin and heal their land.[2]

There is a portal complex. It is another reality through that door
which the community must work to keep open. Where does it come
from, that sacred portal? What are its manifold meanings? How
has it metamorphosed through time and style? It is as new and
newer than Georgia O'Keeffe (1887–1986), and as old as seal impressions from the third millennium B.C.E.

Mircea Eliade (1907–86) writes about the door that opens onto
the interior of the church, that threshold space that separates two
spaces, two ways of being from each other. It is the frontier between the two worlds of the sacred and the profane. Paradoxically,
the threshold is the place where those two worlds meet and communicate. It is also the place where one can pass from one to the
other; the threshold is both the symbol and at the same time, the
vehicle of passage.

Human beings associate these openings with their personal passages from one existential situation to another. So doorways become more than doorways; they acquire the rank of the archetypal
symbols of the human condition. The history of religions identifies
threshold passages with a variety of ritual gestures: a bow, a pros-
tration, or a pious touch of the hand. The threshold also has sacred
guardians who forbid entrance to enemies, pestilence, and demons. Offerings to those guardian divinities, remnants of sacrificial rituals, have been found beneath the threshold.[3]

Portal-awe is not an answer; rather, it is a question of how the
doorway becomes so special to begin with. Looking beyond immediate and ordinary limited human space to access into another
quality of space, human beings connect with the transpersonal
source of their nourishment. The sophistication of the quest ne-
glects its fundamental simplicity. By reaching into space and met-
aphorically poking a hole in it, the Hidden Light is allowed to enter. The very act of reaching brings one to the sacred center, to the
navel of the universe, and connects one to the cosmic umbilical
cord which Eliade called the *axis mundi*.

Georgia O'Keeffe probed the dark passageway to admit the Hidden Light in *Black Abstraction* (1927; Metropolitan Museum of Art, New York).

> I was on a stretcher in a large room, two nurses hovering over me, a very large bright skylight above me. I had decided to be conscious as long as possible. I heard the doctor washing his hands. The skylight began to whirl and slowly became smaller and smaller in a black space. I lifted my right arm overhead and dropped it. As the skylight became a small white dot in a black room, I lifted my left arm over my head. As it started to drop and the white dot became very small, I was gone. A few weeks later all this became the *Black Abstraction*.[4]

Before her surgery, the skylight was O'Keeffe's access to the divine presence. Throughout the history of religions, people sensing that not all space is alike have reached for God in a similar fashion. Some have dreamed of ladders reaching to heaven. One such dreamer cried out,

> What an awesome place this is; surely this is the House of God; and that must be the gate of heaven.[5]

Whether majestic gate or modest skylight, both are versions of the sacred portal that access Hidden Light to one prepared to perceive it.

Hidden Light is the mystical idea of *OR GANUZ*. It is the light of Day One of Creation, and is so uniquely powerful that it obscures the light of the sun.[6] In the thirteenth-century Kabbalistic commentary on the Pentateuch, *The Zohar*, Rabbi Yossi said,

> That light (of Day One) was hidden away, reserved for the just in the world to come, based on the verse, "Light is sown for the just" (Psalm 97.11). R. Yehuda said, it couldn't be completely hidden away, else the world would not exist for a moment. Rather it is hidden away and sown like a seed, which then gives birth and produces seeds and fruits. Every single day a ray of that light shines into the world and keeps everything alive, for with that ray the Holy One, may He be blessed, feeds the world.
>
> And in every place where Torah is studied at night, one thread-thin ray comes out from that hidden light and flows down to those studying. . . . Since the First Day the light has never been fully revealed, but it works in the world. Every day it renews the Act of Creation.[7]

Word, Seed, Light: Psycho-Linguistics, Etymologies, and Relationships

With the dreams that give life to words, and the unconscious fantasies that underlie human speech, psycho-linguistic studies support our intuitive grasp that God and Light are one.[8] The earliest appearance of God as Light, that joyous opening in the dark passageway, is found in *The Sun-God Ascending between Two Mountains* (fig. 8), which is an Akkadian cylinder seal dating around 2800 B.C.E. The proud and regal sun god is in the center of the seal. The three pairs of rays shooting out of each shoulder, celestial rays that become horns of power on his headgear, are his visual identifying marks. His action of stepping out of the dark night between the scalloped mountains also identifies him. In a single godlike giant step, he ascends the mountain and lights up the world. At the same time, flanking him left and right, his stewards roll back the shades of night. This is the unfailing miracle of the daily recreation. At the close of the day, the evening liturgy declares,

Poteah she'arim . . . gollel or mipnay hoshekh veh oshekh mipnay or.

He opens the gates . . . [He] rolls back light before darkness, and darkness before light.

This is the literary-liturgical expression of a much earlier pre-Hebraic visual encounter.

The image of *The Sun-God Ascending Between Two Mountains* is the essence of deity: the body of the god is a central trunk from which emanate the divine functions, in this case, symbolized by three pairs of symmetrical rays. If this was the god of vegetation, his body would produce three pairs of wheat stalks; if the goddess of war, spears; if the god of water, a stream would flow from his shoulders.[9] Such images indicate the primordial recognition of God as a tree, as a Tree of Light, and as a Tree of Life.

The image of the *Sacred Tree* (fig. 7) suggests how the menorah, the seven-branched candlestick envisioned in Exodus 25:31–40, derived both its form and symbolism from the model of the sacred tree in the ancient Near East.[10] The image of the menorah stimulates an "image" of God "who wrapped himself in light as a robe,"[11] a converging of primeval forms of eternal seed and light. For the Hebrew root for menorah, *nur*, means fire.

7. *Sacred Tree. Stone Vase*. Mesopotamia, ca. 3000 B.C.E.

8. *The Sun-God Ascending between Two Mountains* (ca. 2800 B.C.E.;
The Pierpont Morgan Library, New York).

The Tree of Life/Light undergoes another metamorphosis in Proverbs 3:18, where "wisdom [that is, Torah] is a Tree of Life to those who hold fast to it." The carved wooden cylinders on which the Torah scrolls are wrapped are called *atsay chayim*, trees of life.

In Latin, *semen* means the seed of plant as well as the seed of man. In Greek, *sperma* comes from the verb *speiro*, which means to scatter seed, to sow, to spray, to sprinkle, and also, to emit sparks. How does sowing seed become connected with emitting sparks? It comes from the connection with the sowing, engendering, and begetting of children. The Greek verb *spargao* means to be full to bursting, to swell, to be ripe, or to swell with humors. It means that one is full with desire, bursting, and coveting. In Latin, this verb becomes *spargo*, describing the subjective sensation of emitting semen; and in German gives rise to the related words: spring, sprinkle, spray, spark, and speak.[12]

> Behind these words of fertility, discharge, and the rapid rising of new life lies an intensity of emotion invested in the original meaning and repressed. Also, a strange paradox surfaces in those closely related English words sprinkle, spray, and spark. Sprinkle suggests not only the agricultural scattering of seeds but also something fluid. Spark on the other hand, suggests that something fluid is an ignited substance emitted from the body.[13]

Spark was part of the original meaning of scattering seeds.

That there is a visual relationship between plant forms and forms related to fire and light isn't a surprise. There is an acknowledged methodological difficulty as the linguistic evidence presented from Greek and Latin is later than the visual evidence from the Akkadian cylinder seals. However, other evidence attests to the relationship; for example, the Sumerian words *zee* and *izee*, meaning respectively life and fire, are related as are the Egyptian words for seed and word.[14]

The first association between seed and word is through a phallic understanding of the tongue, since the head is the seat not only of intellectual capacity but of human generative power. The word *generate* means to beget in both a physiological and intellectual way. One can generate word and seed. In the Book of Genesis, God creates by speaking, "Let there be . . ." In Egyptian mythology, the god Ptah conceives in thought and creates by commanding speech, with teeth and lips, the creator god, Atum (Totality). In turn, Atum creates Shu and Tefnut, the god of art and the goddess of moisture. But Atum does not create with speech:

> I copulated with my fist, I masturbated with my hand. Then I spewed with my own mouth. I spat out . . . Shu, and I sputtered out . . . Tefnut.[15]

Further, word and seed are related through the Latin words for sow and plant. *Sero* also means to beget, to bring forth, rendering the concept of planting in a *series*, which leads to the Latin word *sermo* and the English word *sermon*. The sower and the speaker perform similar acts whether the words are laid out in orderly discourse or informally scattered in chit-chat. The fantasy of word and seed is expressed through the parables of Jesus, for "the seed is the word of God."[16] The experience of the Christian believer is worded as,

> Being born again, not of corruptible seed, but of incorruptible, by the word of God which lives and abides forever.[17]

The sower sows the word, said Jesus, and the word was "sown in their hearts."[18]

The Sacred Tree

The primacy of the portal image in the human psyche admits the presence of Divine Light breaking through primordial darkness and acquiring the image of God as Tree of Life, as Tree of Light, and as generator of the Divine Word. The psycho-linguistic connection between these seemingly disparate subjects as seed and light and word affirm this imagery. The power of the door as a religious symbol is apparent, but consider that the most prevailing image in that doorway is the tree.

Eliade indicates that the sacred tree is the most widely distributed variant of the symbolism of the center. All sacred trees, natural or artificial, become the cosmic tree at the omphalos of the universe. The sacred tree signifies sanctity in nature, and yields a cluster of symbols embodying the life principle. Three expressions of this tree symbolism are germane to this discussion: the tree as person, the tree as Israel, and the tree as Messiah.[19]

Tree symbolism has a particular appeal in its archetypal imagery. The structure of human experience and imagination is analogous to that of a tree. Human beings are rooted in the threefold structure of the cosmos: heaven, earth, and underworld. The human imagination links us to the luminous world of consciousness as well as to the dark underworld of the unconscious. By drawing nourishment from the heavenly immaterial realm of ideas, human beings are grounded in the material world of sense perception. Like the tree, human beings are subject to cycles of regeneration.

However, the tree is "larger" than human beings are, and so its connection to the generative powers of the divine. Revealed in the tree, God is the source of the hoped-for-life without death which human beings turn to in search of their immortality. Like the portal, the tree becomes a religious symbol since it expresses something beyond itself. The tree as self, and as God, is illustrated by the image of the goddess Isis as a sycamore tree whose breast emerges from the branches to suckle the young Pharoah Thutmose III.[20]

In Frida Kahlo's (1907–54) powerful painting, *My Nurse and I* (1937; Collection of Dolores Olmedo, Mexico City), a nude Indian woman with the calm strong face of a pre-Columbian stone mask suckles Kahlo who has an adult face and a child's body. The lactating transparent breast is filled with flowers whose stems lead out through the nipple.[21] It doesn't matter that these images are separated by three thousand years, their power and authenticity transcend ordinary time.

In another contemporary example, a psychologist indicates that a client undergoing a developmental crisis draws herself as a tree within a womb to envision her rebirth. What is there about the human body that enables the artist and the layperson alike to intuitively express fertility, continuity, and divinity through treelike images within the body? The answer can be found in the anatomical drawings of any proper physiology textbook. There is an *Arbor Vitae*, a tree of life, in the cerebellum and in the cervix. Human lungs have branchi (branches); arms and legs are limbs; kidneys, cardiovascular systems, and nerves are networks of roots and shoots. Human beings record archetypal aborescent images because in fact we *are* trees.

As the individual sees himself or herself as a tree, so in the Hebrew Scriptures, Israel is a tree:

> I will plant them upon their land and they shall never again be plucked up out of the land which I have given them.[22]

> The surviving remnant of the house of Judah shall again take root downward, and bear fruit upward.[23]

> Like the days of a tree shall the days of my people be.[24]

As a corollary to this regrowth of Israel is the restoration of the Davidic throne. The earliest image in Jewish art of the aborescent Messiah is in the Dura-Europos synagogue (244 C.E.).[25] In the reredos is a tree whose roots emanate from the Torah niche and whose crown reaches the feet of the seated messianic king (a mythic composite of Jacob, Judah, and David) flanked by his eleven sons, the two sons of Joseph, and the two scribes. This is the "picture" of restoration as prescribed by the Targum Jonathan,

> Kings and rulers shall not cease . . . nor scribes and teachers of the law from among his descendents.

In Zechariah 4, the lampstand and the tree are combined in a messianic vision,

> The seven lamps are the eyes of Yahweh covering the world . . .
> the two olive trees to the right and left are the two anointed ones,

referring to Zerubabel and Joshua as the restored king and priest. This is the image in a famous manuscript illumination in the fourteenth-century Cervera Bible which preserves the original concept of seed and light forms as imbued with sanctity.[26]

Finally, the Tree of Jesse, a classic prefigure in Christian art, appears for the first time in the twelfth-century miniature from the *Psalter of Henry of Blois* (1140–60; Winchester).[27] The tree graphically springs from the loins of the sleeping Jesse. A crowned King David is the first figure seated in the branches, leading up to Jesus and the Holy Spirit.

> And there shall come forth a shoot from the stock of Jesse and a branch shall flourish from his roots; on him the wisdom of the Lord rests.[28]

The Tree of Life and the Tree of Light both confront the transitory nature of life by giving artistic permanence to plant forms. Both have become symbols of Jewish continuity in their forms as the menorah and as Torah, and are imaged either as flanking or within the sacred portal, the Ark of the Torah. The Tree of Life as Israel's life is rooted in the land of Israel. However, the Tree of Life as Torah was never socially confined. This Tree of Life is a portable *axis mundi*. Its verdant life as a paradoxically portable yet rooted center preserves the viability of the diaspora experience of the Jewish people.

NOTES

1. Rabbi M. Silverman, *The High Holiday Prayer Book* (Hartford: Prayerbook Press, 1951).

2. Rabbi W. Braude and I. Kapstein, *Peskita De Rab Kahan* (Philadelphia: Jewish Publication Society, 1975), p. 435.

3. Mircea Eliade, *The Sacred and the Profane* (New York: Harcourt, Brace, and World, 1959), pp. 25–27, 181; see also B. Goldman, *The Sacred Portal* (Detroit: Wayne State University Press, 1966).

4. Georgia O'Keeffe, *Georgia O'Keeffe* (New York: Viking Press, 1976).

5. Gen. 28:17.

6. The curious fact is that the plain meaning of Gen. 1 reveals that the author(s) fully intended for the Light of Day One to be THE source of the light of the sun and the moon. A close reading discloses that the six days are designed as two pairs of three, and that on the first day of each pair (namely, days 1, 2, 3) the element(s) are created; while on the second day of each pair (days 4, 5, 6) the users of those elements are created. For example, on Day Two, sea and sky are the elements to be used by fish and fowl (created on Day Five). Clearly then, the sun, the moon, and the stars are the USERS of the Light of Day One. They are not the (divine) autonomous sources of their energy. Further corroboration of this polemic is their anonymity. They are called the greater and lesser lights. Were their names to be used, reality would be given to the pagan gods they represent, especially Shamesh, Hebrew for sun.

7. D. Matt, ed. *Zohar, The Book of Enlightenment* (New York: Paulist Press, 1981), p. 52.

8. Th. Thass-Thienemann, *The Interpretation of Language*, 2 vols. (New York: Aronson, 1973), 1:323; 2:159.

As a further example, consider that the Sanskrit root *devi* means bright and is the root for day, divine, and deity. The Sanskrit roots *dyaush, dyu,* and *div* mean sky and day, sometimes called father, *pitar.* Set together these words yield *dyaushpitar,* which becomes *Jupiter,* meaning the great Light-Father. *Dyaush* moves into Latin as both *dies* meaning day and *deus* meaning god.

9. C. Meyers, *The Tabernacle Menorah* (Missoula: Scholars Press, 1976), especially chap. 5, "A Typology of Tree Motifs in Ancient Israel"; and J. B. Pritchard, *Ancient Near East in Pictures* (Princeton: Princeton University Press, 1969), pp. 220–21.

10. See the golden menorah being carried from the Temple during the sack of Jerusalem as inscribed on the Arch of Titus in Rome after 81 c.e.

11. Ps. 104:2.

12. Thass-Thienemann, *The Interpretation of Language*, 1:86–89.

13. Ibid., 1:87.

14. Consultation with Ann Kilmer and Dan Foxvog, Department of Near Eastern Studies, University of California, Berkeley.

15. J. B. Pritchard, *Ancient Near Eastern Texts* (Princeton: Princeton University Press, 1950), pp. 5–6.

16. Luke 8:11.

17. Pet. 1:23.

18. Mark 4:14–15.

19. K. Bolander, *Assessing Personality through Tree Drawings* (New York: Basic Books, 1977).

20. Tomb painting in Thebes, sixteenth to the fourteenth centuries B.C.E. The sycamore fig which exudes a sticky fluid and generates long aerial roots is associated with the fertility of both sexes; see R. Cook, *The Tree of Life* (London: Thames and Hudson, 1974), pp. 8–9, 42–43.

21. Lucy Lippard, *Overlay, Contemporary Art and the Art of Prehistory* (New York: Pantheon Books, 1983), pp. 47–49.

22. Amos 9:15.

23. Isa. 37:31 = 2 Kings 19:30.

24. Isa. 65:22.

25. Erwin R. Goodenough, *Jewish Symbols in the Greco-Roman Period*, Volumes 9–11, *Symbolism in the Dura Synagogue* (Princeton: Princeton University Press, 1964).

26. B. Narkiss, *Hebrew Illuminated Manuscripts* (Jerusalem: Keter, 1969), pp. 52–53.

27. Cook, *The Tree of Life*, p. 85.

28. Isa. 11:1.

5

The Art of Marc Chagall:
An Interpretation of Scripture

STEPHEN BRECK REID

Hans-Georg Gadamer's view of aesthetics as hermeneutics is a difficult concept to teach to students.[1] His point that Being speaks in both the work of art and the work of literature is problematic to present in a way that engages students.[2] This is a pedagogical problem.

The solution to this problem is twofold. The first step is to point out the procedural similarities between art and literary criticism. The second step is to explore how Being is expressed in the analysis of a work of art or literature. The methodological objective is for the student to be able to interpret the similarities between biblical exegesis as a form of literary criticism and the interpretation of Scripture through art criticism.

The lecture which follows is on the art of Marc Chagall (1887–1985). The similarities between art and literary criticism, and their relationship to scriptural exegesis will enable students to interpret other paintings by Chagall (and other artists) in a similar manner.

This lecture is presented in an advanced undergraduate course in literary scriptural criticism. It is also applicable to advanced humanities courses. Familiarity with biblical literature is assumed. The interpretation of scriptural texts is similar to the interpretation of visual art. The demonstration of the methodological and philosophic points of connection demonstrates the cross fertilization between art and literary criticism, and their application to scriptural studies.

The power and potential for using Chagall's art to teach scriptural interpretation as both aesthetics and literary criticism is presented in this lecture. His art indicates the reflexive and reciprocal relationship between the scriptural text and its interpretation in the visual arts. The text shapes the visual art and the visual art reshapes the interpretation of the text. In this way, Chagall's paintings offer a significant context for scriptural interpretation.

This analysis of Chagall's paintings is similar to the exegetical process. The decisions that Chagall made in the construction of his paintings exemplify and embody scriptural interpretation. The reflection of appropriate questions in the analysis of Chagall's art and in his interpretation of Scripture will be the vehicles for clarifying the nature of scriptural exegesis and hermeneutics.

Exegesis of Art

The term *exegesis* comes from the Greek "to lead" or "explain." Therefore one way to understand exegesis is to ask central questions that move toward an understanding of a work of art whether it is visual or textual. The list of questions vary according to the interpreter. This list has been devised to clarify the similarities between art analysis and traditional exegesis.[3]

For Scripture scholars from the Enlightenment through Friedrich Schleiermacher and Wilhelm Dilthey, exegesis was the recapitulation of experience. This experiential emphasis enables the viewer to revision the work of art. This revision unleashed *anamnesis,* the recollection and reexperience of the work of art by the first viewers. This revisioning of the work of art is a catalyst for the transformative elements that determine religious art.[4]

An explanation of the constitutive elements of a work of art is required. Joshua C. Taylor's discussion of "expressive content" is helpful:

> it might be useful to adopt the term "expressive content" to describe that unique fusion of subject matter and specific visual form which characterizes the particular work of art. "Subject matter," then, would be the objects and the incidents represented; "expressive content" would refer to the combined effect of subject matter and visual form.[5]

Exegetes must examine visual form and subject matter before constructing an interpretation that might be called "expressive content" of the work of art or literature.

The similarities between art and literary analysis begin with a recognition of limitations. Truth is beyond method. While exegetes strive to find appropriate methods, the methods do not assure the revelation of truth.

The Central Questions of Analysis

Basically there are two styles of questions. The first style is that which deals with the analysis of visual form. The second style treats the execution of the project using symbols. These two styles complement each other.

Analysis of visual form is analogous to the analysis of genre in form criticism. The premise is that types or forms, whether they be literary or visual, bring to the situation of experience their own logic that must be accommodated by the artist or the writer. The interpreter must be attentive to the form of the work of art. The interpreter is a sculptor of meaning and must be able to go beyond the artist's vision once a particular form or medium has been chosen.

For example, in English literature when a poet decides to write a sonnet there are constraints presented by the genre of a sonnet, namely, fourteen lines in iambic pentameter with a specific rhyme scheme. A similar rubric can be seen in prophetic vision such as Isaiah 6:1–13 or Ezekiel 1:1–3:27. In visual art, there is the relationship between the visual form and the media; so an oil painting has certain qualities that are different from those of a watercolor. The visual form and the media must be examined. To ask questions about visual form is similar to those about genre in literary analysis.

Form criticism maintains that there is a relationship between the genre and the use of the text. In visual art, the relationship between visual form and its utilization should be considered. Such relationships are important in analyzing and studying the art of Marc Chagall. He worked in stained glass, tapestry, mosaics, oil, and watercolor; and used each of these media as he worked with varied scriptural themes. Each of these media and their visual forms has its own integrity. While it is possible to use each of these to reconstruct Chagall's scriptural interpretations, it would be a mistake to fuse them without sufficient attention to their individual characteristics as expressive of scriptural interpretation. These varied media independently shape the expressive content of each work of art, and can be said to reflect Chagall's method of scriptural interpretation.

Chagall's painting *Moses before the Burning Bush* (n.d.; Musée National Message Biblique Marc-Chagall, Nice; fig. 9) will be carefully examined. The fact that this is an oil painting introduces the significance of texture(s) into the analysis. However, the designation of genre does not end with the statement that this is an oil painting.

Genre is related to matters of function which can be represented in two ways. First is the issue of whether Chagall's painting is scriptural interpretation or scriptural illustration.

> The paintings are not, however, mere illustrations of the book, [the Bible], selected episodes that guide us from a beginning to an end. Chagall is not Gustave Doré, he does not use the Bible as a pretext to make illustrations. The Biblical Message reflects a certain number of choices within the rich biblical material, but the choices are independent from the narrative and exist on their own. These notions of cycle and choice must be examined before any in-depth discussion of the Biblical Message can be undertaken.[6]

The distinction between scriptural interpretation and scriptural illustration is an important one. Provoyeur has mistakenly proposed the dichotomy of dependent and independent. Rather, the issue is the reader's response to the complexity of the text, its polyvalent quality, namely, that there is a constellation of meanings in a particular text. Scriptural illustration like bad exegesis seeks to take the complexity of the text and simplify it by generating a single meaning. Provoyeur's metaphor "from a beginning to an end" is appropriate. Scriptural interpretations as exegetical works are successful, whether they be literary or visual, if they refrain from simplifying the scriptural text. Therefore, it is significant that the viewer of Chagall's art be aware that this is interpretation and not illustration. The genre of *Moses before the Burning Bush* is a scriptural interpretation depicted in an oil painting.

There is a relation of the form and the function. Hence the examination of form or genre does not end there. The form process is more complex. Once this painting was designated as scriptural interpretation, the form of this work of art is identified to some degree. The function of this work of art is understood when one enters the Musée National Message Biblique Marc-Chagall. This painting is undated, and cannot be documented as contemporary to the building of the museum. Its size (two by three meters) is too large for the typical living room. This presupposes a gallery or museum as the intended setting. The specific size of this painting approximates that of many of the other paintings in the Musée. Its function as a part of the Musée and as scriptural interpretation establishes a field of meaning that must be considered in an analysis of Chagall's paintings.

Analysis of the Visual Technique

It is not enough to determine merely the genre of a painting. The particulars of technique must also be analyzed. In the analysis of scriptural texts, these are referred to as rhetorical criticisms. They have their counterparts in the analysis of the execution of technique in a given work of art. Chiasm, rhetorical questions, and other literary devices have their counterparts in color, perspective, and composition in visual art. This analysis will proceed with these three criteria as a way into the rhetoric of this painting.

Any discussion of color has three components: hue, saturation, and value.[7] There are five colors in *Moses before the Burning Bush:* yellow, blue, green, red, and white. The tone of this painting is set by the dominant primary color, blue. The function of the blue is to point back to the sense of chaos as in blue water. Water and blue are symbolic of potential crisis. Water can give life or bring death. The community of faith is depicted as blue. At least two-thirds of this painting is blue.

The other primary colors, yellow and red, establish relationships within the painting. The parentheses of red and yellow contain the angel that comes from the burning bush. This focal point informs Chagall's interpretation of this story. Yellow represents the numinous. It encircles Being (or the being) coming out of the bush and the face of Moses before the Torah, tablets of commandments. The latter represents Chagall's rendering of Exodus 34:35, "rays of light came from the face of Moses," (*ci qaran 'or pene Mose*).

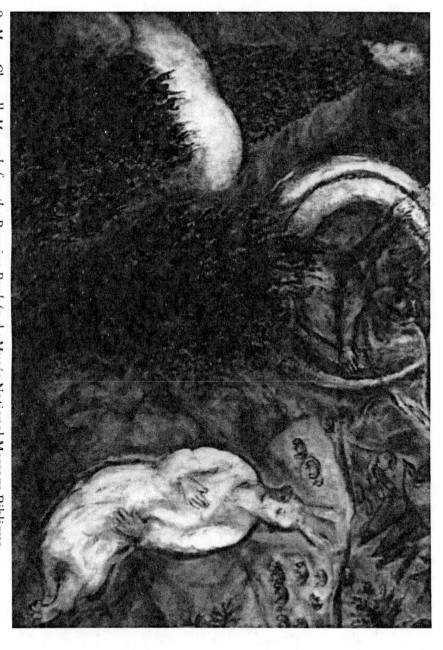

9. Marc Chagall, *Moses before the Burning Bush* (n.d.; Musée National Message Biblique Marc-Chagall, Nice).

The secondary colors signify relationships: the green in the upper part of the painting represents the realm of the divine. It is interesting that yellow (the numinous) and blue (the human) come together to form green (the divine realm). The significance of green is confirmed as Being (as green) emerges from the bush.

The aspect of exegesis called tradition history has its counterpart in symbolic analysis in visual art. Once again the rules of art criticism, literary analysis, and scriptural exegesis are similar. There is a consensus that the nature of a given work of art determines what methods should be used in its interpretation.

In this painting, there are ten symbols which frame five sets of relationships. The painting's central focus is the burning bush itself. At the same time, the painting moves from the right to the left as the storyline is created. The movement from right to left returns the viewer to the center as the focal point of the scriptural story. This is a clear example of art as midrash, the prescientific existential interpretation of Scripture.

On the edge of the painting are two symbols which are difficult to decipher. Aaron is on the lower right side. He is paralleled by the fishes on the lower left side. Aaron is in full ceremonial dress even though his clothing as depicted here is not legislated until later in the Book of Exodus 28:1-43.

Above the image of Aaron, some animals graze on the hillside and reach toward heaven. These animals may represent the sheep that Moses was tending in Exodus 3. In his green heaven, there are the typical Chagall birds. It is difficult to determine whether Chagall is making a theological statement or this is simply artistic whimsy.

Moses is the major figurative symbol to the right of the burning bush (Fig. 10). This figurative symbol is related to the bush as well as to the depiction of Moses on the left side of the bush. The dual representation of Moses implies his transformation as described in Scripture.

The transformed Moses is in the upper left corner. In order to understand the significance of the transformed Moses, the symbolism of the community must be explained. The people of God, the community, are in blue. The people of God are the same color as the earth. They are contrasted to the Egyptians who are depicted in red. They are separated by the white foam of the Reed Sea.[8] A less

10. Detail of Moses from Marc Chagall, *Moses before the Burning Bush*
(n.d.; Musée National Message Biblique Marc-Chagall, Nice).

saturated color rendering of this scene is in Chagall's watercolor *The Israelites Crossing the Red Sea* (1931; Musée National Message Biblique Marc-Chagall, Nice). The color qualities allowed by the medium of oil paint enabled him to depict the distinction and the conflict by the intensity of color symbolism.

The transformed Moses is a face, his body being the people of God, reflecting on the tablets of the Torah. This is a cryptic reference to and midrash on the end of the Book of Deuteronomy 34. Moses does not enter the promised land, but he is resurrected in the community and thereby experiences the promised land. Chagall has used this traditional symbol to reshape the interpretation of the story of the burning bush (Exodus 3). Here the story is not framed within the limits of that single chapter, but extends into the entire Pentateuch through the Book of Deuteronomy.

The center of the painting is the burning bush and the angel. Moses as the leader of the people and as the representative of the people passes through the experience of the burning bush into a new and transformed life. The angel is equated with the burning bush. As a historical particular gives way to the angel, the burning bush is timeless. The angel is a familiar Chagall symbol. A literary analysis of Exodus 3 would maintain that the experience of Moses becomes paradigmatic for the believer as well as a part of the tradition of the believing community.

Methodological Limitations

Any process of analysis has certain limitations. Literary criticism deals with written texts. The medium of these texts is language, for example, Hebrew, Greek, or Aramaic. Often the reader studies these texts in translation. However, translation is like kissing through a screen door. Similarly, our contact with the art of Marc Chagall usually comes from reproductions in art books. These two forms of criticism share analogous limitations: the critic often is not able to read the text in the original language or view the actual work of art.

These limitations lead to the temptation to focus on the author as a way of discerning the meaning of the work. However, Chagall did not provide a commentary on his art. Such a preoccupation does not collaborate with the artistic project; rather, it moves at cross purposes.[9]

Conclusion

The similarities between literary criticism and art criticism are manifold. Both try to recover an original experience of the work of art that will generate a transformation for the viewer or the reader. One path toward transformation through a work of art or of literature is the collaboration of the expressive content and the subject matter. Literary or art criticism also maintains such distinctions without losing the collaboration.

The task is completed by analyzing several central questions. One central question is that of form. This may be compared to the process of form criticism. The genre of oil paint or watercolor is not a sufficient response as there is the generic difference between scriptural interpretation and scriptural illustration. A second question is that of the technique applied in the work of art. In scriptural exegesis, this is called rhetorical criticism. The rhetoric of a painting involves both color and symbols in much the same way that the work of literature involves words and metaphor.

The similarities found in the limitations of analysis represent a useful point of comparison between art and literary criticism. The limitation of photographs of paintings is similar to the limitation of scriptural criticism without benefit of the scriptural languages. Each of these similarities demonstrates an analogous attempt to establish a sense of meaning in the encounter with the work of art or of literature. Art and literary criticism are similar in that they strive to be vehicles in collaboration as literature interprets the visual world; and visual art interprets the Scriptures through the art of Marc Chagall.

NOTES

1. Hans-Georg Gadamer, *Truth and Method* (London: Sheed and Ward, 1975).
2. See also Robert Palmer, *Hermeneutics. Interpretation Theory in Schleiermacher, Dilthey, Heidegger, and Gadamer* (Evanston: Northwestern University Press, 1969), pp. 169–71.
3. The terms *exegesis* and *literary analysis* will be used interchangeably throughout this essay.
4. Doug Adams, "Theological Expression Through Visual Art Forms," in *Art, Creativity, and the Sacred*, ed. Diane Apostolos-Cappadona (New York: Crossroad Publishing Co., 1984), pp. 311–18.
5. Joshua C. Taylor, *Learning to Look. A Handbook for the Visual Arts* (Chicago: University of Chicago Press, 1957), p. 43.
6. P. Provoyeur, *Marc Chagall. Biblical Interpretations* (New York: Alpine Fine Arts Collection, 1983), p. 19.

7. Taylor, *Learning to Look*, p. 61.

8. The Reed Sea is often mistranslated as the Red Sea. The Hebrew text reads *yam sup*, "sea of reeds."

9. Michel Foucault, "What is an Author?" in P. Rabinow, *The Foucault Reader* (New York: Pantheon Books, 1984), pp. 101–20.

6

"The Lord has struck him down by the hand of a woman!" Images of Judith

DIANE APOSTOLOS-CAPPADONA

"The Image of the Jewish Woman in the Arts" is an undergraduate seminar in which students are exposed to the interdisciplinary methodology of religion and the arts, and to the comparative approaches of art history, Judaic studies (including history, law, and literature), music history and theory, and women's studies. Interdisciplinary seminars such as "The Image of the Jewish Woman in the Arts" allow students to explore the essentially unmapped territory of interdisciplinary scholarship, and to create an opportunity for clarification of traditional disciplines and methodologies (e.g., art history vs. religion and the arts).

Guest lectures by scholars in those fields suggest the multiple ways of approaching and analyzing a single question: Whether or not there is an identifiable way of representing the Jewish woman in the arts? The central question of the seminar is complicated by traditional prejudice against visual modality in Judaism. Examinations of the imaging process in Hebrew, Jewish, and Jewish-American literature, and in Western music suggests an analogue for those identifiable visual representations of Jewish women.

The essay which follows serves as the introductory lecture for this seminar. Through an examination of the image of Judith in Western Christian art, it raises the central questions of the seminar: (1) Is there an identifiable way of representing the Jewish woman in the arts that sets her apart from other women; and, (2) if so, what does that visual differentiation mean to Jewish women, to Judaism, to women in general, and to Western culture?

Even though there are numerable visual examples of the image of Judith in Jewish art, my interest is in the way that Western Christian artists have imaged her, and what that imaging indicates about the relationship between Christianity and Judaism, and about the Christian understanding of the Jewish woman in particular and women in general.[1]

The well-known story of the beautiful widow Judith who saves the city of Bethulia from the army of Holofernes has intrigued and fascinated painters, sculptors, poets, writers, and composers for centuries. Some of the fascination with the story of Judith has to do with the fact that the traditional story of the beautiful damsel in distress has been inverted. In the story of Judith, it is the beautiful damsel who saves the day and the city when everyone else has failed.

The story of Judith was written around the turn of the second century B.C.E. in Palestine. As the champion of her people, this heroine's very name means "Jewess." In every way, she becomes symbolic of and for the faith of the Jewish people. Judith is a beautiful and irreproachable young widow who has faithfully mourned her husband, Manasseh, for three years and four months. She has followed the proscribed rites for a pious widow: wearing only sackcloth and weeds, fasting continuously, and never leaving her house.[2]

The city of Bethulia is under siege from the Assyrian general Holofernes, who wishes to conquer the city for his lord, Nebuchadnezzar. Beyond the siege itself, Bethulia suffers from a prolonged drought. The elders have therefore decided to surrender to Holofernes within five days time unless God intervenes to save them. Judith confronts the elders, upbraids them for their cowardice and lack of faith in God. She announces a secret plan by which she will save the city and sends the elders away to pray.

After a long and ardent prayer for the destruction of Israel's enemies and the victory of her God, Judith prepares to put her secret plan into action.[3] She returns to her home, reenters the room set aside for feastdays, and prepares herself to meet Holofernes. She bathes and anoints her body, and dresses in her finest clothing and jewelry.[4] Judith then prepares a sack full of festival foods. Then she and her maid depart Bethulia to confront Holofernes.

As she enters the enemy camp, Judith's beauty astonishes the soldiers who point out the way to Holofernes' tent. "Who could despise a people having women like this?"[5] The soldier's comment is more than meaningful for Judith will come to embody and symbolize the nation as well as the faith of Israel. As she enters Holofernes' tent, Judith falls on her face to do obeisance to him.

Pledging her loyalty to Nebuchadnezzar, Judith seduces Holofernes with her flattery and her beauty. She offers him a secret plan to conquer Bethulia. She tells him, "God has sent me to do things with you at which the world will be astonished."[6] Completely charmed by Judith, Holofernes invites her to drink and eat with him. But Judith must refuse as she must keep her dietary rules. She spends three days in a tent near to Holofernes, and finally he invites her to a banquet.[7]

The sight of Judith arrayed in her "feminine adornments" overwhelms Holofernes. He is determined to seduce her.[8] As the evening progresses, Holofernes proceeds to drink himself into a stupor. At this point in the story, Judith and her maid are alone with Holofernes in his tent. Judith sends her maid from the tent, prays to God for strength, and cuts off Holofernes' head with his own sword. She places his head in the sack in which she had carried the ritual foods. She and her maid then depart the enemy camp without raising any suspicion, as every evening she ventured forth to pray.

Once she returns to Bethulia, Judith displays Holofernes' head and calls the Jews to prayer. She cries, "Praise God! Praise him! The Lord has struck him down by the hand of a woman!"[9] She announces her innocence and her unstinting faith in God. The Israelite army proceeds to massacre the now leaderless Assyrian army. And Judith is praised as the deliverer of her people.

Judith: Basic Symbolism and Imagery

The basic symbolism present in visual representations of Judith are the sword of Holofernes (sometimes a scimitar), the sack, the head of Holofernes, and her maidservant. Judith is usually dressed in fine clothes and jewelry, and is normally represented as a beautiful young woman. There is no iconographic pattern for either the color(s) of her clothing or her hair.[10]

In paintings and sculptures of Judith, there are a series of visual references to other scriptural figures. The most significant and obvious visual reference is in terms of the importance of hair. Hair is symbolic of energy and power. And in the majority of representations of Judith, she holds Holofernes' head by his hair never touching his face or his neck. This visual reference has two immediate connections: the story of Samson and Delilah, and the story of David and Goliath. The connection to Delilah is obvious—just as Delilah destroyed Samson's strength by cutting off his hair, Judith removed the strength of Holofernes' army by cutting off his head and holding it by his hair. The connection to David is both visual and scriptural. In many representations of David and Goliath, David is shown holding the severed head of Goliath by the hair.[11] And of course, both Judith and David become popular symbols of freedom against tyranny and the liberation of the city in the Renaissance.

Another visual and scriptural reference to the story of Judith that should be considered is the inversion of her story: the story of Salome and John the Baptist.[12] Although the actual scriptural passage is brief, the connections between Judith and Salome have long been recognized by visual artists. Salome, the young and beautiful daughter of Herodias, seduces her stepfather by her dancing in order to satisfy her mother's desire to have the prophet, John the Baptist, silenced. The relating of the young Salome who has the Baptist beheaded and the beautiful Judith who herself beheads Holofernes is obvious. The inversion of the story of the moral and virtuous woman who saves her people and justifies her faith through such a gruesome deed to that of the sensuous and amoral . woman satiated by this gruesome deed symbolizes in its own way the two traditional perceptions of *woman* in Western culture: the idealization of virtue and the personification of vice.

Judith becomes not only for the Jews but later for the Christians a symbol of faith, chastity, and virtue. The fact that she is a woman is not ignored, but rather enhances her story, her faith, and what she comes to symbolize in Western art. And as Western history unfolds, Judith becomes more than a religious symbol—a cultural symbol for freedom, democracy, and liberty.

But for Christian artists and theologians, Judith's triumph is an antetype of Mary's triumph over the devil. Both of these noble women remain chaste despite their acts of seduction (Judith) and motherhood (Mary). Judith destroys Israel's, and therefore God's, enemies by decapitating the enemy general, while Mary destroys evil by crushing the head of the serpent. Judith becomes a symbol of salvation as her chastity, piety, and faithfulness highlight her symbolic relationship to Mary the Virgin Mother.[13] And in this regard, Judith finds her place in writings of the church fathers like Jerome, and in medieval Christian texts like the *Speculum Humanae Salvationis*. It is through this typology that Judith enters Western Christian painting and sculpture.

The earliest representation of Judith in Christian art is probably found in the Bible of San Paolo fuori le Mura (ninth century, Rome). And images of Judith in medieval Christian art range from several episodes depicted in the arches of the north portal of Chartres Cathedral (thirteenth century, Chartres) to the stained-glass window in La Sainte-Chapelle, Paris.

In Italian Renaissance art, Judith comes into her own. Almost every major Italian Renaissance artist from Sandro Botticelli (ca. 1445–1510) to Michelangelo Buonarroti (1475–1564) portrays the story of Judith. Perhaps the most famous Renaissance representation of Judith is the bronze sculpture by Donatello (ca. 1386–1466). His *Judith and Holofernes* (1455–57; Piazza della Signoria, Florence) is a classic presentation of Judith as the virtuous woman who for patriotic and religious reasons causes the downfall of a powerful man. Here is a matronly and humble Judith who is about to cut off the head of the man seated at her feet. Judith's humility and chastity are symbolized by the simplicity of her dress and the veil which covers her head (signifying her status as a married woman and her piety). Donatello's *Judith* however signifies civic virtue more than she does Christian piety. As such she represents the City of Florence which saw itself as both the "new Athens" and the conscious symbol of freedom and liberty. Like David, Judith becomes an important scriptural reference for civic and political virtues during the Renaissance.

More typical Renaissance images of Judith represent her as a beautiful and richly adorned young woman who stands almost distant from the gruesome act she has just committed.[14] Renaissance artists like Botticelli and Michelangelo paint the episode either of Judith's placing the head of Holofernes in the foodsack or the return of Judith and her maid with the head of Holofernes. Judith usually stands separate from the action facing the viewer as she

holds the sword of Holofernes in her right hand and places his severed head into the foodsack with her left hand. Her maid who is
holding the foodsack grimaces with disgust. Judith however appears placid and aloof, as if she recognizes the she is not there to
participate in the act of Holofernes' death, but is rather an object
of adoration of female beauty and of admiration of the *noble* heroine by Renaissance artists.

It is in Italian Baroque art that Judith becomes a provocative
and powerful visual image in Christian art. This is the time of the
Reformation and Counter-Reformation, and thus religious tensions and artistic innovations ran in tandem. Like other figures
from the Hebrew Scriptures, Judith finds a renewed and inspired
role in Christian iconography. For the artists of the Protestant
Reformation like Hans Baldung Grien (1484/5–1545), Conrad Meit
(d. 1544), and Jan Sanders van Hemessen (1500–1555), Judith
comes to represent virtue personified. Whereas for artists of the
Roman Catholic tradition like Michelangelo Merisi da Caravaggio
(1571–1610), Orazio Gentileschi (1563–1639) and Peter Paul Rubens (1577–1640), Judith symbolizes salvation through works
tempered by faith. Her act of killing Holofernes, no matter how
gruesomely portrayed, is motivated not by personal lust or for personal gain but out of the depth of her faith in God and her devotion
to God's chosen people.

Italian Baroque artists come to image Judith in the act of cutting
off Holofernes' head.[15] Her maidservant is sometimes present and
turns her head away from the grisly act. The Judith of Italian Baroque art is engaged in the action of slaying Holofernes just as the
Judith of the Italian Renaissance was aloof from her action. The
Baroque was a period of decisive action when one stood clearly on
one side of the religious argument or the other. It was not the time
of contemplation that the Renaissance had been. And the images of
Judith by the artists of both periods clearly reflect this difference
in attitude and posture.

Perhaps the most famous Italian Baroque interpretations of Judith are those painted by Artemesia Gentileschi (ca. 1597–1651/3).
The daughter of the painter, Orazio Gentileschi, Artemesia is one
of the followers of Michelangelo Merisi da Caravaggio. Her paintings of Judith clearly represent her Caravaggesque tendencies toward realism, chiaroscuro (dramatic baroque lighting) and "the

moment of truth." Her skillful and dramatic renderings of the Judith story are accented by the fact that art for the artist becomes autobiography.[16] Artemesia's violent and gruesome paintings of the beheading of Holofernes have been critiqued as the most ferocious and shocking visual representations of this scene. These images are doubly shocking as they come from the hand of a woman. But they come from the hand of a woman who was raped and later further humiliated during her testimony against her violator. Her paintings of the Judith story can be interpreted as a way not simply of "banishing the demons" but also as Artemesia's way of reestablishing her own sense of self.[17]

The art of the artists of the seventeenth and eighteenth centuries became increasingly secular in content. And just as authenticity and inspiration fell away from Christian art in general, so the representations of Judith became few and far between. Interesting images of Judith were painted by Francesco Solimena (1657–1747) (in which Judith symbolizes the propriety of *regio de statio*), Elisabetta Sirani (1638–65), Bernardo Cavallino (1618–56), and Simon Vouet (1590–1649). The theme of Judith was renewed in Austrian art circles by symbolic identification with Empress Maria Theresa (1740–80), who was symbolized as a contemporary Judith standing up to the new Holofernes, Frederick the Great of Prussia (1740–86).

With the beginning of the nineteenth century and its pluralistic styles of art and philosophy, the image of Judith is retrieved by artists in both a secular and sacred fashion. Of course Eugène Delacroix's (1798–1863) romantic interpretations of *Liberty Leading the People* (1830; Louvre, Paris) and *Greece Dying on the Ruins of Missolonghi* (1826; Musée des Beaux Arts, Bordeaux) are related to interpretations of "woman" as liberty, democracy, freedom, and nation, and thus to the earliest images (verbal and visual) of Judith as the deliverer of her people.

With development of the *femme fatale* in nineteenth-century literature and art, Judith like other women from Scripture and history including Mary Magdalene, Cleopatra, and Salome become imaged as exemplars of female eroticism. From the academic images that William Etty (1787–1849) exhibited at the Royal Academy in 1827 to 1831 to the oil sketches of James Ensor (1860–1949) to the eroticism of Gustav Klimt's (1862–1918) paintings at the turn of the century, the Judith image emerges in multiple transformations in Western art.

In the early part of the twentieth century, Judith was represented in a series of controversial drawings by Thomas Theodor Heine (1867–1948), which were illustrations for Friedrich Hebbel's play, Judith (1908), and also by Frederick von Stuck (1863–1928). And more recently, Judy Chicago (b. 1939) created a Judith Plate for The Dinner Party (1979; Collection of the artist). And choreographer Martha Graham (b. 1895) has created three dances interpreting Judith's story from her solo work (1950) to Legend of Judith (1963) to Judith (1963). Still photographs of these dances are works of art in their own right. In her "secularized" imagery as the armed maiden whose virtue triumphs over tyranny, the Judith type has journeyed through the twentieth century as Wonder Woman and Princess Leia Organa, among other heroines of popular culture.[18]

Judith's journey through Western Christian art has seen her characterized as a prefigure of Mary, as virtue triumphant over lust, as a humble matron, as civic virtue, as faith triumphant, as object of male admiration, as lady liberty, as artist's alter ego, as armed maiden, and as femme fatale. In this journey, Judith has encompassed through the imaging process the fullness of the female experience with the single exception of motherhood.

Judith: Renaissance and Modern Interpretations

Perhaps one of the clearest ways to understand and critique the image of Judith in terms of its relationship to the central questions of this seminar is to carefully compare and contrast two historically distinctive images of Judith. In this case, comparative analysis will focus on a typical Renaissance interpretation, Andrea Mantegna's (ca. 1431–1506) Judith and Holofernes (ca. 1495; National Gallery of Art, Washington, D.C.; fig. 11), and a typical modern interpretation, Klimt's Judith I/Judith and Holofernes (1901; Österreichische Galerie, Vienna; fig. 12).

Mantegna's image of Judith is typically Renaissance. This is the beautiful and virtuous young widow who stands with her maidservant within the tent of the now dead Holofernes. Dressed in classical Greek garments, Judith is decently covered yet seductive

11. Andrea Mantegna, *Judith and Holofernes* (ca. 1495; The National Gallery of Art, Washington, D.C.).

in both her dress and her demeanor. At the same time, she is calm and composed as she places the severed head of Holofernes into the foodsack held by her maid who grimaces in disgust. But Judith in typical Renaissance fashion is almost contemplative in her aloofness. Here is a Judith who is the object of admiration and adoration both for her beauty and her action.

The grisly act of Holofernes' beheading is almost lost to those viewers who concentrate their gaze upon Judith. In following the diagonal which begins with the maid's bent right knee up toward Judith's sword (which is paralleled by Holofernes' head), the viewer's eye reaches the pinned-back right corner of the tent and spies the bare foot of Holofernes lying on his bed. Mantegna's genius takes over as the viewer recognizes the subtle but careful and intricate details throughout this small painting. The crumbling floor of Holofernes' tent signifies the destruction of the Assyrian army. The shape of Judith's sword is distinct, neither pointed nor curved but either blunted or squared off, or else broken.[19] If it is broken, it is perhaps logical to suggest that the act of severing Holofernes' neck was so violent that the sword broke during one of two strokes it took Judith to complete her bloody deed.

The image of Judith stands in the center of the painting as if to indicate not only her central position in the story but in this act. Her central position is emphasized by the visual parallel of the tent's central pillar (which is compositionally off center), which symbolizes that which is simultaneously the orientation point of the tent and the central support of the canopy. Mantegna paints his Judith in classical Greek garments of blue and white. Her blue cloak is dramatically wrapped around her right arm and the lower portion of her body, emphasizing both her pelvic area and her bent right knee which parallels the bent left knee of her maidservant. The pyramidal shape which is formed between these two bent knees with the pleats of Judith's cloak and the pose of her sword lead the viewer's eye first to the head of Holofernes with its back turned away from the viewer, signifying an end, and then to the face of Judith which is turned to the left as she stares into the future beyond the bounds of the painting.

And when the viewer's eye rests on Judith's face, one understands the powerful influence of Greek and Roman art on the artists of the Renaissance. The classical head which Mantegna has painted on Judith echoes her metaphoric relationship to Pallas Athena who was both the protectress of Athens, and the goddess of wisdom and war.[20] Even the pose that Judith affects is classical and sculptural both in position and execution. In this way, Mantegna has made a series of visual references to his interpretation of Judith, relating her to classical Greek virtues and spirituality in keeping with the Renaissance temperament, and not to a traditional Hebraic context. There is nothing in Judith's demeanor, dress, or physical presentation to indicate her "Jewishness." The only possible connection to "Jewishness" is that the painting is entitled *Judith and Holofernes,* thus creating a link to the apocryphal story of the Book of Judith.

From this painting, the viewer can infer several things about the Renaissance and about the position of woman in the Renaissance world. First of all, one recognizes the influence of the classical world upon the Renaissance and its art. Second, one realizes the importance of sculpture in the Renaissance aesthetic, both in the influence of sculpture on Renaissance art in general and the central place of sculpture among the great Renaissance artists who were either inspired by individual sculptural works or by the concept of sculpture. Third, the image of Judith suggests the passive demeanor expected of women who were objects to be seen, admired, and perhaps adored and respected. Even though Judith is an active character in this story, she appears in this representation to be "divorced" from the act of the action and "posed" within its context. And finally, the viewer recognizes the interest and importance that Renaissance artists placed not merely on the subtlety of details but upon the symbolic import of those details.

On the other hand, Klimt's interpretations of Judith suggest modern fascination with the destructive and seductive natures of female personality. His *Judith I* is a typical representation of Judith as *femme fatale.* As opposed to Mantegna's representation of the scene within Holofernes' tent, which includes the presence of the maid, Klimt centers his attention solely on Judith and the head of Holofernes.

His Judith is the height of sensuality, from the pose of her body to her revealing garments and her facial expression. Even the way this Judith caresses rather than holds the severed head of Holofernes is distinctively different from earlier versions of Judith. The diaphanous lavender and gold garment she wears clearly exposes one breast and suggestively covers the other. The thick gold collar and arm band heighten the erotic quality of the figure of Judith. The lavender highlights in her exposed torso and facial flesh accent the overall sensuality of the painting by juxtaposing the coolness of purple tonalities with the warmth of flesh and gold tones. The lavender accents in Judith's flesh are reminiscent of the lavender-blue tonalities John Singer Sargent (1856–1925) painted earlier in the flesh of *Madame X* (1884; Metropolitan Museum of Art, New York). Perhaps, the most famous *femme fatale* of her day, *Madame X* was a scandalous painting which reeked of the erotic and the sensual. Judith's facial expression with her partially closed eyes and slightly open mouth, and the tilted back position of her head heighten the sense of orgasmic vitality of this painting.

In a typical nineteenth-century fashion, Klimt has given an exotic aura to the painting by the "oriental" costume on Judith, her jewelry, and the background screen. And in both this decorative mode and the erotic character of the painting and of Judith's person, Klimt clearly conflates the image of Judith with that of Salome. In fact, in a later version titled *Judith II/Salome* (1909; Galerie d'Arte Moderne, Venice), Klimt extends the conflation not only to the title itself, but to the evil and destructive quality of the almost demonic *Judith II/Salome* whose clawlike hands grip the severed head of Holofernes by the hair. This later version focuses more on the evil and destructive nature of the feminine, whereas *Judith I* clearly emphasizes the sensual and the erotic.

Of course the viewer must recognize that just as Mantegna's *Judith and Holofernes* reflects the Renaissance, so Klimt's *Judith I* reflects turn-of-the-century Vienna. The sense of imminent destruction, the exaltation of the sensual, the interest in the exotic, and emphasis on the decorative combine with the atmosphere of Freudian discoveries. Klimt's painting is also completed many years after the emancipation of the Jews in Western Europe and after the French Revolution. These two historical factors greatly influence the representation of the Jewish woman in the arts, including music and theater as well as painting and sculpture.

From Klimt's *Judith I*, the viewer can suggest several factors about the modern interpretation of religion and of women in Western culture. First and foremost, the role of women is clearly seen as

12. Gustav Klimt, *Judith and Holofernes*
(1901; Österreichische Galerie, Vienna).

sexual object. She is an active and aggressive sexual creature. In his emphasis on the sensual and erotic in *Judith I*, Klimt suggests an interpretation of Judith as a castrating female—not in the act of physically castrating Holofernes—but rather in terms of "castration anxiety" for the male viewer who fears entrusting himself to a woman and thereby losing his identity. Second, the conflation of Judith with Salome indicates the loss of scriptural clarity that might have been present to earlier generations of Jewish and Christians artists who were more firmly rooted in their respective faith traditions. This conflation, then, suggests two things about modern culture: the loss of a religious center, and the loss of separate identities for these scriptural women who are compressed into a singular type, in this case, the *femme fatale.*

Third, the French Revolution and the emancipation of the Jews throughout Western Europe in the eighteenth and nineteenth centuries opened up a new world and signaled the end of the old world of meaning and value. One of the results of the French Revolution, and the loss of a center it brought about in terms of political, civic, and social mores, was the change in roles of men and women. This change is reflected in the variety of ways that women were interpreted in nineteenth-century art from the romanticism of Delacroix to the symbolism of Klimt. The emancipation of Jews resulted in a renewal of and increase in anti-Semitic feelings, especially among Christian families whose sons were in danger of being "entrapped" in marriage by Jewish women.[21] Such an unconscious fear may be made visible in interpretations of the Jewish woman as the exemplary *femme fatale* in Klimt's paintings.

In this comparison between a Renaissance and a modern interpretation of Judith, differences and similarities in artistic visions have been suggested. The emphasis in both portrayals has clearly been in terms of the image of woman more than in terms of religious inspiration or authenticity of scriptural portrayal. Neither painting suggests an identifiable distinction between Jewish women and other women, in terms of physical representation, dress, or comportment. The major distinction, if any, between Jewish women and Christian women, for example, would be in terms of the activities these two images of Judith suggest. Neither the qualities of *femme fatale*, castrating female, nor aggressive "doer" are usually represented in portrayals of Christian women who emulate the virtues of the Virgin Mary.[22]

Therefore the identification of the image of the Jewish woman in the arts is neither through the title of the work of art nor its scriptural or religious referent, but through the action of the female figure. For example, it is possible to suggest that general male fear of women is visually represented in and through the vehicle of the Jewish woman, especially during those centuries of Christian domination over Western culture or during pronounced periods of anti-Semitism. It is also possible to suggest that it is more appropriate and perhaps "safer" for an artist to represent the Jewish woman performing negative or threatening acts, such as the beheading of a general, than it is to portray virtuous Christian women as castrating, destructive, or erotic creatures.

This preliminary study of the image of Judith in Western Christian art has been more suggestive than definitive. It indicates a series of relationships between the role of the visual in the formation and reflection of religious and societal values in Western culture, and the ways that the visual theologically reflects and interprets Scripture. In tandem, the concentrated study of any visual image like Judith indicates the different "readings" and interpretations that reflect different moments in Western cultural history. The simple fact that the image of Judith has been a constant source of interest and inspiration for Western artists from the early Christian period into the present argues for the classic stature of Judith.

NOTES

1. For a preliminary discussion of the image of Judith in Jewish art, see the entry "Book of Judith," in the *Encyclopedia Judaica* (Jerusalem: Keter Publishing House, 1974), 10:451–62.

2. Jdt. 8:7–8.

3. Jdt. 9:10–11.

4. Jdt. 10:3–4.

5. Jdt. 10:19.

6. Jdt. 11:16.

7. This passage of time is significant and controversial. According to some interpreters this passage of five days signifies Judith's menstrual period during which time it would have been forbidden for her to have sexual intercourse. In this case, her entry to Holofernes' tent for a banquet on the last evening just prior to her beheading him would indicate that she was chaste during her days and nights in the enemy camp, as Judith testifies upon her return to Bethulia (Jdt. 13:16).

8. Jdt. 12:16.

9. Jdt. 13:16.

10. This separates Judith from the Christian iconographic tradition of symbolizing major saints (male and female) through the symbolic use of colors.

11. For example, consider Michelangelo Merisi da Caravaggio, *David with the Head of Goliath* (ca.1605; Galleria Borghese, Rome).

12. This inversion was clarified for me by Lilien F. Robinson, professor of art history, during her guest lecture for "The Image of the Jewish Woman in the Arts." Further clarification was later found in Marina Warner, *Monuments and Maidens: The Allegory of the Female Form* (New York: Atheneum, 1985), esp. 166–68.

13. In studying the imagery of Judith, I have come to differ with Elisabeth Moltmann-Wendell's position that "Women in the Bible are not allowed any beauty, independence, or originality of their own, and are made to fulfill the function of whatever image of womanhood Christianity may desire. Where this does not work—for example, with the women of the Old Testament who engaged in politics and made history, Deborah, Judith, and Miriam—the women concerned went off to find a place in literature and were lost to the church's tradition" (*The Women Around Jesus* [Crossroad Publishing Co., 1982], p. 8). Rather, the visual evidence is so strong and prolific, especially in Judith's case, to argue for a recognized awareness of her in Christian theology and spirituality.

14. In this category the following Italian Renaissance artists have imaged Judith: Giorgione (1477/8–1510), Andrea Mantegna, Titian (1485–1576), and Paolo Veronese (1528–88). And the German Renaissance painter, Lucas Cranach the Younger (1515–86) painted several versions of Judith in a similar symbolic pose.

15. In this category one would find representations by Caravaggio, Artemesia Gentileschi, Orazio Gentileschi, Francesco del Cairo (1607–65), Fede Galizia (1578–1630), and Rubens.

16. Other artists have used the Judith story as reflective of art as autobiography. For example, Cristofano Allori's (1577–1621) masterpiece, *Judith with the Head of Holofernes* (1613; Galleria Palatina, Palazzo Pitti, Florence), is said to portray the artist's mistress as Judith and himself as the dead Holofernes.

17. Artemesia Gentileschi's versions of Judith can be found in the following museum collections: Detroit Institute of Art, Palazzo Pitti, National Gallery of Oslo, and the Uffizi. A good source for a discussion of Gentileschi's life and her paintings is Germain Greer, *The Obstacle Race* (New York: Farrar, Straus, and Giroux, 1979); see esp. her chap., "The Magnificent Exception," pp. 189–207.

18. For a full discussion of the image of the armed maiden in popular culture of the twentieth century, see Marina Warner, *Monuments and Maidens*, esp. 173–74. Her discussion of Judith is complimentary but not identical to mine; see *Monuments and Maidens*, pp. 160–74.

19. My intuitive response to this unusual sword is that Mantegna is suggesting a parallel between the sword and Holofernes, both of which have lost their points. In this symbolic parallel, I would suggest the possible further interpretation of the act of a strong woman beheading a man as a metaphor for castration; thus Judith symbolizes the image of the castrating female. However, I am cautioned in this interpretation by correspondence with Leo Steinberg, Benjamin Franklin Professor of the History of Art, the University of Pennsylvania. Readers are referred to sect. 3, chap. 2, "Judith, Holofernes, and the Phallic Woman," in Mary Jacobus's *Reading Woman, Essays in Feminist Criticism* (New York: Columbia University Press, 1986), pp. 110–36; for a Freudian and feminist interpretation of the Judith story and its representation in art, see esp. pp. 122–34.

20. It is Judith's conflation with other female figures both historical and mythological which allows her image and her story to survive into the twentieth century. Along with Pallas Athena, Judith has a relationship to the Virgin Mary, Salome, Delilah, and Joan of Arc, as well as with the ideals of civic virtue, freedom, the city, and religious piety. A lengthy and in-depth study of Judith's image in the arts (dance, drama, music, painting, poetry, prose, and sculpture) would suggest these connections and how the image of Judith is a classic representation for a series of civic and religious ideals as well as of the Jewish woman. For an introductory over-

view to such a study of Judith, see "Interlude: Judith and Holofernes," in Lawrence Cunningham and John Reich, *Culture and Values*, vol. 1 (New York: Holt, Rhinehart, and Winston, 1982), pp. 81–89.

21. For an enlightening discussion of this issue, especially in terms of literary and dramatic sources, see Livia Bitton-Jackson, *Madonna or Courtesan* (New York: Seabury Press, 1983).

22. Of course, the one possible and regular exception to this rule are representations of Mary Magdalene and Joan of Arc. For a discussion of the Magdalene in art, see Jane Dillenberger, "The Magdalene: Reflections on the Image and Sinner in Christian Art," in *Women, Religion and Social Change*, ed. Yvonne Yazbeck Haddad and Ellison Banks Findly (Albany: SUNY Press, 1985), pp. 115–45; and Diane Apostolos-Cappadona, "Images, Interpretations and Traditions: A Study of the Magdalene," in *Interpreting Tradition*, ed. Jane Kopas (Chico: Scholars Press, 1984), 109–23. For a thorough discussion of the symbolism and interpretations of Joan of Arc in Western culture, see Marina Warner, *Joan of Arc: A Model of the Female Hero* (New York: Knopf, 1981).

PART II

VISUAL ARTS IN CHRISTIANITY

7

Nudity, Gender, and Religious Meaning in the Italian Renaissance

MARGARET R. MILES

The catalogue description for "The Role of Visual Images in Historic Christianity":

> *An exploration of the relation of image and word, verbal and visual modes in the development of the Christian churches. The course focuses on understanding and interpreting the central role of images in Western Christianity and in the Orthodox Church in liturgy, piety, and theology with the aid of relevant texts (in translation) and slides. Special attention is paid to visual communications as they expressed and trained attitudes to race, gender, and class.*

The central assumption of the course is that visual images provide the most immediate and direct communication of messages about the participation of human beings as bodies in Christian worship and piety. Visual images of divine, scriptural, and historic human beings model for the worshipper attitudes, emotions, and intensity of engagement. From the house churches of the late Roman world to the whirling images of Baroque cathedrals, Christian worship has entailed very different visual experiences with different theological values and rationales. These experiences were also, within communities, significantly different for different individuals, according to gender, lifestyle, time of life, and class in ways that we can sometimes understand through analysis of visual images. The following lecture is from the last section of the course, which deals with the visual changes that occurred in the Renaissance and in the Protestant and Catholic reformations of the sixteenth century.

Why is history, as most of us have studied it—and as some of us teach it—so boring? Certainly the past was, in Plotinus's phrase, "boiling with life," an unimaginably rich mixture of the energies, ideas, and passions of people of the past. What happens in the course of identifying and describing all this life that makes it feel to us so eviscerated of the "stuff" of life? How do historians manage to eliminate all sense of the richness of the mixture?

It is, on the one hand a problem of sources: the ideas of the culturally and educationally privileged members of historical communities, though these people were the most atypical members of their communities, receive the attention of historians because they wrote texts. Their ideas became available to us through written language while the self-images, ideas of relatedness, community, and world of people who did not write—or even read—are much less accessible.

But there is an even more fundamental reason why history as most of us have studied it is so boring. Historians are motivated by a need to recover, to uncover, the historical antecedents of the sort of person the *historian* is—the people of the past who had similar values, a similar lifestyle, and similar interests and skills. And so the general answer to my question has a great deal to do with who the historian is, and with the historian's idea of what part or activity of human beings is self-constituting, normative, and interesting.

These two factors—the problem of sources and the problem of the historian's perspective—lie at the heart of the elite, intellectual history that claims to be simply "human" history. The second factor—the perspective of the historian—can be addressed by inviting, encouraging, and supporting people who have not traditionally shared in historical reconstruction. The perspectives, interests, and concerns of women, of black women and men, and of people of the Third World are not merely "nice to have." Since there is no absolute or universal perspective from which an accurate picture of historical situations can be made, contributions from a variety of perspectives are necessary in order to mutually correct one another's blind spots.

The problem of sources can be similarly addressed. If we would like to know what *most* of the people of a fifteenth-century Italian community thought, for example, we need to explore information they used in order to construct their self-images, and ideas of relationship, community, world, and God. The search for a different kind of people of the past than those who wrote and read texts, leads us to look for evidence closer to these people than written texts. For predominantly illiterate people, this information must include the visual images that accompanied and focused their worship. The visual images on the walls and ceilings of churches were the primary "media" for most people until at least the sixteenth century. Visual images—available to the whole community on a daily basis—must then be carefully studied and analyzed when we study a particular community. A range of messages—both theological and social—can be suggested as likely to have been received by a particular medieval worshipper. For people who did not, and often could not, read, who probably received scanty catechetical instruction and who frequently could not, in large churches without public address systems, hear the words of the liturgy, visual images formed a major share of their religious orientation. We can support our interpretations of the messages communicated by visual images with popularly accessible materials such as devotional texts, sermons, religious drama, liturgy, Scripture, and hymns. In short, we can explode the boundaries of text-oriented historical theology, gaining access to the material used for religious orientation by people who neither wrote nor read theological texts.

The question of the perspective of the historian and the use of visual images as historical evidence can be explored in the following extended example. Several years ago, Leo Steinberg's book, *The Sexuality of Christ in Renaissance Art and in Modern Oblivion*[1] attracted a great deal of public attention with a startling thesis. Steinberg's thesis is that a massive "education to incomprehension" has kept modern viewers from recognizing the premeditated theological significance of a large number of Renaissance paintings and sculptures. In a discussion lavishly documented by illustrations of European religious painting and sculpture from the fourteenth, fifteenth, and sixteenth centuries, he argues that in Renaissance imagery the male genitals of Christ became the focus of a new pictorial presentation of the Christian doctrine of the Incarnation (fig. 13). Paintings and sculptures of the infant Christ, the crucified Christ, the dead Christ, and the resurrected Christ have "an emphasis on the genitalia of Christ that is assertive and central."

Provocative as it is, Steinberg's thesis raises questions that lie at the heart of the interpretation of religious visual images. Three of the most pressing of these questions are: first, the relation of a new subject of visual imagery to the visual associations and interpretive tools of people in the culture for which these new depictions were created; second, the necessity of employing gender as a category of analysis; and third, the importance of exploring the visual and/or religious problems inscribed in the new depiction. I will discuss these questions as they pertain to Steinberg's thesis and the visual texts that document the thesis, but let us first examine the thesis itself.

Steinberg argues against naturalistic interpretations of depictions of Christ with uncovered genitals. It is not enough, he insists, to claim that paintings of the infant Christ simply display an unclothed baby. In Renaissance paintings in which every detail of the painting carries strongly conditioned visual associations, it is not possible that the inclusion of Christ's genitals was accidental or haphazard. Rather, he urges that the nudity of Christ carries a specific doctrinal message: "To profess that God once embodied himself in a human nature is to confess that the eternal, there and then, became mortal and sexual. . . . The evidence of Christ's sexual member serves as a pledge of God's humanation."[2] Supporting his interpretation with a group of sermons delivered at the papal court between 1450 and 1521, Steinberg claims that before the Renaissance, the full humanity of Christ had not been adequately represented in visual images. His thesis is dramatic and succinct:

> The Incarnation of the Trinity's Second Person is the centrum of Christian orthodoxy. . . . This much Christendom has professed at all times. Not so Christian art. . . . For those western Christians who would revere the Logos in its human presence, it was precisely an "admixture of earthly realism" that was needed. . . . And because Renaissance culture not only advanced an Incarnational theology . . . but evolved representational modes adequate to its expression, we may take Renaissance art to be the first and last phase of Christian art that can claim full Christian orthodoxy. . . . It became the first Christian art in a thousand years to confront the Incarnation entire, the upper and lower body together, not excluding even the body's sexual component.[3]

13. Pietro Perugino, *Madonna and Child* (1500; The National Gallery of Art, Washington, D.C.).

Steinberg's illustrations are as startling as is his explanation of their theological import. Christ is repeatedly depicted with deliberately featured genitals in paintings of the Epiphany and circumcision scenes, in paintings and sculptures of Christ on the cross, in depositions and lamentations, and in resurrected glory. In scenes treating the years of Christ's ministry, however, nudity is absent; Steinberg reasons that during this time in his life, Christ's sexuality "matters in its abeyance: Jesus as exemplar and teacher prevails over concupiscence to consecrate the Christian ideal of chastity."[4] A particularly striking group of paintings shows the risen Christ with a draped, but unmistakable, erection. Steinberg finds that there are theological grounds for these potentially shocking images; the phallus, he writes, "is reasonably equated with power. [And] the supreme power is the power that prevails over mortality."[5] Could not, then, the "truth of the Anastasis, the resuscitation, be proved" by Christ's erection? "Would not this be the body's best show of power?"[6]

This is Professor Steinberg's thesis. Let us now take up the questions raised by it: first, an essentially art historical question with devotional significance—the relationship of the painting and sculpture discussed by Steinberg to visual depictions of the Incarnation of Christ prior to the Renaissance. Steinberg describes earlier—and later—treatments of the Incarnation as inadequate, "evasive," and even unorthodox. What were these visual depictions?

Prior to the Renaissance paintings of the nude Christ, the full humanity of Christ had been demonstrated and supported by reference to his human birth from a human mother, the Virgin Mother, Mary. As a continuous stream of late classical and medieval theologians insisted, she was "the great proof of Christ's true humanity."[7] It was her "pure blood" that supplied his flesh; it was she who gave the Word a body. By the time of the Renaissance, the pivotal significance of Mary's role in the Incarnation had repeatedly been articulated visually. Medieval paintings show her presenting the child Christ to the world, his body surrounded by her body, and sometimes even enclosed in an egg-shaped casement that signified her womb. At the beginning of the fourteenth century, Giotto di Bondone's (1266–1336) scenes on opposite walls of the Scrovegni Chapel in Padua show parallel scenes from Christ's life

and from the life of the Virgin. Christ's miraculous conception was
paralleled by Mary's Immaculate Conception, an unscriptural doctrine that was rejected by Thomas Aquinas and heavily contested
and defended by theologians from the fourth century onward.
Christ's birth and Mary's birth both receive their full share of visual as well as verbal attention. Christ's circumcision finds its parallel in Mary's purification; neither was necessary, yet both were
willingly accepted. Christ's presentation in the temple is matched
by the apocryphal account, depicted by Giotto, of the Virgin's presentation in the temple at the age of three years. The ministry years
of Christ's life do not always find iconographic parallels in the Virgin's life, but in popular devotional works, as well as in Giotto's
paintings, scenes of Christ's ministry were interspersed with accounts of the Virgin's activities and emotions. The Virgin was an
indispensable spectator in Crucifixion scenes. She and her more
flamboyant counterpart, Mary of Magdala, provided the hearer of
devotional stories or the viewer of paintings of the Crucifixion
with models of the emotions they were instructed to experience—
the dignified, heavy grief of the Virgin or the Magdalen's histrionic
lamentation. Because Christ's bodily Ascension was taught in
Scripture, the bodily Assumption of Mary, although unscriptural
and contested until it became dogma in 1950, was a devotional requirement as a parallel for Christ's Ascension.

In fact, all evidence suggests that at no time had popular Marian
devotion been more prominent in Italian culture than immediately preceeding the Renaissance. Never had theologians argued
more heatedly about the Virgin's specific attributes and powers
than in the thirteenth and fourteenth centuries. Councils invoked
Mary's presence and guidance; theologians like Jean Gerson
(1363–1429), chancellor of the University of Paris, attested her
participation in the Last Supper and Pentecost. Affirming her appointment to the priesthood, Gerson called her "the Mother of the
Eucharist," the one who made possible the offering of Christ to the
world. Bernardino of Siena (1380–1444), the fiery evangelist of the
first half of the fifteenth century, waxed eloquent over the "un-
thinkable power of the Virgin Mother":

> Only the blessed Virgin Mary has done more for God, or just as
> much, as God has done for all humankind . . . God fashioned us

from the soil, but Mary formed him from her pure blood; God impressed on us his image, but Mary impressed hers on God. . . . God taught us wisdom, but Mary taught Christ to flee from the hurtful and follow her; God nourished us with the fruits of paradise, but she nourished him with her most holy milk, so that I may say this for the blessed virgin, whom, however, God made himself, God is in some way under a greater obligation to us through her than we to God.[8]

Inflated as such rhetoric may sound to us, it accurately represents popular interests of the time in the role and power of the Virgin. Visually also, Christ's physical dependence on his mother was emphasized in many paintings that show her with one breast bared, either nursing or preparing to nurse the infant Christ (fig. 14). In these paintings, the Christ child often turns while he nurses to engage the viewer's eye, inviting the viewer to share in the Virgin's nourishment. Her power to request and receive mercy for the sinners frequently depicted as huddling in her cloak also comes from her provision of human nourishment for Christ, as an early fourteenth-century anonymous painting makes clear. Redemption of the sinners who have taken shelter in Mary's robes begins with her exposure of the breast that nourished Christ; the adult Christ, in turn, shows his wounds to the Father, while the Father, persuaded by these legitimate claims on his mercy, sends down the dove, the Holy Spirit, to bring redemption to those who have entreated Mary for help.[9]

This strong visual and verbal popular interest in the role and power of the Virgin is the immediate context for the images of the nude Christ discussed by Steinberg. Images of the nude Christ did not replace images emphasizing the Virgin's role in guaranteeing the full humanity of Christ; rather, images of Mary's power continued to be popular through the Italian Renaissance and to the time of the Council of Trent. There, some of the most vivid of these images were proscribed, such as the so-called Madonna of Mercy, that shows Mary protecting, and securing the redemption of, sinners covered by her cloak. Even after the proscription of this image, however, earlier depictions of the theme were not removed from churches where worshippers could see them daily. The persistence of interest in the Virgin's power, obtained through her essential role in the Incarnation, brings us to consideration of the

14. Andrea di Bartolo, *Madonna and Child* (ca. 1415; The National Gallery of Art, Washington, D.C.).

second question raised by Steinberg's argument, the question of the gender assumptions that underlie his argument.

I suspect it was not theological arguments, but the devotional need of women and men for symbolic representations that supplied a rich provision of parallel male and female images that was decisive. Theologians might protest "abuses" and offer strained definitions of the precise function of the Virgin at each moment of Christ's life, but artists continued to paint the images in a devotionally compelling manner. It is important to remember that religious images did not merely delight the predominantly illiterate congregations of late medieval churches; they also supplied images that articulated and supported spiritual life and that directed religious affections in fundamental ways understood as essential for salvation.

Moreover, the class and gender affiliations of the Italian Renaissance cannot be overlooked if we are to understand the context and audience of the images Steinberg has gathered. Although historians have often written as if "the Renaissance" were a term that could accurately designate the whole of Italian society in a certain time period, a closer analysis of those actually participating in the scholarly and artistic excitement of the rediscovery of classical antiquity reveals the participation of about two hundred people. In *The Social History of Art* Arnold Hauser has written that the Renaissance was the "jealously guarded possession of a highbrow and latinized elite."[10] Involvement in the scholarly activities of the Renaissance required the social class and privileged leisure necessary for a long and intensive education; even artistic participation, though potentially more accessible to men of talent, was not open to all artists, but only to those who were unusually gifted and who came to the notice of wealthy patrons. Furthermore, the Italian Renaissance was a male movement: "Nearly everywhere . . . the patrons and friends of art were men."[11] Asking, "Did women have a Renaissance?" Joan Kelly-Gadol found that women lost ground in all the categories she examined.

> Women as a group, especially among the classes that dominated Italian urban life, experienced a contraction of social and personal options that men of their classes either did not, as was the case with the bourgeoisie, or did not experience as markedly, as was the case with the nobility.[12]

Steinberg does not tell us *why* it suddenly became imperative to find a new and more vivid expression of the Incarnation of Christ to "full humanation." In fact, images of the nude Christ probably did not arise from the devotional needs of the vast majority of people who lived and worshipped in Italy at the time of the Italian Renaissance. These images may even present a conscious protest to contemporary visual and verbal interest in the Virgin, and perhaps not only the Virgin but also a host of scriptural and historical female saints. Images of the nude Christ may have served, rather, to provide for "Renaissance man" visual images that confirmed his precariously inflated self-image.

Moreover, the appearance of God in the male sex was understood as privileging that sex. Explicit visual depictions of Christ's male genitals reinforced the identification of men with Christ more forcefully and dramatically than did theological writings, although this identification was also urged in texts. The first manual on the identification and examination of suspected witches, the *Malleus Maleficarum* (1484), states that most witches are women because men are much less likely to associate with the devil than women because they belong to Christ's sex: "And blessed be the Highest who has so far preserved the male sex from so great a crime: for since He was willing to be born and to suffer for us, therefore He has granted to men this privilege."[13]

Nude images of Christ reinforced and extended the "dignity of man" theme so dear to Renaissance men. It is likely that these images were relatively successful in communicating this message to their chosen limited audience. However, we need to address our last issue concerning the religious and social problems associated with these images. The first of these problems concerns the representation of nude or partially nude bodies in religious art.

In *Seeing Through Clothes* Ann Hollander has argued that nudity in art always carries a sexual message; visual depictions of a nude body are never so thoroughly devoid of sexual meanings as to become a perfect vehicle for an abstract theological message. At the same time, nudity can intensify the narrative, doctrinal, or devotional message of the painting by evoking subliminal erotic associations. In a religious painting that intends to stimulate in viewers a complex response of affective piety, nudity must be carefully balanced with other visual content so that an erotic response does not dominate, causing the viewer's engagement with the painting to collapse into "mere" sexual interest. On one hand, then, nudity must be depicted realistically enough to evoke the viewer's erotic interest; on the other hand, it must not be dominant enough to make this erotic attraction primary. The religious message must dominate, with the erotic component in a subordinate and supportive role.[14]

Did nude paintings of Christ achieve the delicate balance of eroticism and theology that Steinberg claims for them? Apparently not; some of them were criticized, draped, and overpainted almost immediately, and a wave of negative reaction to them culminated in a proscription against nudes in religious art at the Council of Trent in 1563. This reaction, usually explained by art historians as attributable to the priggishness of the Counter-Reformation, may have come from many contemporary viewers' sense that, rather than stimulating piety, nude images of Christ stimulated erotic voyeurism. Michelangelo Buonarroti's (1475–1564) painting of *The Last Judgment* (1534–41; Sistine Chapel, Vatican City)—the largest fresco in Rome—originally contained many nude bodies. Pietro Aretino wrote an open letter accusing Michelangelo of being irreverent. "Such things might be painted," he wrote, "in a voluptuous bathroom, but not in the choir of the highest chapel."[15] After the decree of the Council of Trent, Michelangelo's painting was overpainted by his pupil, Daniele da Volterra; the figures were given additional clothing in 1572, and again in 1625, 1712, and 1762. Aretino, Biagio da Cesena, and other theologians who complained of the nudity in the painting may have been concerned that the balance of eroticism and piety was not maintained. If this interpretation is correct, it raises a welter of difficult issues that require further examination. To whom were images of male nudes erotic? Were they seen by whole communities in their places of worship, or were they largely inaccessible to the public due to placement in the Vatican or in the homes of wealthy noblemen?

The second concern about the problems implicit in Renaissance depictions of a nude Christ concerns the religious messages of the paintings. Were these paintings not only "a major phenomenon in historic Christianity"[16] but also "the first and last phase of Christian art that can claim full Christian orthodoxy?"[17] Many people of Renaissance societies were not nourished devotionally by depictions in which the gender balance had been tipped so heavily toward a male symbol and in which the mother of Christ was relegated to marginality from her former role of "proving" the Incarnation.

There is both textual and visual evidence throughout Christian history to the time of the Italian Renaissance that theologians as well as painters understood the importance of the Virgin for the devotional needs of communities. It was the figure of the Virgin which guaranteed—along with Christ's full humanity—that the devotional needs of women and men for gender parallelism in Christian verbal and visual symbols would be met. For example, Thomas Aquinas (1225–74) quotes Augustine (356–430) in his answer to his question "whether the matter of Christ's body should have been taken from a woman:"

> Because the male sex exceeds the female sex, Christ assumed a man's nature. So that people should not think little of the female sex, it was fitting that he should take flesh from a woman. Hence Augustine says, "Despise not yourselves, men, the son of God became a man; despise not yourselves, women, the son of God was born of a woman."[18]

Despite the explicit gender assumptions of a patriarchal society that are evident in this quotation, concern for affirmation of both women and men emerges as a religious value. Although the "place" of women and men in medieval society was not only different but was also asymmetrically valued, women's participation in worship and piety was encouraged and cultivated for purposes of social control as well as for women's challenge and comfort. A different historical subject must be imagined and sought than "Renaissance man" if we are to understand the affective valence of images painted, not primarily for their artistic creativity, but for the spiritual nurture of communities. The multivalence and ambiguity of images of the Virgin becomes apparent when we try to imagine the possible meaning, for a married woman who might reasonably expect to die in childbirth as a teenager or young woman, of paintings of a human woman, like herself, who managed to live the events of a woman's life while maintaining both her spiritual energy and her power.

If a delicate balance of gender imagery was disrupted by nude images of Christ, as I have suggested, might it have been possible to present visual images of Mary that reestablished that balance? Could artists have found subjects and styles that similarly raised the intensity of devotional paintings of Mary? If nude paintings of Christ added a conscious or subliminal erotic attraction to the viewer's engagement with the painting, might a similar device have strengthened depictions of Mary? As Steinberg states, the nudity of Christ was made possible theologically by Christ's innocence; his sinlessness and freedom from any taint of concupiscence ensured the guiltlessness of his body which could then be displayed without shame. Even the Virgin/mother did not participate to the same extent in sinlessness, although popular devotional texts, like Jacobus da Voragine's *Golden Legend* insisted that Mary, despite her consummate beauty, did not arouse sexual desire:

> Such indeed was Mary's innocence that it shone forth even outside of her, and quelled any urgency of the flesh of others. . . . Although Mary was surpassing fair, no man could look upon her with desire.[19]

Yet visual depiction of the innocence of Mary remained difficult to imagine and present. Giotto's painting of the sexless kiss of Joachim and Anna at the Golden Gate, the kiss by which Mary was conceived, was certainly a less-than-vivid demonstration of her Immaculate Conception. Apparently, the only part of her body that could be uncovered was the breast at which the infant Christ was nourished. Paintings of the Virgin with one bared breast show careful effort by the painter to overcome the potential erotic attraction of the sight of a naked breast. The two most frequent conventions by which this was done were: first, rendering the covered breast perfectly flat, without contour so that the large bared breast appears to be an appendage to Mary's body, not an exposed part of it; and second, Mary's clothing is never disheveled, giving the impression of a suddenly revealed nakedness; buttons and ties remain closed at the neck of the dress, while the breast juts from the middle of the chest. In spite of theologians' agreement on her innocence — though they differed over the details of her sinlessness — Mary's nudity was apparently too problematical to represent visually. Thus, no fully satisfying visual portrayal of Mary's sinlessness was found to balance the nude portrayals of Christ.

Finally, Steinberg's claim that paintings of the resurrected Christ with an erect phallus depict "the body's best show of power," is loaded with the gender assumptions of our contemporary culture. "The body" is, first of all, unquestionably a male body: the male body is normative for human experience. Female bodies, as Aristotle said, are a deviation from the male norm. And Augustine had written, in *De mendacio*: "The body of a man is as superior to that of a woman as the soul is to the body."[20] Second, that the erect phallus is the natural symbol of "the body's best show of power" is not evident. If "the body" were not assumed to be male, would not the female body's capacity for conceiving, giving birth, and nourishing human life seem the strongest and most obvious candidate for the human body's most dramatic power? In fact, reproduction, the process by which the Virgin gave God human flesh, was visually represented throughout Christian tradition to the time of the Italian Renaissance as "the body's best show of power." Visual presentation of the male genitals of Christ, in the context of late medieval art, then, was not the first Christian art to present the Incarnation of Christ in "full Christian orthodoxy." Steinberg's interpretation of Renaissance images of the nude Christ illustrates the inadequacy of descriptions of religious art that do not take into account the gender assumptions of the interpreter as well as those of the society from which the art came and within which it had meaning.   ·

This example of the use of visual images as historical evidence and the perspectival bias—Steinberg's and mine—inevitably engaged in historical interpretation, permits us to glimpse the fruitfulness and excitement of new historiographical methods and to recognize that historical reconstruction, in common with all domains of knowledge, always bears the pervasive coloring of the historian's education, perspective, and interest. Moreover, perspective operates at every stage of the work, in the choice of subject matter, in method, in kinds of evidence taken into account, and in conclusions.

The limited and complementary evidence of texts and images will become evident only when those who study the past have developed the ability to explore both texts and images in their full

nuanced complexity. When we have developed skill in the interpretation of visual images we may become fascinated by the singular effectiveness with which human life, the life of bodies, has been
represented and expressed by visual images, just as language for-
mulates and communicates human life as the life of the mind.

NOTES

1. Leo Steinberg, *The Sexuality of Christ in Renaissance Art and in Modern Obliv-ion* (New York: Pantheon Books, 1984). This discussion of Steinberg's book is re-vised from my review of *The Sexuality of Christ* that appeared in *Christianity and Crisis* 44, no. 17 (17 September 1984): 333–34.
2. Steinberg, *The Sexuality of Christ*, p. 13.
3. Ibid., pp. 71–72.
4. Ibid., p. 23.
5. Ibid., p. 90.
6. Ibid., p. 91.
7. Tertullian, *De Carne Christi*, 17: "Christ received flesh from the Virgin . . . cer-tain proof that his flesh was human, if he derived its substance from his mother's womb." Translation from *The Ante-Nicene Fathers*, vol. 3, p. 536.
8. Cited in Hilda Graef, *Mary, a History of Doctrine and Devotion*, (New York: Sheed and Ward, 1963), 1:316–17.
9. See my essay, "The Virgin's One Bare Breast: Female Nudity and Religious Meaning in Tuscan Early Renaissance Culture," in *The Female Body in Western Cul-ture*, ed. Susan Rubin Sueliman (Cambridge, MA: Harvard University Press, 1986), pp. 193–208.
10. Arnold Hauser, *The Social History of Art*, 2 vols. (New York: Vintage Books), 2:51.
11. Ibid., p. 48.
12. Joan Kelly-Gadol, "Did Women Have a Renaissance?" in *Becoming Visible, Women in European History*, ed. Bridenthal and Koonz (Boston: Houghton Mifflin, 1977), p. 39.
13. Kramer and Sprenger, *The Malleus Maleficarum*, trans. Montague Summers (New York: Dover, 1971), p. 47.
14. Anne Hollander, *Seeing Through Clothes* (New York: Viking, 1980), pp. 178–79.
15. Quoted in Ludwig Goldscheider, *Michelangelo, Painting, Sculptures, Architec-ture*, 4th ed. (London: Phaidon Press, 1962), p. 20, col. 1.
16. Steinberg, *The Sexuality of Christ*, p. 109.
17. Ibid., p. 72.
18. Thomas Aquinas, *Summa Theologiae*, 3a, q. 31, art. 4; translation from the Blackfriars ed. (New York: McGraw-Hill, 1969) vol. 52, p. 23.
19. Jacobus di Voragine, *The Golden Legend*, trans. Granger Ryan and Helmut Ripperger (New York: Arno Press, 1969), p. 150.
20. Augustine of Hippo, *De mendacio* 10, in J. B. Migne, ed., *Patrologiae cursus completus*, Series Latina (Paris), vol. 40, p. 195, col. 2.

8

From Overwhelming Power to Suffering Love: Tracing Transformations in Michelangelo's Art and Theology

NICHOLAS PIEDISCALZI

"Religion and Ethics in the Arts" is one of several interdisciplinary courses offered by the Department of Religion at Wright State University. The rationale for this course is twofold: first, knowledge is wholistic; all of its forms are interrelated. The multiplicity and exclusiveness of disciplines in the contemporary university deny this fact and present students with distorted interpretations of their own experiences and reality. It is incumbent upon scholars to correct this error. A way to do this is through interdisciplinary courses which focus upon the interrelatedness and interdependence of all academic endeavors.

Second, the arts are replete with religious and ethical themes. They are embodiments of the wholistic nature of knowledge. They provide a unique opportunity for demonstrating this point and gaining insights into the nature and functions of religion and ethics and their interrelationships in ways which are not available to those who study them as separate entities.

"Religion and Ethics in the Arts" usually includes four selected art forms, for example, the visual arts, music, dance, and cinema. Each one is studied within its own context. Specific works within each form are allowed to speak for themselves. Students are taught to avoid using heteronomous criteria in their analyses. They are trained to discover the specific world view and/or ethical themes embodied in or

communicated through specific works of art. By so doing, they respect the integrity of the artistic creations under study.

The following bibliographic essay is used as the major source for a slide lecture on Michelangelo Buonarroti (1475–1564) which is presented in a unit on the visual arts. It is preceded by sessions on the nature of the visual arts; various ways to analyze them and their religious and ethical content; and the classical and biblical roots of Renaissance art in addition to its character, style, content, and development.

Charles de Tolnay,[1] Frederick Hartt,[2] and Leo Steinberg[3] have studied changes which occurred in Michelangelo's works. They also have singled out transformations in his own religious experiences and theology as two of the major causes of these significant developments. De Tolnay uncovered three major periods in the artistic career of Michelangelo.[4] Each stage is dominated by a specific religio-philosophical theme. This essay summarizes these three periods and delineates the theology and/or philosophy which undergirds each. However, before this is done, Michelangelo's philosophical and religious roots will be summarized.

Religious and Philosophical Roots

Seven separate religious and/or philosophical traditions may be found intermingled in the life and works of Michelangelo: the traditional Roman Catholicism of his family; ancient Greek views of supernatural powers; the early Hebrew vision of God; the Neo-Platonism of his intellectual peers; the prophetic message of Girolamo Savonarola (1452–98); Juan de Valdés's (1500?–41) Pauline theology; and the thought of Ignatius of Loyola (1491–1556).

Michelangelo's letters to his family reveal the traditional Roman Catholic side of his life. Here we find him asking people to pray for the success of his specific works; requesting his brother to arrange for the administration of extreme unction to his seriously ill father; and inviting a nephew to offer alms for the salvation of his soul and the souls of other family members. According to de Tolnay, this form of religiosity remained with him throughout his life.[5]

Ancient Greek views of supernatural powers which determine the course of the world and the fate of humanity influenced Michelangelo's early life. So did a conceptualization of Yahweh as an exacting and demanding God who punishes severely those who break his laws. The former came from his introduction to the myths of ancient Greece and the latter from the Roman Catholic church's interpretation of Hebrew Scripture.

Erwin Panofsky holds that Michelangelo is the only sixteenth-century Italian artist who adopted Neo-Platonism not only as a meaningful world view but also as a philosophical justification of his own existence.[6] Three aspects of Neo-Platonic thought were of special importance to his life and work. First, the doctrine of the immanence of the divine undergirded Michelangelo's theory of aesthetics and love of beauty. Second, the interpretation of human existence as the painful imprisonment of a soul in a material body justified his lifelong discomfort with himself and the world. Third, the Neo-Platonic goal of releasing the soul from its bondage to the body and returning the soul to its original divine source counterbalanced his basic dissatisfactions and inspired some of his most significant works.

Drawing heavily upon the prophets of the Hebrew Scriptures and the prophetic sections of the Christian Scriptures, Savonarola called a corrupt church and immoral Florence to repentance. He predicted doom for those who did not heed his words. These themes may be found in Michelangelo's "Prophets, the Sibyls, and the *Flood* of the Sistine Ceiling, in the *Moses* of the Tomb of Julius II, and in the apocalyptic vision of the *Last Judgment*."[7]

Michelangelo also was influenced by Savonarola's belief that the prayers of the interior heart are superior to external rituals. This theme is found in Michelangelo's later works which eschew external beauty in favor of the spiritual beauty of internal suffering and humility.

Contrary to the Roman Catholic theology of his day, Juan de Valdés, a follower of Erasmus and student of the Bible, taught that one is saved by faith alone. He influenced a small group of men and women, including clergy, who adopted and disseminated his basic teachings. One of these, Vittoria Colonna (1490–1547), introduced Michelangelo to the Pauline doctrine of "justification by faith alone" which she was taught by Valdés. De Tolnay reports:

In one of his letters, probably written in 1540, addressed to the
Marchesa Colonna, Michelangelo said: . . . I now understand and
see that the grace of God cannot be bought, and that it is a very
great sin to find this grace oppressive.[8]

Like Savonarola, Valdés also elevated the life of meditation and
private prayer above external ceremonies. He taught that these
acts of personal piety should center on the internal images of the
suffering of the crucified Christ. These evoke a special type of faith
and loving attitude in the believer which cannot be inspired by an
external portrayal of his suffering. These two themes are found in
the sonnets, sculpture, and frescoes of Michelangelo's last period.

Michelangelo admired Ignatius of Loyola's theology and his
program of reform. He appears to have been influenced most by
Loyola's call for Christians to meditate in seclusion on the life, Passion, and Resurrection of the savior; his plans to rid the church of
moral corruption; and his desire to reestablish true faith in the
hearts of all believers. According to Leo Steinberg, during his last
ten years, Michelangelo, like Loyola, made piety and contemplation of the divine "not a distinct form of activity but the tone of all
his activity, including all drawing, designing and carving."[9] It
was in this spirit that Michelangelo wrote to Loyola in 1554 offering to prepare gratuitously the plans and model for the Jesuits'
new church, Il Gesù, in Rome.

De Tolnay argues that, even though Michelangelo held Loyola in
high esteem, he never relinquished, like Vittoria Colonna, his lib-
eral, humanist Catholic ideas in order to survive the Inquisition.
Moreover, even though some individuals accused him of heresy, he
neither was investigated by the Holy Office nor required to choose
between the Roman Catholic church and the Reformation.[10] To
the very end of his life he maintained a high degree of independence from institutional authority—both religious and artistic—
even though he strove to humble himself before his God.

These are the major religious and philosophical sources of the
changes in Michelangelo's works. At times each was expressed individually in a specific sculpture, painting, drawing, or sonnet. On
other occasions they were intermingled. The following paragraphs
will describe how these themes found expression in the three major periods of Michelangelo's creative years outlined by de Tolnay.

First Period

The first period of Michelangelo's creative work stretches from his earliest works until about his forty-fifth year (ca. 1490–1520). During this period, two different types of divinity are portrayed. In one, ancient Greek and early Hebrew themes predominate. Human beings are presented under the governance of unseen supernatural forces, "the *ananke* and *fatum* of ancient Greece or the terrifying power of Jehovah."[11] At this time Michelangelo was able to interchange ancient Greek and Hebrew types with those of the Christian tradition without any philosophical or theological conflict. For example, we find the Virgin represented as a Sibyl, Christ the judge portrayed as Apollo, and the Last Judgment originating with the fall of Phaeton.[12] Roland Bainton in his essay, "Man, God, and the Church in the Age of the Renaissance," explained how and why this interchange was possible not only in Michelangelo but many other artistic and intellectual leaders of this period. The Renaissance's emphasis on the immanence of God made it possible to discover God everywhere. In turn, this made it possible "to discover confirmation of Christian doctrines in other religions. . . . Much of the borrowing from classical mythology aspired to be no more than a restating in a new set of symbols of the traditional affirmations."[13]

At this stage when classical Greek and ancient Hebrew themes were intermingled by Michelangelo, he presented the divine powers as stern judges who expect human beings to accept their fate with a stoic resignation. This theme is found in many of his Virgins and the *Pietà* (1500; St. Peter's Basilica, Rome; fig. 15). In the latter, Mary does not express any deep emotion. Rather, she appears to accept without tears the Crucifixion of her son as the fulfillment of God's will. "With a restrained gesture of her hand, expressing obedience to a superior will, she yields to destiny."[14] Frederick Hartt supports de Tolnay's conclusion: "Not maternal grief but grateful reverence in the presence of an unspeakable mystery, in which Mary gently participates, is the theme of Michelangelo's *Pietà*."[15]

Another theme, according to de Tolnay, that of pre-Christian ecstasy may be found in Michelangelo's portrayals of individuals under the dominion of divine powers. In these works, wind billows "around them, the divine afflatus can be read on their faces, in their violent gestures, and in their garments."[16] These individuals presented by Michelangelo are possessed totally by God. In fact, the divine power removes them from their attachment to their historical moment and binds them to his eternal realm.

The second portrayal of God by Michelangelo during this period reflects his acceptance of Neo-Platonic thought. God is presented as the Idea of Man, an immanent rather than a transcendent divinity. He is the true source and essence of the human soul and he is the true reality with which the soul seeks reunion. This is the Neo-Platonic concept of *deificatio*—by reuniting with God, the human soul becomes divine.[17]

At the center of Michelangelo's works during this period is the power of God's love. According to Panofsky, the Neo-Platonic philosophy which Michelangelo embraced taught that

> Love is the motive . . . by which God causes Himself . . . to effuse His essence into the world, and which, inversely, causes His creatures to seek a reunion with Him. According to Ficino, *amor* is only another name for that self-reverting current (*circuitus spiritualis*) from God to the world and from the world to God. The loving individual inserts himself into this mystical circuit.[18]

This view of divine love is a rational concept. Love without a rational goal, according to the Neo-Platonists, is merely a blind power. Neo-Platonists such as Ficino held that God's ultimate rational goal is the creation of beauty. This is what makes his creative power love. For this reason, "celestial love or *amor divinus* possesses itself of the highest faculty in man, i.e. [sic] the Mind or intellect, and impels it to contemplate the intelligible splendour of divine beauty."[19]

De Tolnay claims that on the ceiling of the Sistine Chapel Michelangelo painted a Neo-Platonic view of God and, at the same time, portrayed God as evolving. On the one hand, God is presented anthropomorphically as the Idea of Man and the goal toward which the human soul aspires, through escape from the imprisoning body.[20] God also is presented as evolving from an anthropomorphic to a uranian divinity. This is where one sees God emerging out of chaos. He is portrayed as transforming himself from matter into spirit.[21] In the final scene, God becomes divine

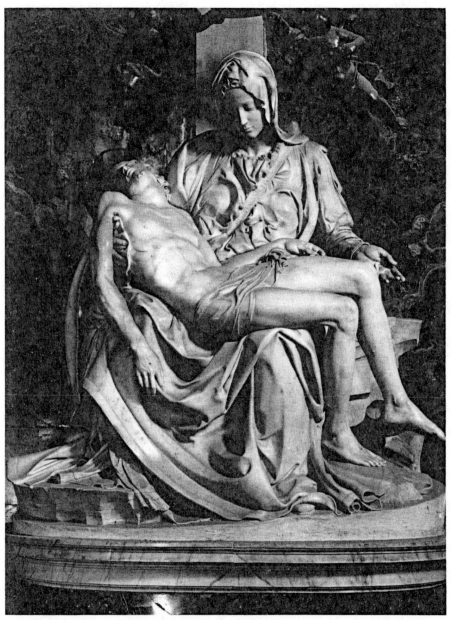

15. Michelangelo, *The Pietà* (1500; Basilica Church of St. Peter, Vatican City).

intelligence. This takes place first in God's creation of Eve which, according to de Tolnay, represents the emergence of limited intelligence. Next God transcends himself by creating Adam, an act which represents unlimited intelligence and omniscience.[22] This self-transcendence by God as represented in the creation of Adam illustrates that "God is more powerful when He creates greater works. His creative force determines not only the work but His own form. . . . He is the creative force, the 'absolute artist.'"[23]

Second Period

The second period of Michelangelo's work (ca. 1520–ca. 1535/ 36), according to de Tolnay, is one of transition. It represents his gradual movement from ancient Greek, Hebrew, and Neo-Platonic forms to symbols of the Christian faith. Savonarola's prophetic faith and the Pauline theology of Valdés start to take hold, and he begins to merge ancient Greek and Christian themes. *Christ of Santa Maria sopra Minerva* (1520; Santa Maria sopra Minerva, Rome) is from this second stage of Michelangelo's development. Although Christ is represented by Apollo, a new interpretation of his saving work is introduced. On the one hand, Christ is presented as "enduring and concealing his suffering behind a noble serenity."[24] On the other, Christ joins his destiny with man against a secular and corrupt church.

According to de Tolnay, the major theme of this figure is found in a poem which Michelangelo wrote in 1512. In it he accuses the. church of corruption and calls for immediate reform.[25]

Through *Christ of Santa Maria sopra Minerva*, Michelangelo

> criticized the corrupt, avaricious, and secularized Church, and the practice of Simony. In an emphatic contrast to the Antichrist, who was adored in the Rome of that time, Michelangelo tried to erect the image of the true Christ, the Christ of goodness, suffering and patience. So this statue. . . . had a special meaning: It was a sort of monument commemorating the true Christ in the midst of the greedy and perverted city. Savonarola's ideas for the internal reform of the Church came to life again. Let us not forget that the statue was made for . . . the Dominican Church in Rome.[26]

The *Pietà* (1538–40; Isabella Stewart Gardner Museum, Boston) which Michelangelo drew for Vittoria Colonna also comes from this period of transition. It is quite different from the *Pietà* which is in St. Peter's Basilica. In the latter, all attention is on the Virgin. In the former, attention is on Christ. At the same time, Mary "is expressing her grief in a despairing gesture, and seems to be calling attention to the immensity of the sacrifice."[27]

Michelangelo made a similar statement in the *Crucifixion* (1540; British Museum, London) which he produced for Vittoria Colonna. He presented the crucified Christ alive and suffering and the attending angels weeping—neither of which are found in previous Renaissance portrayals of the Crucifixion. Once again, Michelangelo focused on the suffering of Christ and the high cost he paid for humanity's salvation.

In both of these works Michelangelo gave expression to the Pauline theology of Valdés which he learned from Vittoria Colonna. One of her sonnets, according to de Tolnay, contains the major theological themes in the *Pietà* and *Crucifixion* which were executed by Michelangelo in this period: "Man must serve his true Lord, not by indolent intentions and tardy good works, but by the cross, by blood and sweat, by his ardent spirit always prepared for danger."[28] Michelangelo repeated this theme in several of his own sonnets: "Only your blood, Lord, can wash me and cleanse me of my sins. . . . With your blood cleanse the soul and heal it of the infinite vices and human desires."[29]

Third Period

When Michelangelo signed the contract for the *Pietà* in St. Peter's Basilica, he stated that he would produce "the finest work in marble which Rome today can show, and that no master of our day shall be able to produce better."[30] Writing to Pope Julius II in 1506 about the tomb he was to make for him, Michelangelo claimed that, if the work is completed, "there will be nothing to equal it the world over."[31] According to Steinberg, "an introverted aestheticism had ruled Michelangelo's art during this period. His figures tended to turn in on themselves—in the sufficiency of their beauty, in their cyclical structure and their emotional self-absorption."[32]

In 1554 Michelangelo wrote:

> To paint and carve no longer calms
> The soul turned to that Love divine
> Who to embrace us on the cross opens his arms.[33]

The juxtaposition of the quotations from Michelangelo's early period (1498 and 1506) with this sonnet from 1554 reveals the dramatic changes which occurred in Michelangelo's professional goal and his theology. These developments may be attributed in part to at least four causes. First, the disruptive changes in society which tempered the unlimited optimism of the early years of the Renaissance. Second, Michelangelo's conversion to the theology of Valdés and his followers. Third, the influence of Ignatius of Loyola. Fourth, his personal struggles with aging and the threat of death.

The changes are found in the *Florentine Pietà* (1547–54; Museo dell' Opera del Duomo, Florence), a drawing which depicts the savior on the cross between the Madonna and St. John (ca. 1556; British Museum, London), the Pauline frescoes (1542–49; Capella Paolina, Vatican City), and the *Rondanini Pietà* (1564; Castello Sforesca, Milan; fig. 16). A dominant theme in these works, according to de Tolnay, is a mystical vision of a suffering God in Christ which inspired him to subordinate "physical beauty to the inner radiance of the soul. . . . The external and material image of Christ is supplanted by the internal spiritual image, directly inspired—as the Italian reformers would say—by the Holy Ghost."[34]

Steinberg adds another theme—"the servant or friend bending over to help."[35] This helper serves as a mediator of communion between God and the others. He reflects Michelangelo's new faith in the transforming power of empathetic, suffering love. Frederick Hartt confirms this interpretation when he analyzes the positioning of the individuals in the *Florentine Pietà*: they represent "the ultimate union of man and God . . . which Michelangelo so deeply desired and which this group celebrates, all individualities are merged to the point of transfusion. . . . Currents of sacrificial love flow like ocean tides throughout the group."[36] The communion of suffering saints replaces the individualism of the Renaissance.

Steinberg adds that Michelangelo's portrayal of Peter's crucifixion in the second Pauline fresco and his plan for St. Peter's Basilica both contain pleas for a reformation of the church by recalling how the church's life began with and was sustained in purity by martyrdom:

> In the lustihood of his youth, he had dreamt of seeing his masterwork rise three storeys high under the vault of a new choir, over-

16. Michelangelo, *The Rondanini Pietà* (1564; Castello Sforesca, Milan).

looking St. Peter's tomb and giving the Church a spatial climax that would have prolonged and commended its longitudinal axis. "Once I had hoped to raise me by thy height," he had written in a sonnet to Julius II. Counting on the omnipotence of the Pope, he had meant to use St. Peter's as an exalting frame for his art. Now, after a life of punished hubris, he would use his art to exalt St. Peter. . . . He begins by enforcing the central plan that honors the sepulchre of the martyred Apostle—and in the very year of the crucial decision, diverts the subject of the second Pauline fresco from Christ's charge to St. Peter to the consummation of Peter's mission in crucifixion.[37]

These two works along with his *Last Judgment* (1536–41; Sistine Chapel, Vatican City) and the *Florentine* and *Rondanini Pietàs* reflect the culmination of Michelangelo's conversion to the theologies of the Catholic reformers led by Valdés on one end of the spectrum and Ignatius of Loyola on the other. In these final works there is, according to Steinberg, an absence of pagan and sensuous themes. At the same time, there is "a new directness of address to the viewer, a concept almost apostolic of the role his art must now play in the world."[38] This is especially evident in the way St. Peter confronts the viewer in the second Pauline fresco, *The Crucifixion of St. Peter*. Steinberg also believes that this newly adopted cause represents a switch of allegiance from Florentine "patriotism to religious faith. Now the all seeing, all summoning power is not the state but the Church, here personified in its founder."[39]

Conclusion

Erik H. Erikson claims in *Young Man Luther* that Martin Luther (1483–1546) formed his mature Christian identity when he gave up his substitutionary theology of Christ's death, abandoned his goal to imitate Christ as an ideal, and discovered that the suffering Christ within him was the core of his Christian identity. This new perspective taught him that his suffering and faith introduced him to the suffering Christ who is God's face.[40]

Like Luther, Michelangelo came to a new understanding of God and formed a new religious identity based on an identification of his suffering with the suffering of Christ.[41] De Tolnay asserts that in his final works, Michelangelo, in profound solitude, beyond the world and the Church, . . . sought alone the road which would lead him to beatitude. It is those long soul-searchings and those long gropings which give to these works their moving depth. The feeling of bliss seems always to be tinged with the suffering which he endured to attain it.[42]

This final transformation in his religious life and artistic works made Michelangelo a prophetic reformer and a new role-model for artists. In his works he presented his reformed spirituality and morality, which were prophetic condemnations of the individual and institutional corruption of his day and calls for reform. And, according to Frank La Brasca, "he was probably the prototype of the modern artist for he was the first to intermingle Life and Art in an existential and suffering unity, liberating definitely the plastic arts . . . from the status of purely mechanical skills."[43]

NOTES

1. Charles de Tolnay, *The Art and Thought of Michelangelo*, trans. Nan Buranelli (New York: Pantheon Books, 1964); and *Michelangelo: Sculptor, Painter, Architect*, trans. Gaynor Woodhouse (Princeton: Princeton University Press, 1975).

2. Frederick Hartt, *Michelangelo's Three Pietàs*, photographic study by David Finn (New York: Harry N. Abrams, 1975).

3. Leo Steinberg, *Michelangelo's Last Paintings: The Conversion of St. Paul and the Crucifixion of St. Peter in the Cappella Paolina, Vatican Palace* (London: Phaidon, 1975).

4. De Tolnay, *The Art and Thought of Michelangelo*, pp. 56ff.

5. Ibid., p. 57.

6. Erwin Panofsky, *Studies in Iconology: Humanistic Themes in the Art of the Renaissance* (New York: Harper & Row, 1972), p. 180.

7. De Tolnay, *The Art and Thought of Michelangelo*, p. 63.

8. Ibid., p. 71.

9. Steinberg, *Michelangelo's Last Paintings*, p. 52.

10. De Tolnay, *Michelangelo: Sculptor, Painter, Architect*, p. 114.

11. De Tolnay, *The Art and Thought of Michelangelo*, p. 58.

12. Ibid.

13. In Wallace K. Ferguson et al., *Six Essays: The Renaissance* (New York: Harper & Row, 1953), p. 88.

14. De Tolnay, *The Art and Thought of Michelangelo*, p. 57.

15. Hartt, *Michelangelo's Three Pietàs*, p. 30.

16. Ibid., p. 59.

17. Ibid., p. 43.

18. Panofsky, *Studies in Iconology*, p. 141.

19. Ibid., pp. 142–43.

20. De Tolnay, *The Art and Thought of Michelangelo*, pp. 41–42.

21. Ibid., p. 46.

22. Ibid., p. 44.

23. Ibid., pp. 47–48.

24. Ibid., p. 64.

25. Ibid., pp. 63–64.

26. Ibid., pp. 64–65.

27. Ibid., pp. 65–66.

28. Ibid., p. 69.

29. Ibid., p. 70.

30. Steinberg, *Michelangelo's Last Paintings*, p. 40.

31. Ibid.

32. Ibid.

33. Ibid., p. 52.

34. Charles de Tolnay, *Michelangelo, Vol. 5: The Final Period* (Princeton: Princeton University Press, 1960), p. 93.

35. Steinberg, *Michelangelo's Last Paintings*, p. 26.

36. Hartt, *Michelangelo's Three Pietàs*, p. 105.

37. Steinberg, *Michelangelo's Last Paintings*, p. 44.

38. Ibid., p. 40.

39. Ibid., p. 49.

40. Erik H. Erikson, *Young Man Luther* (New York: W. W. Norton and Co., 1962), pp. 212–13.

41. In a letter to the author dated 17 June, 1986, Frank La Brasca, a lecturer in Italian history and literature at the University of Paris, states, "this fusion . . . [of] the Creator and his creature, or as I would put it, of reflexivity between . . . a commentator and his 'auctor' . . . is one of the great themes of the Italian Renaissance."

42. De Tolnay, *The Art and Thought of Michelangelo*, p. 81.

43. Frank La Brasca's letter of 17 June 1986.

9

El Greco's Art in Counter-Reformation Spain

JOHN W. COOK

Spain is a country where thinkers and artists
have forever striven for the translation of
reality into the miraculous and of the
miraculous into reality. El Greco possessed
that capacity.[1]

The following lecture on the art of El Greco is one part of a two-semes-
ter course entitled "Christianity and the Arts" given at Yale University.
As professor of religion and the arts, I have been developing this
course for fifteen years. The material presented is organized chrono-
logically, covering the role of the arts in the Christian tradition from their
origins to the end of the eighteenth century. El Greco is studied in the
second semester. Meeting one and a half hours, twice a week, there
are fifty-two sessions in one academic year. Each lecture is illustrated
with slides. Outside the class, field trips are made to local museums as
well as relevant centers in New York City and Boston.

A variation of this lecture has also become a facet of the "History of
Christianity" course at Yale, an interdisciplinary course taught by four
professors (historian, theologian, art historian, and patristics scholar).

I was invited to give this lecture in a series of presentations that ac-
companied the touring exhibition of El Greco's paintings in the United
States in 1982 and 1983. The exhibition appeared at the National Gal-
lery of Art, Washington, DC, the Toledo Museum of Art, Ohio, and the
Museum of Fine Arts, Dallas, Texas. The catalogue, El Greco of Toledo
(Boston, MA: New York Graphic Society, 1982), is the best single
source of color prints of the works discussed in this lecture.

In order to appreciate fully El Greco's art, one must consider the religious atmosphere in which it was created and the purposes it served. The purpose of this lecture is to encourage the consideration of El Greco's paintings in relation to the religious climate in which they were created and, more specifically, to the spaces for which they were designed. While we are accustomed to viewing works of art as isolated pieces in the clarity and neutrality of an art museum, many of El Greco's paintings, especially those done for altarpieces, need to be seen within their original groupings and considered in relation to their function.

El Greco's painting of the *Burial of the Count of Orgaz* (1586–88; Santo Tomé, Toledo; fig. 17) illustrates how he composed a work in relation to its location. The upper portion of the composition presents a heavenly scene in which a "cloud of witnesses" attends the burial scene taking place in the lower portion. The late sixteenth-century grouping of figures, civic and religious, observes the moment that Sts. Stephen and Augustine deliver the body of the dead count to his tomb. A representation of El Greco's son, Jorge Manuel, stands to the left of St. Stephen. The composition suggests that the saints from heaven have entered the earthly world of Toledo to accompany local citizens to the burial of a local hero. On the wall of a chapel, this large painting visually represents one moment in time when a death that occurred in a previous century is presented in a sixteenth-century setting as two saints of the early church usher the count to his eternal reward. The actual tomb that will receive the count's body is below the painting. The organization of the picture takes the viewer from the multiple historical referents painted to the space of the chapel itself. Thus the setting in which the composition appears is a necessary part of a proper reading of the painting.[2]

Prior to considering specific examples of religious uses of El Greco's mannerist style and characteristics of his altarpiece compositions, two aspects of the religious situation in Spain provide a context within which he was working; namely, the Counter-Reformation and the Spanish Inquisition.

El Greco in the Counter-Reformation

The religious world of Toledo that El Greco experienced after he arrived (ca. 1577) consisted of factors that were shaping Europe at the time, as well as attitudes that were peculiarly Spanish.

17. El Greco, *The Burial of the Count of Orgaz* (1586–88; Santo Tomé, Toledo).

The Counter-Reformation movement within the Roman Catholic church counteracted charges of the Protestant Reformers, especially those made in Germany and Switzerland. The Roman Catholic church called a general council, the Council of Trent, meeting between 1545 and 1563, that produced doctrinal clarification and guidelines. In the council's final sessions, the church's position concerning the arts was promulgated.

The Tridentine teachings were enforced in Spain under the action of Philip II and maintained by each local bishop. Three different attitudes concerning the arts are specifically expressed in the orders from Trent and appear to relate to El Greco's work. These have to do with the images of the saints, the sacrament of penance, and the discussions concerning the Real Presence in the celebration of the Mass.

We shall consider how the following excerpts from the council's position on the arts relate to El Greco's work in Toledo.

> . . . the holy council decrees that no one is permitted to erect or cause to be erected in any place or church, howsoever exempt, any unusual image unless it has been approved by the bishop.[3]

> . . . images shall not be painted and adorned with a seductive charm.[4]

> . . . no representation of false doctrines and such as might be the occasion of grave error to the uneducated [shall] be exhibited.[5]

> . . . by means of the stories of the mysteries of our redemption portrayed in paintings and other representations, the people are instructed and confirmed in the articles of faith, which ought to be borne in mind and constantly reflected upon; also that great profit is derived from all holy images, not only because the people are thereby reminded of the benefits and gifts bestowed on them by Christ, but also because through the saints the miracles of God and salutary examples are set before the eyes of the faithful, so that they may give God thanks for those things, may fashion their own life and conduct in imitation of the saints and be moved to adore and love God and cultivate piety.[6]

These teachings suggest a pastoral function for the visual arts in that they are to lead believers to order their lives, to imitate the saints, to adore and love God, and to cultivate piety.

A large number of paintings of saints by El Greco, in which "their salutary examples are set before the eyes of the faithful," present pairs of saints with their attributes in order to inspire imitation and contemplation. For example, the famous study of Sts. Andrew and Francis (ca. 1590–95; Museo del Prado, Madrid) is one of this type. Andrew on the left and Francis on the right are paired in this composition outside of real time and place. Although they are historically separated by centuries, they are presented as though in dialogue. St. Andrew holds an X-shaped cross, the symbol of his own martyrdom. Tradition records that he was crucified upside down on this cross for his faithfulness. An example of obedience, chastity, and poverty, St. Francis exposes the wounds of Christ, the stigmata, which he received as a sign of his faithfulness. The literal presence of a cross and the wounds of Christ identify saints who have experienced Christ's sufferings in their own lives to be viewed as salutary examples.

Numerous paintings El Greco did of saints in an attitude of penance are more directly related to the teachings of Trent; compositions in which familiar saints are seen in the act of penance. Although the penance of St. Jerome had been a popular Italian theme, El Greco was presumably the first artist to paint St. Francis in this attitude. St. Francis kneels contemplating a crucifix, beneath which rests a skull (1585–90; Torello Collection, Barcelona). The moment represented refers to the Roman Catholic sacrament of penance, where one confesses one's sins and is reminded of Christ's sacrifice on the cross when Adam (the former self), symbolized by the skull, is replaced by a new being realized in Christ. The sacrament of penance was instituted by Christ for the remission of sins that were committed after baptism, and required outward acts of contrition on the part of the baptized faithful, whereby sorrow for sin was demonstrated.

The Council of Trent had reinforced the sacrament of penance in opposition to Reformation leaders who had eliminated penance as a sacrament and who stressed that salvation was by faith alone and for all time. Paintings like this reinforced the role of the sacrament of penance in the Counter-Reformation church in Spain.

St. Peter in Tears (1580–85; Bowes Museum, County Durham, England) is a Counter-Reformation hero. He who denied Christ is seen in penance. Even the humble chief of the apostles and the rock on whom the church was built is seen in contrition for his sin. In this panel, he is an example set before the faithful. In the left background of the painting, a shining angel sits on an empty tomb as one of the three Marys appears to be rushing away to "tell the others" of the Resurrection. Contemplating life, death, and the Resurrection, St. Peter looks heavenward as an example for piety.

These paintings provided models for believers who meditated upon them. The work of art served in a manner similar to the way the Spanish theologian, Diego de la Vega, wrote about the saints. He wanted to show "how the lives of saints could serve as mirrors from whose light and example we can compose and adorn our own."[7] El Greco's numerous paintings of saints relate in this regard to the spirit of the Tridentine rulings.

The Spanish Inquisition

A major factor of religious culture in Spain in the fifteenth and sixteenth centuries, the Spanish Inquisition was an established aspect of life in Toledo when El Greco arrived in Spain around 1577. The Inquisition had rooted itself in the Spanish culture during the reign of Queen Isabella, whose own hatred of the Moslems and the Jews was well known, and whose strict and dogmatic control was carried out by her inquisitor general, Tomas de Torquemada, between 1483 and 1493. By the end of the sixteenth century the Inquisition had become "hardened by the logic of its own system."[8] The spirit of free inquiry concerning beliefs and institutions had been stifled. In 1559 and 1561 there had been public executions of persons related to the Protestant Reformation, for example, the Lutherans at Seville and Vallodolid, and the Waldensians. By the end of the sixteenth century, Spanish Catholicism had been shaped in great measure by its refutation and conflict with its religious enemies—Judaism, Islam, Erasmianism, and various forms of Protestantism.

The Purity of Blood Issue

In 1547, thirty years prior to El Greco's arrival, the situation reached a dramatic stage at the Cathedral Church of Toledo (the premier church in Spain) when a statute concerning the "Purity of Blood" was endorsed, a statute that involved the exclusion of general heretical influences while attempting to purify its own interior leadership. The controversy concerning the Purity of Blood had to do with so-called new Christians whose families had been Jewish or Moslem. The intention was to exclude converted Jews and Moslems who had become Christians, especially those who had entered one of the monastic communities. This restrictive attitude toward non-Christian backgrounds spread throughout Spanish society, reaching its peak between 1590 and 1600, coincidentally, a decade of high productivity for El Greco who by then was in residence in Toledo.

Nothing in El Greco's art or documentation about him reflects the Purity of Blood controversy, even though he was obviously of foreign origin. With a background in the Greek Orthodox church, he seems not to have been suspect on any religious or racial grounds. Nothing in his art directly reflects the attitudes of the Spanish Inquisition or the specific restrictions of the Purity of Blood issue. He does not appear to have shaped his art to serve the negative influences of those seeking to purify the doctrinal and institutional structures of the church. On the contrary, El Greco's religious art is affirmative in the manner in which it treats history and religious heroes. As illustrated above, there are characteristics in his work that correspond to the spirit of the Council of Trent, but he appears to avoid explicit connections with the more negative aspects of the Spanish Inquisition.

El Greco's Mannerist Icons

El Greco's origins as a painter can be traced back to Greece, and to Crete where as a young man he painted icons. In Greek Orthodox worship icons provided access beyond themselves to the reality of the event or person imaged. Icon means image. In that tradition, images rested on stands or hung in an iconostasis in the main worship space. In an icon the figure is often presented as a portrait bust composed in stark frontality, engaging the observer in direct eye-to-eye contact. El Greco's Christ-figure painting, completed in Spain by about 1614 (1610–14; Museo del Greco, Toledo), reminds one of the traditional Greek Pantocrator, a figure that presented Christ as equal to God the Father and a powerful, if severe, presence in worship. Theologically, the Pantocrator image, according to Greek tradition, affirmed the consubstantiality of the Father and the Son. In the hands of El Greco this traditional subject is presented in Spain in an early seventeenth-century mannerist style that reflects his background as a Greek Orthodox icon painter. The Christ figure is one of a series of apostle paintings by El Greco, called *Apostolodos*. Each of the portraitlike panels presents a single apostle figure with an attribute related to his identity.

For instance, in a white robe of martyrdom *St. Bartholomew* (1610–14; Museo del Greco, Toledo) holds a knife in his right hand. (The knife refers to the means by which he was martyred, being skinned alive.) In his left hand he holds a chain looped around the head of a demon who is subdued by the saint's power—an image of domesticated, constrained evil. The treatment of the drapery in this painting draws attention to itself and reflects earlier Italian mannerist influences on El Greco. In this instance the voluminous white robe appears to be deep folds of stiff material. The robe is treated as a symbol and stands out as an almost separate entity within the composition. It is a mannerist device in painting that symbolizes martyrdom. There is an element of exaggeration in the treatment of the robe (a mannered treatment) that becomes an attribute of the significance of the figure.

Although *Saint Luke* (1605–10; Toledo Cathedral) was not one of the original twelve apostles, El Greco has included him in the series for obvious reasons. St. Luke is an evangelist-artist. He is the patron saint of artists due to the tradition that he did several portraits of the Virgin Mary and the child Jesus. El Greco has included a Virgin and Child portrait in this painting as though it were a page in an illuminated manuscript, a reference perhaps to El Greco's own past as a miniaturist, the vocation by which he was registered in Rome. Again the symbol for the saint represented calls attention to itself in a method typical of mannerism. Although these single figures are iconlike in scale and composition, they are decidedly mannerist in style.

Two additional paintings illustrate how he uses mannerist elements for religious purposes. The first of these is the *Espolio* or *Disrobing of Christ* (1577–79; Toledo Cathedral), painted shortly after El Greco's arrival in Toledo. It is often discussed because of the controversy about the appearance of the three Marys in the lower left corner. Their appearance in this scene is not consistent with the scriptural source (see Matt. 27:27–31). More interesting, however, is the manner in which this painting treats the subject matter in an emblematic and symbolic way. The narrative moment painted represents Christ among his accusers when his garment is about to be torn from him. It anticipates the moment he will be left naked prior to the Crucifixion. At the same time, the heavy blood-red garment with thick folds pulsates at the optical center of the composition in an elliptical shape that stands out away from the somber tones of brown, gray, and dull gold of the framing figures. The attention of the gray-brown crowd of human confusion is focused in the turmoil of the event itself. The attention of the Christ figure transcends the human turmoil and concentrates on a light from heaven. Spiritual presence contrasts with human presence. The color red stands out from the gray-brown tones. The formal elements of the work enhance the narration of the subject matter.

Furthermore, the painting hangs in the sacristy, a place where vesting, "robing" and preparation for the Eucharist takes place, the place where clergy prepare to go out to the altar where Christ's sacrifice will constantly be reenacted in the Eucharist. This painting hangs as a reminder and enactment of preparation for sacrifice. In three different aspects—narrative force, language of form, and placement—this painting is a remarkable work of mannerist liturgical art that served not the worshipping community directly but the clergy in preparation for the liturgy.

The second example of mannerist elements in a religious painting by El Greco is *Agony in the Garden* (1590–95; Toledo Museum of Art, Toledo, Ohio). El Greco relates a moment that combines Gospel texts[9] (see Matt. 26:36–47; Mark 14:32–43; Luke 22:40–47). Christ is at the center in a posture of prayer. The gestures of the hands and the facial expression denote receptivity to the will of God, suggesting the response of Christ, "Thy will be done." An angel of God, hovering on the surface of a cloud in a golden robe, holds the cup of sacrifice. Beneath the angel, in an elliptical opening of the cloud, the three apostles sleep. A divine light shines directly on Christ, and its brilliance changes the deep maroon of his robe into patches of luminous milky pink. Christ seems suspended from the hard surface of the earth as do the apostles and the angel. The right side of the painting is bathed in a different light, a strong moonlight that dots the landscape and reveals a

group of soldiers carrying torches and following the figure of
Judas.

The painting is a visual presentation of different "realities," as
well as the juxtaposition of episodes from the Gospel texts. In this
work, one observes real and unreal space, light, color, and weight.
As far as the space is concerned, compare the "real" landscape
with Judas to the ambiguous area of the sleeping apostles. Note
the way El Greco breaks up the foreground-middle ground-back-
ground regions of the painting by having incongruous elements
overlap; for example, the cloud around the moon at the right is in
front of the mound in the center. The sleeping apostles appear to
be displaced from the landscape. Three kinds of light illumine the
scene, moonlight, torchlight, and "divine radiance." Exceptional
treatment of color is illustrated in the surfaces of Christ's robe; the
deep colors contrast with the dissolving tones in the highlights.
Real and unreal weight are suggested by the rocky mound as the
backdrop behind the "sliding, hovering" figure of Christ in the center, who is also in contrast with the stable position of the kneeling
angel on the cloud. All of these compositional devices give the
painting a spiritual quality that emphasizes a sense of mystery.
Martin Soria comments on these qualities: "Cervantes's *Don Qui-
xote* succeeded in making the incredible so real that it became a
way of life, and El Greco likewise possessed that capacity for transforming the supernatural into intangible truth."[10] El Greco continued to develop these characteristics until his fully mature mannerist style appeared in the great altarpieces he painted in Toledo.

Altarpieces

Retables, or altar backdrops, had taken on a peculiarly Spanish
character in the fifteenth century, not exactly reproduced in any
other part of Europe. El Greco knew the art world of Venice inti-
mately, and there are large retables from that period created by
his teachers, especially Titian. However, in none of these is the
scale, program of painting, or doctrinal preoccupation, a direct antecedent to El Greco's Spanish altarpieces.

The traditional medieval altarpiece composed in a tripartite
fashion had been commonplace until the first half of the fifteenth
century in Spain. For instance, the Altarpiece of Fray Bonifacio

Ferrer (ca. 1400; San Carlos Museum, Valencia) is divided into three parts with a raised central panel painting of the Crucifixion. Its sharply silhouetted figures and flat graphic form reflect its medieval antecedents.

Almost fifty years later, the Altarpiece of the Transfiguration (ca. 1450, Barcelona Cathedral) was organized in a similar fashion, although planes of perspective and chiaroscuro modeling are introduced. Some elements suggest, within the tripartite arrangement, influences from Northern European painting.

A transitional phase of altarpiece construction in Spain is illustrated in the Altarpiece of the Holy Spirit (1394; Church of Santa Maria, Manresa). Here the painted surface is broken into multiple panels relating horizontally and vertically to a central theme. These narrative niches anticipate the schematic arrangement, if not the scale, of things to come.

Between 1431 and 1480 the alabaster altarpiece of the Saragossa Cathedral was completed, presenting a grand architectural Gothic screen where Christ stands in openings to the left and right of a nativity scene. The complete retable resembles an architectural facade framing sacred figures.

These ideas take on extended monumental proportions in the altarpiece for the Toledo Cathedral, completed between 1498 and 1504. Constructed from larchwood, the filigree facade opens in windows framing scenes of the sacred story. The figures are pulled out to the surface of the screen for visual clarity, painted in colors that distinguish them from the gold frames. A detail of the base of the Toledo altarpiece at the height of the altar suggests an architectural model in which a miniature portal under a Gothic canopy opens onto a grouping of figures. This is the altar El Greco saw when he first visited the Toledo Cathedral. Schematically, similar ideas will appear later in his own altarpieces. The evolution of form suggested in these few examples appears to be toward altarpieces that stand as architectural screens in which scenes of holy figures reside in windowlike openings to attract the imagination of the worshipper.

By 1563 Gaspar Becerra had designed an altarpiece for the high altar of the Astorga Cathedral. In a preliminary drawing, the framework for the figures is conceived as an architectural facade with windows. The buildinglike qualities are boldly articulated.

The multistory building opens at the ground level (altar level) through a miniature central door. The windows on each "floor" open as settings for sacred scenes. The "roof" is crowned with a cornice and pediment. The total effect suggests that the altarpiece is a facade placed in front of a heavenly mansion approached through the small door at the top of the altar, for example, the level of the sacraments. Sacred events are revealed in its windows. In the drawing by Becerra, the evolution of form from 1400 to 1560 has reached a distinctive design concept based on architectural motifs.

El Greco was particularly responsive to this design concept. From his Greek background he was accustomed to framing religious pictures in an iconostasis inside worship spaces. In Spain he created mannerist icons to be hung in great retable facades. If the traditional Byzantine icon brings the spiritual universe into the historic moment of the observer, El Greco's mannerist icons appear in grand architectural screens where the religiously historic episodes are presented as moments of great spiritual insight.

The altarpieces he created in Spain are multimedia presentations of painting, sculpture, and architecture that include many of the mannerist aspects described previously. A view toward the altar in the interior of Santo Domingo el Antiguo at Toledo reveals an elaborate architectural framework for a series of paintings. Each relates to the large central image entitled *Assumption of the Virgin* (1577–79; Art Institute, Chicago) that presents the Virgin of the Immaculate Conception at the moment of her Assumption into heaven. The doctrine of the Immaculate Conception was of major theological concern for Spanish theologians in the sixteenth century who had pressed the Council of Trent to formulate and standardize the doctrine for the Roman Catholic church. Although the Spaniards at the Council of Trent did not succeed in getting a major reformation of the doctrine into the final documents, the doctrine remained a vital expression of the Roman Catholic church in Spain. This altarpiece illustrates the artist's attempt to visualize in one painting two major doctrines concerning Mary—her purity and her Assumption. The full assemblage of this altarpiece includes seven paintings: the Assumption in the center, flanked on the lower left and right by full length images of Sts. John the Baptist and John the Evangelist. Above them, on the left and right respectively, are the half-figure images of Sts. Bernard and Benedict. On a central axis above the Assumption is a cartouche with a portrait face of Christ. These six are surmounted by the large and exceedingly beautiful painting of the Trinity.

Each composition relates to subjects outside its own pictorial frame. Attended by Gospel writers and saints who sing her praises, Mary rises from earth toward heaven to reside in the Trinitarian cosmos flooded with golden light. She appears here as the Blessed Virgin of the Immaculate Conception, but the grouping of the pictures suggests a narrative progression that anticipates her coronation as Queen of Heaven. The individual paintings of this altarpiece have been removed from this original setting and sold to various institutions. Only by considering the original relationships of all seven does one enjoy the full meaning of each.[11]

Being the first major project that El Greco realized upon his arrival in Toledo, this altarpiece program illustrates his confidence and expertise in handling complex theological subject matter for liturgical settings. Architecturally, the total concept suggests a facade with windowlike openings through which one views holy scenes and figures.

Many of his large panel paintings were originally composed for groupings in altarpiece frames. The evidence suggests that El Greco's painterly style took formative shape in Venice and later in Rome under the Italian mannerists, as mentioned above. However, in Spain as he shaped his style in a highly individual manner, he appears to have been influenced by Spanish retable builders to enlarge the scale of his works.

The best illustration is given in a full view of the collected panels painted for the College of Doña María de Aragon.[12] Originally, the windows of the retable presented six scenes. The upper three panels, an arrangement suggested by Alfonso E. Perez Sanchez, are, left to right, the Resurrection, the Crucifixion, and Pentecost. The lower three, left to right, are the Nativity, the Annunciation (fig. 18), and the Baptism. Each composition presents the major figures at the surface of the panel for visual clarity. Each grouping includes clearly delineated major figures, ambiguous clusters of crowded, moving figures, and, finally, amorphous forms that appear to take shape and dissolve in light.

In the Resurrection scene, the distorted and tumbling bodies in the lower half of the picture seem chaotic as they writhe in the cool, stable presence of the elevated, resurrected Christ who gently supports an enormous banner of victory. The contrast between stable central axis and contorted confusion sets up a tension between the world and Christ in the composition.

In the Crucifixion scene, the silent anguish of the three figures at the foot of the cross—Mary the mother of Jesus on the left, John the Beloved Disciple on the right, and Mary Magdalene kneeling in the center, is complemented by the three angels, one related to each of these figures. Above Mary an angel catches the blood of the wound in Christ's side, while above John an angel attempts to catch drops from the left hand of Christ. At the foot of the cross, the angel near Mary Magdalene is viewed from behind and holds a sponge as though retaining the blood from the wounds in Christ's feet. Christ appears to be watching enigmatically as the world beneath him takes the blood of his sacrifice. The composition and placement of the painting relate directly to the liturgy of the Eucharist continuously reenacted on the table beneath the scenes.

In the Pentecost scene, tongues of flame hover over each head of the fifteen figures. As the dove of the Holy Spirit soars in a burst of light at the top of the painting, the surrounding space darkens as the quietly ecstatic figures receive the Holy Spirit. The center of the group opens beyond the tilted heads of the two lower figures. The gestures indicate a posture of willing receptivity. The composition seems to anticipate the presence of the Holy Spirit in their midst, and consequently, in the midst of the church building in . which the painting appears. The Nativity scene composes the figures around the figure of the Christ Child and highlights the various elements from a central radiance. Iconographically, Christ is presented to those who approach him in the painting (or, simultaneously, at the altar) as the light of the world.

Heaven and earth seem simultaneously present in the Baptism scene. The narrative elements of water and earth at the feet of John the Baptist and Jesus are caught up into a larger context, a spiritual universe of celebration and praise. This is an excellent example of El Greco's uses of reality subjected to the force of his iconographic inventions. Once the theme of the altarpiece was determined by the commissioner, the church, the compositional and painterly inventions of the artist gave the program its distinctive

18. El Greco, *The Annunciation* (1596–1600; Prado, Madrid).

character. In this painting of the baptism, the real setting of a baptism on a river bank is transfixed as a heavenly pageant with motifs of transcendence suggested by the airy light atmosphere with floating forms.

The central panel of the lower zone of these paintings in this altarpiece is the Annunciation scene (fig. 18). It is, to my mind, the masterpiece of his later years, splendid, particular, and mysterious. Mary kneels on the left gesturing in a posture of willing acceptance as the angel of the Lord enters on the right. The furnishings in her room are indicated, including her sewing basket in the center. All is bathed in a divine light. The humble maiden's chamber is transformed into a miraculous vision of a heavenly realm. Heaven and earth meet, colors burst forth, forms swim and dissolve, and light breaks in. Above the basket in the center, a bush is in flame but does not burn, another symbol of the Virgin's Immaculate Conception and her continual purity. The painting appears to be a historic moment simultaneously caught up in another world of mysterious light, activity, and celestial beings.

We are told that El Greco worked his canvasses for a long time, continuing to achieve a sense of spontaneity and vibrancy. A close inspection of this canvas reveals passages of some of his most expressive surfaces and freest color work. Note the area to the right of the burning bush and in front of the angel. There is a kind of dance of colorful strokes reflecting a sense of spontaneity and delight, yet kept in harmony with the formal elements of the composition. The surface of this painting dances with painterly expressions that articulate the spirit of its iconography.

In this altarpiece these paintings appear to be windows of divine presence, not in the form of rigid, frontal figures staring at the viewer from another world, but as scenes of real historical moments caught up in a spiritual universe. As visually stated, they also reinforce a doctrine of the Real Presence, a presence viewed and continually reenacted in the liturgy, hence another reflection of the priorities of the Council of Trent. During the celebration of the Eucharist, the painted history of Christ's sacrifice is caught up in a spiritual universe. The salvation of the human soul is affected as the historical event reenacted and celebrated in the bread and wine at the altar as the Real Presence is present in the painterly visions in the altarpiece.[13]

The significance of El Greco's achievement is further illustrated when one remembers how the central most important habit in late sixteenth- and early seventeenth-century life in Spain was the so-called Life in the Sacrament. The pervasive nature of the Catholic faith in Spain shaped the cultural and economic life. "Daily life was saturated with religion"[14] and in that context practice of the sacraments, or continued life in the sacraments, was necessary for salvation. Spanish temperament acceded to this persuasion and the teachings of the Counter-Reformation church enforced it. Persons who refrained from taking the sacrament regularly were accused of scandalous behavior. Ongoing life in the sacrament as a priority for a total society placed new significance on the liturgy and the setting for the liturgy, the altarpiece. It is fair, therefore, to suggest that during El Greco's time, the composition, construction and completion of an altarpiece was religiously and culturally significant in the society. El Greco was creating appropriate images for a major aspect of that society's values. His altarpieces were settings for the liturgical actions that were necessary for the salvation of the soul and the society. Considered in this light, El Greco's altarpieces sum up, articulate, and direct a public social consciousness and a pious religious consciousness that, escaping from the heresies of Protestantism and from Judaism and Islam, needed the continuous presence of mystical images that affirmed holy Christian history. Seen in their original settings, these altarpiece paintings visualize the mystical world view of the Counter-Reformation in Spain and illustrate the genius of El Greco's art.

NOTES

1. George Kubler and Martin Soria, *Art and Architecture in Spain and Portugal and Their American Dominions, 1500–1880* (Baltimore, MD: Penguin, 1959), p. 215.

2. For a detailed iconographic interpretation of this painting, see the essay by Jonathan Brown, "El Greco: Between the Renaissance and the Counter Reformation," in a forthcoming collection, *Art and Religion: Faith, Form, and Reform* (Columbia, University of Missouri, 1986), p. 57-60.

3. Henry J. Schroeder, trans., *Canons and Decrees of the Council of Trent* (St. Louis and London: B. Herder Book Co., 1941), p. 217.

4. Ibid., p. 216.

5. Ibid.

6. Ibid.

7. Diego de la Vega, *Paraiso de la gloria de los santos* (Toledo, 1602), in Richard L. Kagan, "The Toledo of El Greco," *El Greco of Toledo* (Boston: New York Graphic Society, 1982), p. 57.

8. B. Bennassar, *The Spanish Character* (Berkeley: University of California Press, 1979), p. 80.

9. I continue to return to this as one of the most visually stunning works in the history of Western art. See William Jordan, "Catalogue of the Exhibition," *El Greco of Toledo*, p. 237.

10. Kubler and Soria, *Art and Architecture in Spain and Portugal*, p. 214. For a thorough study and more recent interpretation of the complexity of El Greco's altarpiece compositions, see Richard G. Mann, *El Greco and His Patrons: Three Major Projects* (Cambridge: Cambridge University Press, 1986).

11. It should be noted that this collection of paintings over the main altar is flanked by two side altars. Each originally had paintings by El Greco—left, *Adoration of the Shepherds* and right, *Resurrection*—that increased the complexity of the total iconographic program.

12. I am indebted to Alfonso E. Perez Sanchez for this reconstruction of the program of paintings. His arrangement is not uniformly accepted by scholars, but the fact that these panels were painted for altarpieces, regardless of their particular relationships, must be kept in mind.

13. Jonathan Brown has recently claimed that "El Greco became one of the most convincing interpreters of the mysteries of the Catholic faith ever to paint." "El Greco: Between the Renaissance and the Counter Reformation," p. 57.

14. B. Bennassar, *The Spanish Character*, p. 256. See also, William A. Christian, Jr., *Local Religion in Sixteenth-Century Spain* (Princeton: Princeton University Press, 1981).

10

Two Faces of Christ:
What Makes Religious Art Good Art?

WILLIAM HENDRICKS

The Puritan proscriptions against theater, dance, and frivolous embel-
lishments were taken seriously by the churches of the Southern Baptist
Convention. In the nineteenth century many of our churches were
built predicated upon the assumption that God loved ugly. Until re-
cently the mention of liturgical dance created a furor which gave more
trouble than the tempos were worth. Even now discreet euphemisms
such as interpretive movement or the use of the body in worship are
used to allay anxiety. Visual art is confined to the romantic reconstruc-
tions of Bernard Plockhorst (1825–1907), Haym Saloman (1740–85),
and the Sunday School leaflet genre. If one combines this general
anticultural posture with an exclusive concern for the verbal mode
of worship, then one has fertile mission territory for propagating an
adequate understanding of the word of God as eikon *rather than as*
logos.

In response to an interest in the visual mode, I was asked to initiate
courses in religion and the arts at the Southern Baptist Theological
Seminary. Additionally, a Center for Religion and the Arts was estab-
lished. Its purpose is to create an interface for the various fine arts with
the religious heritage, contemporary experiences, and multiple minis-
tries of the Christian community. This is accomplished through classes
and seminars, workshops, presentations, exhibitions, and dramatic,
musical, and multimedia productions.

The basic course, "Christianity and the Arts," is a theological elec-
tive in our curriculum. The introductory class is a general overview with
lectures by architects, musicians, painters, sculptors, theater produc-
ers/directors, denominational representatives assigned to ministry in-

volving art forms, media producers, ballet directors, creative writers, and literature professors. Field trips are made to local museums, art galleries, and a stained-glass window studio. One of the visual arts presentations I offer is a slide lecture entitled "The Faces of Christ," which stresses various media and which is multiethnic and contemporary in nature. The slides from that group provide an interesting comparison. Two of these paintings give focus to the question, What makes religious art "good" art? Or what is the distinction between "great" religious art and merely "good" religious art?[1]

The question, What makes religious art good art? can be preemptorily answered by an artist. It is less easily answered by a theologian. This is true because theologians who are not artists, first of all, are unaware of the skill and technique required to produce "good painting"; second, often bring more agenda to a religious painting than the artist did; and third, are guided by critics who set the "rules" as to what is and what is not "great" and "good" art. Good artists possess the necessary skill and technique developed through a discipline of training. The majority of artists have a minimal interest in a theological agenda and tend to ignore critics. I am *homo theologicus*. Therefore I must struggle with the double agenda of "good" theology and "good" art. Both are at a premium.

In this analysis of two paintings, I hope to raise central issues for those interested in religion and the visual arts. With malice aforethought, two opposite, contrasting, and utterly disparate examples of thematically intentional and representational Christian works of art have been chosen: Dante Gabriel Rossetti's (1828–82) *The Passover in the Holy Family: Gathering Bitter Herbs* (1855; Tate Gallery, London; fig. 19) and Georges Rouault's (1871–1958) *Christ and the High Priest* (1937; Phillips Collection, Washington, DC; fig. 20).[2] An initial narrative of each work is in order. This Rossetti painting was commissioned by Sir John Ruskin (1819–1900) in 1854. Rossetti had proposed two sketches, *Gathering Bitter Herbs* and *Eating of the Passover*, to Ruskin who preferred the general details of the first and even selected a model for the youthful Jesus, a very nice little fellow whom I picked out from the Saint Martin's School, the other day. He has a lovely head, and such a beautiful forehead.[3]

The scene of the resultant painting, *The Passover in the Holy Family*, depicts a youthful Jesus, whose head Rossetti repainted three times. Finally, the artist cut the canvas and patched in the final "fine head." The youthful Jesus holds a bowl of blood from which Zechariah sprinkles the door posts. A compliant John the Baptist latches the sandal of Jesus while Mary gathers the bitter herbs. On an interior table are the bread and wine for the Passover meal. Joseph brings in the lamb, and Elizabeth lights the pyre. By the well are sticks shaped in a cross. The opening of the chamber is framed by a grapevine. A memorial window using the design of this picture was executed in 1883 for the Holy Trinity Church, Birchington-on-Sea. The painting passed from Ruskin's collection to the Ashmolean Museum, Oxford, to its current home.[4]

Georges Rouault's *Christ and the High Priest* presents a striking figure of Christ facing the audience. Banded by a block of color which renders him impervious to the malevolent, malignant attitude of the doctor/high priest, Christ's frontal image contrasts to his antagonist's profile. As in all of Rouault's later works, each figure is graphically contained in its own bands of black and its own field of color. The coarse stroking of the paint points to the stained-glass effect which is Rouault's trademark and reflects his earliest training as a worker in stained glass.

I recently studied this painting at first hand, observed it from every vantage, and was grasped by the placid contentment of the Christ and the vivid hostility of his adversary. Even skillful reproductions and photographs do not do the painting justice. The three dimensional effect of built-up paint cannot be captured by the flatness of a photograph. Neither can the subtle richness of the field of color that marks the distinction between the two figures be conveyed. This is an electrifying picture, and its painter deserves the accolades which have been heaped upon him, including the epithet, greatest religious painter of the twentieth century.[5] Conversely, in our current setting, the Pre-Raphaelites are neglected and damned with faint praise.[6]

Why is Rouault's painting considered "great religious art" and Rossetti's merely "good religious art"? Is it a question of subject matter, of artistic temperament, of character, or of technical skill? Is Rouault "great" and Rossetti "maudlin" simply because the critics say so? Does the age and its aesthetic tastes and religious sensibilities determine such a judgment, set the standards, or assign the accolades? Is beauty in the eye of the beholder, the fancy of an era, or inherent in the work of art itself?

It is a reductionist perspective which affirms that art is merely "paint on canvas." Painting is also technique. Rossetti's technique is fine, intense; his colors are luminous and bold; and his details are precise and exact. His figures are pretty, romantic, larger than life, and ethereal in quality.

George Chabot (1890–1975) says that Rouault's paintings give the effect of

> congealed lava, in which luminous tones . . . crackle among dark, rugged impastos. . . . The light does not come from without, does not fall upon the forms, but emerges from the canvas itself.[7]

Rouault's works are stark, imprecise, surreal via his postimpressionist style. There is no romance here. There are no soft and gentle children; only the passionate, suffering Christ of the *Miserere*. Rossetti is specific while Rouault is suggestive. Both paint on canvas, but the simple description of "paint on canvas" does not explain why one painting is preferable to or better than the other.

Even the most grudging modern art critic must grant Rossetti's skill, if not in the *Passover of the Holy Family*, then surely in *The Day Dream* (1880; Victoria and Albert, London) or the *Astarte Syriaca* (1877; City of Manchester Art Galleries), romanticized portraits of Janey Morris, or the *Beata Beatrix* (1864; Tate Gallery, London), a posthumous portrait of Elizabeth Siddal. Likewise, even the most stubborn representationalist must acknowledge the skill and power apparent in Rouault's *Miserere*.

One might suppose that the moral character and spiritual temperament of the painter resulted in a good or great work of religious art. However, the principle of cause and effect is inoperative here. If the Victorians were "more religious" or "more moral" than persons in the twentieth century (a highly dubious, even if widely

19. Dante Gabriel Rossetti, *The Passover in the Holy Family: Gathering Bitter Herbs* (1855; The Tate Gallery, London).

held, supposition), Dante Gabriel Rossetti would have been more at home with modern mores. Conversely, Georges Rouault's conservatism would have "amused" even Queen Victoria, who would have been pleased enormously by his moral character and familial piety.

As different as Rossetti and Rouault were in their lifestyles, they shared a mutuality in the relationship of their painting with their poetry. In fact, Rossetti penned a sonnet, "The Passover in the Holy Family," about his painting by the same title:

> Here meet together the prefiguring day
> And day prefigured, "Eating, thou shalt stand,
> Feet shod, loins girt, thy road-staff in thine hand,
> With blood-stained door and lintel,"—did God say
> By Moses' mouth in ages passed away.
> And now, where this poor household doth comprise
> At Paschal-Feast two kindred families,—
> Lo! the slain lamb confronts the Lamb to slay.
> The pyre is piled. What agony's crown attained,
> What shadow of Death the Boy's fair brow subdues
> Who holds that blood wherewith the porch is stained
> By Zachary the priest? John binds the shoes
> He deemed himself not worthy to unloose;
> And Mary culls the bitter herbs ordained.[8]

Rouault wrote sublimely and expressively, although he is not celebrated for his poetry as Rossetti was. Rouault wrote:

> You shall celebrate all living things:
> The smile of the newborn infant
> When he begins to stammer
> The first buds in spring
> The first work you created
> Apprentice, even if it was a failure
> In the hope of doing better.
> Don't conceal your pleasure
> Over a color harmony
> Even if you hit on it by chance.
> Celebrate the long road
> In the golden summer sun
> The friendly white house
> The little path
> And its cheerful occupants

20. Georges Rouault, *Christ and the High Priest* (1937; The Phillips Collection, Washington, D.C.).

Who rejoice over
Your imaginary successes
First fruits of a lifework
Slow to be born
But steadily growing
Some new trouble every day.
Celebrate the living source
The bark that drifts by noiselessly
Over the sleeping waters
The wheat swaying under the wind
Which is to be harvested tomorrow
Everything is occasion
For serene joy or toil
According as your heart and mind decree
The tiniest flower fades and dies.
In the desolate meadows of Unhappiness.

Be by turns
Romantic
Fauve
Cubist
Orphist
Futurist
Rhomboidist
Classical tomorrow—why not?
See how rich you are
My dear son!
I am but a will-o'-the-wisp
Which trembles in the wind and vanishes
Then is reborn once
To vanish forever.
There are also difficult victories
Very somber defeats
And famous retreats
More glorious than victories
Blessed meditations
Long infinite patiences
Dumb victims
Thanksgiving after childbirth
And obscure loves
In this beloved art.
Some are pampered
Other excommunicated
But no matter—provided your heart
Unhappy artist
Keeps holiday![9]

Different eras do have diverse tastes. How else could we style them "different" eras? The Victorian era preferred the romantic and the sentimental. The impressionists showed first in the radical Le Salon Refusée, and the postimpressionists sought a return to reality via impressionist techniques. Rouault spoke to a visual audience conditioned by Pablo Picasso (1881–1973) and Georges Braque (1882–1963). It may be that Rouault is "great" because he is in style and Rossetti is merely "good" because he is passé. Might we suppose that Rossetti can come back in favor and Rouault become declassé? Given the sweeping wave of nostalgia in our culture, this is not inconceivable.

It seems to me that two factors enable us to make some determination in evaluating these two examples of religious art. These are: the subject matter and the subtlety of the painterly treatment. Rossetti gives us a cloyingly sweet treatment of tender youth, whereas Charles Dickens's portrayal of Fagan's juveniles was more realistic, even in its own day. Rouault's Christ of the Passion is a man for all seasons. What is at issue is more than a separation of the man (Christ) and the boy (Jesus). Rossetti's sweet and pretty youth is basically unbelievable either as a first-century Jew, a nineteenth-century lad, or a twentieth-century child. Even in his quasi-impressionist pastiche, Rouault's Christ presents a poignant figure who is a man of sorrows, acquainted with grief, a man who is in the first-century style, but one who evokes the timeless response of pathos in the face of innocent suffering, of passive resistance to powerful intolerance and hatred. It is subject matter which, in my opinion, makes Rouault's *Christ and the High Priest* "great" and Rossetti's *The Passover in the Holy Family: Gathering Bitter Herbs* "good."

The second factor in the judgment of Rouault as "great" and Rossetti as "good" is the subtlety of the painterly treatment. Rossetti says too much, too openly and too patently. In a letter, Pre-Raphaelite poet Coventry Patmore (1823–86) criticized Rossetti's painting because: "The symbolism is too remote and unobvious to strike me as effective."[10] John Ruskin was more direct, "Patmore is very nice; but what the mischief does he mean by symbolism? I call the Passover plain prosy fact. No symbolism at all."[11] Plain prosy fact does not lend itself to greatness. Rossetti shows all, depicts too much, and leaves nothing in the shadows.

Art historian, Christian Zervos (1889–1970) said of Rouault's works:

> This art, as Rouault conceived it, results in a humanism situated
> halfway between spirituality and materiality, between the dream
> and knowledge. This humanism obliged him . . . to restore the ties
> of mutual balance and reciprocal penetration between the artist
> and the cosmos. . . . However sincere his religious feelings may
> have been, Rouault never overdid their manifestation.[12]

It is in the balance, the not overdoing that we find Rouault's "unbearable lightness of being."[13]

In the midst of these distinctions between "great" religious art and "good" religious art, we have analyzed two disparate paintings. Even in their disparity, both of these artists exercised commonality in their technical skill and poetic sensibilities; they are separated by different lifestyles, and the spirit and temper of their individual audiences. The most telling criteria for evaluating Rossetti's *The Passover in the Holy Family: Gathering Bitter Herbs* and Rouault's *Christ and the High Priest* were the subject matter and the subtlety of the painterly treatment. Substance and subtlety, subject and style make a decided difference.

NOTES

1. The substance of the following is used by permission of the Owensboro Art Museum, Owensboro, KY. See *Christianity and the Visual Arts: Kentucky Collections* (exhibition catalogue, n.p., n.d.), pp. 30-33.

2. See Pierre Courthion, *Georges Rouault* (New York: Harry N. Abrams Inc., Publisher, n.d.), p. 427 (cat. no. 228). Courthion refers to this painting as *Christ and the Doctor.*

3. See Virginia Surtrées, *The Paintings and Drawings of Dante Gabriel Rossetti (1828–1882): A Catalogue Raisonné,* 2 vols. (London: Oxford University Press, 1971), 1:84 (cat. no. 78), for the picture; 2:40-41, for the description.

4. Ibid., 2:40.

5. See G. di San Lazzaro, ed., *Homage to Georges Rouault* (New York: Tudor Publishing Co., 1971); and Courthion, *Georges Rouault,* "Greatness and Accomplishment," sect. 6, pp. 233–389, and "Salvation and Redemption," sect. 8, pp. 341–73.

6. See Katharine Morrison McClinton, *Christian Church Art Through the Ages* (New York: Macmillan Co., 1962), pp. 118–19.

For a more appreciative view, see *The Pre-Raphaelites: A Catalogue of the Tate Gallery Exhibition 7 March–28 May 1984,* (ed. Alan Bowness (London: Tate Gallery/ Penguin Books, 1984). For Rouault's poetry, see Courthion, *Georges Rouault,* pp. 341ff. For an extensive evaluation of Rossetti's art and poetry with bibliographical references, see William E. Fredeman *Pre-Raphaelitism: A Bibliocritical Study* (Cambridge: Harvard University Press, 1965), pp. 90–132.

7. In Courthion, *Georges Rouault,* p. 236.

8. See *Rossetti's Poems,* ed. Oswald Doughty (London: J. M. Dent and Sons, Ltd., 1961), p. 140. Quoted also in Surtrées, *Paintings and Drawings,* p. 41.

For an acknowledgement that Rossetti's poetry took precedence over his painting, see *The Pre-Raphaelites,* ed. Bowness, p. 13.

9. From *Soliloquis,* Neuchatel, *Ides et Calendes,* 1944, in Corthion, *Georges Rouault,* pp. 399–400.

10. In Surtrées, *Paintings and Drawings,* p. 41.

11. Ibid.

12. San Lazzaro, *Homage to George Rouault,* p. 97.

13. The title of a novel by Milan Kundera, translated from the Czech by Michael Henry Hein (New York: Harper & Row, 1984).

PART III

VISUAL ARTS IN
RELIGIOUS PRAXIS

11

Art and Social Justice

JAMES L. EMPEREUR

The purpose of "Aesthetic Theology" is to investigate the relationship between art and religion/theology. In particular, the course seeks to answer the questions: Is art a form of theology? In what way can art be a method of theologizing? The hermeneutical issues involved are raised through a study of Image as Insight *by Margaret R. Miles.¹ Then the course proceeds to trace historically how religion and art have been expressions of each other, how religious beliefs have been embodied in art forms, and how art is a parallel activity to theology. Extensive readings in* Arts and Ideas *by William Fleming² and* Art, Creativity, and the Sacred, *edited by Diane Apostolos-Cappadona,³ provide the structure and content for this section of the course.* Feeling and Form *by Susanne Langer⁴ is the main text for dealing with the individual art forms as ways of theologizing. Several other issues such as the importance of the imagination in theology and art, art as a form of religious inculturation, and the relationship of art to liturgy are part of the course. The relationship of art to social justice is an important dimension of the course. A sample lecture on that topic follows.*

That there is a relationship between the arts and society is neither new nor surprising. However, this concern has emerged only in the second half of the twentieth century. The history of the visual arts presents us with some well-known and often dramatic examples of the artist as critic of society. There is a way in which all artists, to the degree that they occupy a somewhat marginal existence vis-á-vis ordinary society, actually function as social critics. Usually when we connect social criticism with art, we have specific works of art in mind. These are remembered more for their subject matter or the response of those who were the object of the critique than the quality of the works of art themselves. These works often become relativized once the occasions which motivated their creation have passed. If such works of art are to be significant today, we need to become acquainted with their historical contexts.

When speaking of art- and justice-oriented issues, there are some great paintings which have transcended and continue to transcend their origins. For instance, we think of paintings such as Francisco Goya's *The Execution of the Third of May* (1814–15; Prado, Madrid) or Eugene Delacroix's *Liberty Leading the People* (1830; Louvre, Paris). If we were more artistically literate, we would review the American scene by moving from John Trumbull's *The Declaration of Independence* (1786–94; Yale University Art Gallery) to Ben Shahn's *The Passion of Sacco and Vanzetti* (1931–32; Whitney Museum, New York). According to tastes, others might include such diverse works as Jacques Louis David's *The Death of Socrates* (1787; Metropolitan Museum of Art, New York) or Diego Rivera's *The Liberation of the Peon* (1931; Philadelphia Museum of Art). And for those who have only a superficial acquaintance with the arts, there is always Pablo Picasso's *Guernica* (1937; Prado, Madrid) which has now become a paradigm of the call for justice incarnated in an art object.

Many contemporary painters carry on the tradition of social critic by championing the cause of the weak, the poor, and the oppressed. Often this means exploring areas of human ugliness previously considered by many as unacceptable as the subject matter for painting. For instance, in several works of Georges Rouault (1871–1958), a depth of human compassion for those who suffer from various forms of exploitation is found. Anyone who is acquainted with some of the plates of his *Miserere* series knows how the artist's paintbrush has "lowered the mighty from their thrones." The Mexican muralists, such as Jose Clemente Orozco (1883–1949), identified with their country's revolution against exploitative capitalism in ways that are now being reiterated by the literary artists of Latin America such as the Uruguayan, Eduardo Galeano, in his *Days and Nights of Love and War*.

Such artists take up the cause of victims of social injustice with the explicitness and starkness of a Ben Shahn whose *Miner's Wives*

(1948; Philadelphia Museum of Art) captures the constant fear and anxiety of those whose livelihood depends on such a dangerous occupation. In the Museum of Modern Art, New York, one can experience *The Butcher* by the English painter Francis Bacon (b. 1910). In a somewhat surrealistic fashion, Bacon continues his judgment on the dehumanizing effects of urban life and mass media. Less forceful, but still compelling, the work of Andrew Wyeth (b. 1917) draws our attention to a decaying society and its unfulfilled expectations.

Since certain paintings are contextualized by specific situations which call for human justice, it cannot be presumed that they are weaker aesthetically or rendered less communicative because of their origins. Paul Tillich argued that the simple fact that the criticism of injustice in our world is presented in works of art "elevates critical realism above mere negativity."[5] Tillich's attitude is verified in Goya's *The Execution of the Third of May* (fig. 21). The historical background for the picture is Napoleon's conquest of Spain in 1808. Apparently the French invasion entailed considerable brutality. An attack on the invaders on the second of May resulted in severe reprisals on the day following. Many innocent people were executed and people were indiscriminantly killed. Goya's work depicts a group of Spaniards facing the firing squad. Several have already been shot and are lying at the feet of those awaiting execution. Beyond them, another group of victims stand in line. With its barren ground and darkened buildings, the landscape seems ominous.

This history is helpful, but the painting has a meaning which transcends these details. Long before I knew the historical background, this picture had great import for me. One senses that something cruel and meaningless is occurring, that human rights and life are being violated. At the center of the picture, the young man who flings open his arms in a gesture of vulnerability, moves forward with his companion to meet the bullets. There is energy, life, and humanity visible in these victims. On the other hand, the executioners, with their faces hidden, depict inhumanity. Their anonymity and facelessness identify them as victims of another kind, victims of forces which they blindly follow.

Had Goya let the humanity of the soldiers shine through, the painting would have been less effective. What we have is the direct

21. Francisco de Goya, *The Execution of the Third of May* (1814–15; Prado, Madrid).

22. Pablo Picasso, *Guernica* (1937; Prado, Madrid).

confrontation of the passionate desire for freedom challenging the symbols of unfeeling, unreflective power. This picture of the human desire for justice transcends both the nineteenth century and Spain. Twentieth-century people in El Salvador, Lebanon, or Ireland could find here an appropriate aesthetic expression of their own quest for liberation.

The world today is in even greater need of art which can move us in the direction of human liberation. Art can bring us together in ways that social programs, government policies, or ideological designs cannot. Art can help us to find solidarity in the beautiful rather than in systems. Art speaks for those who will not speak or who cannot speak. Art can help us take the first step in building bridges between hostile powers.

The prime example of such a work of art is *Guernica* (fig. 22). Picasso employed his expressionist and abstract techniques to render his dramatic protest against the cruel and inhuman air raid on the defenseless Basque town by the German air force. This great painting became a wall of the Spanish pavillion at the World's Fair in 1937. The fact that it was as much visual propaganda and social protest as anything done by either Mexican muralists or Goya in no way subtracts from its greatness as a painting. It is both allegorical and highly symbolic. It communicates victimization, brutality, and barbarism. At the top of the painting is an arm which holds a lamp—a light of truth is to be found. At the bottom of the painting the tiny blooming plant amidst the severed arm and broken sword signals hope. *Guernica* is a vivid expression of the conflicts of recent times.

The critical depth of works of art like these by Goya and Picasso makes us aware that a more just world depends upon the realization of a justice-oriented spirituality. *The Execution of the Third of May* and *Guernica* prove that art can be the symbolic enactment of such a spirituality. The way that art and spirituality actually relate reveals how art can be an expression of social justice. This is a very intimate relationship, because aesthetic experience is "understanding with feeling." The emotional quality which we describe as aesthetic brings order into ordinary experience. We find pattern and structure in aesthetic experience. Our relationship to art is precisely one of encounter, not merely of recognition.

> There is an energy now available which assists in the reconstitu-
> tion of reality for the perceiving person. . . . The aesthetic experi-
> ence is not a matter of pure passivity, mere receptivity from the
> art object. The perceiver must enter into the creation of the expe-
> rience. . . . And in this dialectical process human transformation
> takes place.[6]

Our response to works of art is more than simple undifferenti-
ated emotion. We rework emotion in our imaginations. The artist
refashions the raw material of creation in the creative process and
is transformed. "This transformation also takes place for the per-
ceiver in that emotions are clarified in the aesthetic perception.
When we know our emotions and desires with an aesthetic knowing, we and they are transformed."[7] Such transformation is the
conditio sine qua non of justice-directed spirituality, of a way that
"the world will be saved by beauty."

Consider the new Coventry Cathedral (1962) as an example of
how art challenges us to social justice through its transformative
power and its ability to articulate this spirituality of justice. The
old Coventry Cathedral was destroyed in the Second World War by
a German air attack on 14 November 1940, only a few years after
Guernica was demolished in a similar manner. This destruction
was so thorough that a new word entered our vocabulary, "to co-
ventrate," meaning "to destroy utterly." The new cathedral was far
more than a replacement for the older building. One of the book-
lets that explains the story of Coventry puts it like this:

> The new cathedral is not merely a beautiful building. It is a sym-
> bol of faith and of hope. It is a laboratory of experiment in Chris-
> tian renewal. It is the center of a multilateral and worldwide
> ministry. It is the spiritual base for a disciplined and committed
> community and the spiritual home of hundreds of thousands
> throughout the world.[8]

The ruins of the old cathedral were purposely left in place to constitute a sanctuary of meditation alongside the new building. One
enters the new cathedral through the ruins of the old. Once inside
one discovers the glass of the west window portraying Hebrew
and Christian scriptural figures, English saints, and joyful angels.
Beautifying the building within are the cross on the high altar, the
floor of the Chapel of Unity, the Chapel of Industry, and, of course,

the tapestry of Christ in Glory by Graham Sutherland (1903). Although Coventry contains many art objects, it is not an art gallery. Rather it is a place of worship and prayer within an artistic environment. It continually proclaims the word of God through the Tablets of the Word which are visible as one moves through the building. Across the entry way one can read the words which sum up the relationship between the two cathedrals: "To the Glory of God the Cathedral Burnt."

> The designers of Coventry saw that cathedral as the great act of faith that we can achieve something better than international hate and the possibility of worldwide destruction due to nuclear bombs. They rightly point out that the cathedral costs only 1/15th the price of building a bombing airplane. The cathedral stands in judgment on those values which entail war and human devastation.[9]

By juxtaposing the beauties of the new with the devastation of the old, the builders of Coventry created a declaration that we need places where we can recover the vision of something better for humanity. Coventry is a living symbol of how we may join with others in promoting those values which lessen suspicion, hatred, and decrease the possibilities for war.

Coventry Cathedral is not principally a local parish church. The personal spiritual lives of the worshippers are transcended as they are invited to address humanity's common problems of morality, faith, and despair. By assisting people with their integration into a confusing society and by addressing the conflicts among groups and communities, Coventry Cathedral explicates the mutual accord between spirituality and art. In the secular arena, there is a great deal that is aesthetic. However, it is often without any honest commitment to human values. The human imagination is transformed by the Coventry "cathedrals" in the way that spiritual prayerful and aesthetic persons are called to that kind of commitment that breaks through their personal limitations and confines. When we separate our spirituality from our experiences of art, we diminish our power of self-symbolization. The social transformation of our world becomes an empty and unattainable ideal. Like the new Coventry Cathedral we must not be just a building, but rather the "laboratory of experiment in Christian renewal."

Among humans and societies, it is true that there are norms for justice that are relatively universal. The ways in which these universal ideals for justice will be expressed differ throughout history. What may have been a significant concern at one time, such as slavery, might become quite insignificant at another. Other issues will move into prominence such as sexism or apartheid. Art reflects these changing emphases. Some works of art are clearly focused on matters of injustice which have recessed into the historical past. Other works of art which call for social justice may continue to be relevant in specific areas but may not address more contemporary concerns. For example, one of my students has made a most cogent case for this in his work on the relationship of the visual arts to social justice. He compared Leonardo da Vinci's (1452–1519) *Last Supper* (1495–98; Santa Maria della Grazia, Milan) and Judy Chicago's (b. 1939) *The Dinner Party* (1979; Collection of the artist). In this comparison Father Patrick Negri, S.S., argues that social justice is celebrated in both works of art but in different ways.

No one needs to defend Leonardo's masterpiece as a preeminent example of religious and human drama. Most of us continue to recall his work when someone mentions this penultimate event in the life of Jesus Christ. Accepted opinion is that the painting offers us the moment at the supper when Christ said, "One of you will betray me." The disciples are reacting with considerable shock: "Is it I, Lord?" The painting is a manifestation of the presence and power of greed in the face of overwhelming generosity. There are the multiple gestures with eucharistic overtones: for example, Jesus' hands clearly pointing to the bread and wine, the *orantes* position of the hands of Andrew (third from left), and Jesus' right hand which is turned down over the cup evoking one of the traditional gestures of the Roman Mass. There is also the upraised finger of Thomas as a reminder of the Resurrection and the union with Christ when the doubting Thomas put his finger in Christ's right side. Finally, there is the cupped left hand of Thaddeus into which his right hand will be placed. Making a "throne" of the right hand by placing it into the left was the way of receiving communion in the early church. It is now the practice again today.

These eucharistic gestures are contradicted by the divided gesture of Judas. As his right hand moves forward his whole body recoils. His left hand holds on tightly to the bag of money. The gesture of Judas is one of withholding, selfishness, and of refusing to share. Such an attitude was counter to the spirituality of the early Christians. Tightly grasping the bag of money, Judas is a warning to those who view the painting today that we must not be coopted by our affluent society, that greed is a devisive and destructive emotion. We are challenged to live more justly.

"Where are the women?" Patrick Negri has asked. Leonardo's Milanese world was all male. Father Negri is not suggesting that the painting is diminished either aesthetically or religiously because it does not speak to feminist concerns. Rather, it is a stunning example that every art object is historically contextualized, and its availability to communicate on the level of justice is determined by its historicity. The absence of women in the *Last Supper* cannot be explained by maintaining that Leonardo did not paint women. He was the creator of the Mona Lisa. Leonardo would have followed the prevailing view of the time which did not question why there is no mention in the Christian Scriptures of women at the Last Supper. The point is simply that Leonardo's *Last Supper* challenges greed and selfishness, and yet is oblivious to sexism. Protests against sexism in the visual arts were yet to come.

Judy Chicago is an artist who is concerned with the equality of the sexes. Critical of the fact that the history of art has devalued the contributions of women, she is not hesitant to assert that the reason that men reject women artists' views is the denial of their own femininity, especially their vulnerability. According to Chicago, men move to control the world by controlling art.

Judy Chicago's *The Dinner Party* received considerable notoriety a few years ago and is a fine example of what Leonardo's *Last Supper* could not be. She explicitly intended a reinterpretation of the Last Supper from a feminist perspective. Here women would be honored guests, not merely servants. They are represented through the form of thirty-nine plates set on a triangular table. The number of plates comes from a supposition that there were thirteen people at the Last Supper. This number is multiplied by three. Thirteen is also the number of members in a witches' coven. Witches have been associated with feminine evil. This gave a double meaning, both positive and negative, to *The Dinner Party*, which expresses both the achievements and the oppression of women. Along with the plates on this triangular table one finds glasses, napkins, silverware, and tablecloths. The table, its needlework, and settings rest on a triangular Heritage floor which is made of twenty-three hundred handcast porcelain tiles. The names of 999 women are inscribed in gold luster on these tiles. The continual repetition of the triangular form is a significant feminine symbol.

Intentional eucharistic references are found in the chalicelike goblets at each place setting. The cups are gold on the inside, a former indispensable requirement for chalices used in the Roman Catholic Mass. The tablecloth and the runners at each place setting signify the humble service of women through the centuries, and recall the humble service of Christ himself at the Last Supper when he washed the feet of those who were at table with him. A central principle of eucharistic theology is "commemoration." In both the Jewish and Christian traditions, "to remember" is to render present, to make effective in the here and now. There is a great deal of such effective recall, *anamnesis,* in *The Dinner Party,* from the plates, which symbolically represent significant women who embody the feminine experience throughout history, to the more numerous list of Western women whose names are etched into the Heritage floor.

In the fifteenth century Leonardo put into space and scene the experience of good confronting human greed. In the twentieth century Judy Chicago has created another space and scene which challenges the accepted view of women. Obviously, it would be inappropriate to put Chicago and Leonardo on the same level. In fact some critics, while responding positively to *The Dinner Party,* consider it more intellectually than aesthetically convincing. In any case, it is a fine example of "art that does justice."

The relationship between the visual arts and social justice goes beyond these paintings and sculptures whose subject matter deals with inhumanity and oppressiveness. The connection between art and justice is not exhausted by the examples discussed above. Social justice itself has a more comprehensive meaning. It is more than the procedural justice which is the juridical fairness of rules by which society operates. It is more than the justice involved in the fair distribution of goods and opportunities. Rather, it is the fairness of the institutional order of society as a whole. This larger concept of justice is difficult to grasp. It can be defined negatively as the opposite of oppression.

But oppression itself also has many meanings such as burdening someone with cruel and unjust impositions and restraints, or subjecting someone to an excessive exercise of authority or power. When we speak of "social" injustice the oppression usually intended is that caused by an unjust imbalance of power in human social interactions. This form of oppression is often so institutionalized that it becomes a part of the fabric of life. Oppression is so "inculturated" that it becomes a cultural way of thinking. This was the case with slavery and the marginalization of women, and is the current bias against some ethnic groups and homosexuals.

There are clearly negative effects of this kind of oppression. Persons and groups develop a negative self-definition when they have internalized the opinion of their oppressors. The low self-esteem of persons of a different color of skin would be a case in point. The question is how can they break out of this debilitating self-image? How can they believe in themselves? How can they deal with the anger and self-hurt which are the result of being treated as marginal people by the larger society?

Other degrading effects of oppression are the *emotional dependence* in which the oppressed want to resemble and imitate their oppressors; *grief and depression* brought about by the experience of hopelessness to stop tyranny; *rage and anger* which stem from envy, lack of trust of the outside world, feelings of individual aggressiveness, and fear and doubt because of discrimination; and finally, the *fear* of freedom and of taking risks.

How is it possible to counteract this network of dehumanization? How can we promote social justice when social injustice is part of the texture of human living? One way is the human imaginative process wherein we can find the resources for the victims of history to change the web of power and self-depreciation in which they are caught. A just world order presupposes a transformation not only of individuals but of groups and their world views. In a religious context we are saying that spirituality cannot be isolated from the ministry of justice. But what does this mean concretely in terms of the human imagination?

It means first of all that through the workings of the human imagination, that is, through symbols, images, and myths, we can turn away from sexism, racism, environmental destruction, or economic exploitation. We need the human imagination because our empirical sciences and industrial technology cannot save humanity from the horrors of massive destruction. Human imaginations can be the places where this more wholistic conversion can take place.

Human imaginations have this ability because of the nature of symbols which are born in and fed by the imaginative process. There are several reasons why symbols enable individual and communal freedom. First of all, they have the ability to point to several different meanings at the same time. Second, they call for a response; indifference to them is impossible. Third, they are the seemingly irrational causes of our emotions and desires. Fourth, one symbol leads to another and so can lead one into a symbol system. Fifth, symbols produce presence through the concentration of awareness. In short, this means that symbols make it possible for us to live in another way. The symbols which are nourished by the human imagination provide us with an alternative world, which is emotionally meaningful, a raised consciousness, and more intense relationality.

To live in a world of symbols means that there is the possibility that the social and individual dimensions of life are brought together and that an intimacy is created through which the participants feel a nearness to themselves. Because of the way symbols operate, the human imagination provides balance and equilibrium for us. Symbols relativize our experiences of oppression. This is more than intellectual equilibrium or emotional adjustment. It is an integrative process wherein past, present, and future are brought together: where one can step out of pure chronological time by breaking away from fixation on the past, avoiding stagnation in the present, and letting go of preoccupation with the future.

For those living in oppressive situations social justice means integration. The human imagination contributes to this personal integration through interiorization. To be imaginative means that we have the ability to respond to the reality around us. The visual arts are a way in which we can modify our world (with its oppressive structures) so that we can responsibly engage it. If the world of sinful structures dominates, we may be forced to come to a standstill. Through the human imagination, art provides movement by generating a sense of being at home with ourselves, of being familiar with ourselves. The way we can be just to ourselves and just for others is by acquiring this sense of intimacy that allows us to move out of ourselves because we experience our goodness in our inner selves. Such intimacy is possible in the imaginative life nurtured by the visual arts.

To be integrated means to have a sense of balance in our lives. We need not give into denigrating circumstances. When we find ourselves more than usually fragmented, when we feel threatened by dangers both inside and out, the imagination comes to our rescue. It summons up from its repertory images of goodness, positive self-regard, and supportive relationships. An imagination nourished by the visual arts can enhance our personhood, restore balance to our lives, and help us deal with oppressiveness. This is social justice through the arts.

The arts can supply the imagination with counter images. These affirmative images can reduce the power of oppressive images. Anxiety can be relieved by the transformation of a threatening image. Inhibitions can be moved to another area of consciousness. The human imagination's principle of operation is to divide and conquer.

Another way in which the human imagination can undercut oppressive influences is by building up inner security. The repetition of mobilizing images relativizes a menacing situation. The sense of familiarity can dissipate some of the fear. The imagination has the ability to pile one image upon another. The mass of images has a triggering effect by which a whole network of meaning is constructed. We are less overwhelmed by unjust situations and structures when we have an alternative world of meaning. The imagination also fuses many images into one. Any individual image may be frightening and lead to despair, but this can be kept within bounds when several images qualify each other.

The extensive symbolic character of the visual arts allows the imagination full play. Painting as well as the other arts can contribute to that human integration which is characterized by the balanced personality, the overcoming of anxiety, and the inner feelings of personal dignity and intimacy. This is possible because aesthetic symbols are imagined but not logical. Through continual contact with the visual arts we can enhance the quality of our lives and can become more immediate to ourselves. Social justice through the visual arts is achieved when they intensify our self-dignity and enable us to create the sense of closeness and reassurance which is our protection from oppression.

To illustrate this interpretation of the human imagination, social justice, and the visual arts, I shall focus on a later work of
Rembrandt van Rijn (1606–69). I am indebted to my student Caroline Goeser, for her analysis of Rembrandt's artistic progress as a
parable and the parabolic character of his works. In his artistic
journey, Rembrandt moved through his theatrical phase to the
point where he rejected overt drama in his painting. Although his
later works include specifically biblical subjects, they are not in-
dicative of specific times in history, but are symbolic in character.
These later works are fine examples of how visual art triggers the
human imagination to personal and social transformation. These
works of art affect their viewers as the parables of the Gospels affect their listeners. That is, they involve some twist, some upset-
ting of our world view. These paintings and sculptures draw us
into themselves and catch us so that we are forced to confront ourselves.

Rembrandt's portrait of the biblical character, Bathsheba, is entitled *Bathsheba with King David's Letter* (1654; Louvre, Paris). She
is in a position of contemplation, staring pensively into space and
tilting her head to one side. Bathsheba is faced with a great decision. Rembrandt allows us to enter into her thought process. We
know the outcome of the story. Bathsheba responds to King David's invitation. She commits adultery with him. Her husband,
Uriah, is disposed of by the king's soldiers. David is confronted and
condemned by the prophet Nathan. None of this is found in the
painting.

What we are privy to is only the decision-making itself. Brought
into the painting we begin to wonder what decision she will make.
We are absorbed into her absorption. We have been faced with
analogous situations and we can identify with Bathsheba. We ask
ourselves: What would *we* do were we in her place? We are caught
up into her decision-making process and are challenged by the possibilities of what *we* might decide. In this imaginative process, personal (as well as communal) transformation can take place.

Rembrandt's parabolic approach is exhibited in the etching of
Ecce Homo or *Christ Presented to the People* (1655; National Gallery, London). He reworked the etching eight times, the seventh
and eighth states being considerably changed from the first. These
transformations include certain theological shifts made by Rembrandt. For our purpose, what is significant is an omission made in

the final states. In the original etching there is a stage on which Christ, Pilate, and Barabbas as well as a number of witnesses stand. There are also bystanders on the ground below, and on the sides and front of the stage. In the final etchings Rembrandt removed the group of figures in the foreground. With these people missing only a few witnesses to the event remain. The central figures of Christ, Pilate, and Barabbas still face outward. But now they look not out on the foreground witnesses in the etching but into empty space. The etching is still entitled, *Christ Presented to the People*. But where are the people? Caroline Goeser has astutely observed that in the early state of the etchings Rembrandt recorded a group of people who once witnessed this event, whereas the last etching becomes an event each time *we* experience it.

What happens is that *we* the viewers assume the role of the witnesses. Christ is being presented to us. Pilate is addressing us. The etching works like a parable. It tricks us into this illusion and challenges us. Rembrandt has caught us in his symbolic space. We are not seeing an event of the past which brings sorrow and anger to our hearts. We are there. Or, perhaps, better, the *Ecce Homo* is here in our world. Are we calling for Barabbas's release? Do we cry for Christ's Crucifixion? The world of the etching, the world in front of the etching, is confronting our world. One participates in the other. We are drawn into a confrontation and now have the possibility for transformation.

There is a death to our old understandings and the emergence of a new awareness. Like the parables of Jesus Christ we are shocked into new understanding. Visual art as parable refers to the way it promotes imaginative living, the kind of living which is presupposed by a justice-oriented spirituality. Such a spirituality creates the proper context for the transformation of the world. This is the way that art does justice.

Social justice happens when we participate in the process of transformation which moves us from an experience of alienation to a sense of completion or fulfillment. When we accept reality as it is presented in a work of art, our transformation has begun. We are encouraged to expand our world in order to accommodate the new world offered in the work of art. Art enables us to distance ourselves from our old understandings and prejudices. Art creates the condition where we have the possibility of new experiences and new understandings. But we must both surrender our preconceived notions as well as surrender to the work of art.

All of the art discussed above alters reality in some way. All the works of art mentioned require surrender on our part if we are to increase our awareness and move away from areas of alienation in our lives. Some of these works of art require more surrender than others. But because the visual arts can provide us with the means of overcoming alienation, we would urge that the visual arts become part of our theological programs for a more just world.

NOTES

1. Margaret Miles, *Image As Insight* (Boston: Beacon Press, 1985).

2. William Fleming, *Arts and Ideas*, 7th ed. (San Francisco: Holt, Rinehart, and, Winston, 1986).

3. Diane Apostolos-Cappadona, ed., *Art, Creativity, and the Sacred* (New York: Crossroad Publishing Co., 1984).

4. Susanne Langer, *Feeling and Form* (New York: Charles Scribner's Sons, 1953).

5. Paul Tillich, "Art and Ultimate Reality," in *Art, Creativity, and the Sacred*, ed. Diane Apostolos-Cappadona (New York: Crossroad Publishing Co., 1984), p. 229.

6. James L. Empereur, S. J., "Liturgy, Spirituality, and the Arts," *The National Institute for Campus Ministries Journal* 7, no. 4 (Fall 1982):57.

7. Ibid.

8. H. C. N. Williams, *The Story of Coventry Cathedral—The Latter Glory*, (Manchester: Whitethorn Press, n.d.), p.3.

9. Empereur, "Liturgy, Spirituality, and the Arts," p. 59.

12

Classical Paintings in the Teaching of Pastoral Care

ARCHIE SMITH, JR.

During a recent sabbatical in London, I took a course called "The High Renaissance." Although offered through the University of London, this course was on site at the National Gallery, London. At the same time, I was working with families at the Institute of Family Therapy and observing family therapy at the Tavistock Clinic. I began to appreciate the similarities in observing a painting and a family's interaction.

This exploratory essay will suggest how classical paintings, depicted through slides, can aid in the teaching of pastoral care and counseling; the linkage between the perception and reality in works of art and the ways in which perception and reality are "framed" in pastoral situations; and how learning to enter into a slide of a classical painting is analogous to entering into a pastoral care or family counseling situation.

The term *frame* is analogous to the frame around a picture. A frame may be an arbitrary boundary drawn around an event or a series of events by an observer in order to organize a dimension of experience and give it meaning. For example, there may be a legal frame which highlights the legal issues in particular contexts, or a medical frame which emphasizes the medical consequences of particular actions. As well, there may be a pastoral frame to enable pastoral care-givers to discern God's self-disclosure in the lives of parishioners; to mobilize resources of religious faith in times of trouble and help bring salvation to the human spirit. Frame refers to the way in which experience is delimited within a certain organization of space and time. The frame is part of the message conveyed in a painting as it includes certain perspectives while simultaneously excluding others. The principle of psychological frames is useful when we wish to see relationships or sets of relationships more clearly and to lift up a sequence of activity for closer scrutiny or analysis.[1] For example, therapy within the family group is based on close observation and analysis of the process in a room: The small repeated transactions between any two members of a family are taken as material for examination by the therapist in order to understand the family's overall pattern of behavior.[2] The term *frame*, therefore, will be used to refer to any experience of the stream of ongoing activity that is arbitrarily chosen and isolated for the purpose of examining the organization of that experience.[3] The meaning that any event has depends upon the "frames" in which we perceive it. To reframe an event is to think about things differently or to see a new point of view.[4]

Family therapists are trained to observe the interactions between family members by identifying patterns, themes, and sequences of behaviors that bind family members together. Guided by theoretical understandings and observations of family transactions, family therapists are continually framing and reframing the raw data they see. Just as Blake could see "life in a grain of sand," so the therapist can learn to see the essence of the family system in the minutiae of one repeated behavioral sequence.[5] Visual perception, then, is an important part of the therapist's skill of making sense out of a family's transactions. Learning to see the whole in the detail is difficult, but the use of art slides may facilitate this learning process.

If the family therapist is fortunate enough to have a video recording of a session, then the therapist has an opportunity to observe a still frame of the interaction between family members. This increases her or his ability to see what is going on within the therapeutic context. A still frame draws "attention to the paradox of capturing life in a still, of freezing the play of features in an arrested moment of which we may never be aware in the flux of events."[6]

Learning to observe a still frame is made possible by the use of an art slide. Again, learning to enter into an art slide is analogous to entering into a pastoral care or family-counseling situation. When we "see" a landscape, for example, we imaginatively situate ourselves in it. Our appreciation of what we see depends upon our own way of seeing, or construing the world. In order to enter the color slide of a painting with heightened appreciation one needs to raise certain key questions:

1. How is the painting framed?
2. What do you see inside the frame?
3. Is there movement in the painting?
4. What or where is the light source?
5. What relationship or sets of relationships do you see?
6. Which colors are used and with what effect? Are colors used to achieve contrast? to create shade? to unify? to balance? to focus?
7. How is space used? Is there a rational organization of space?
8. Where is the focus?
9. What moods are created?
10. What feelings and or themes are evoked?

These are some questions that will help the observer to enter into the painting, and by analogy to enter into situations of pastoral care and family counseling. For example, when family therapists first meet the family group, there are certain things they have to achieve in order to begin working with that family. Therapists have to get to know individual family members and the issues each is presenting; they have to understand interaction within the family group—how they side with one another, and undermine one another.[7] The pastoral family therapist might ask of any pastoral situation: "How is reality being described or framed by the participants?" "What do we see inside the frame?" "What or where is the light source or sources of meaning inside the frame?" "What relationships or sets of relationships do you see and how have the actors positioned themselves relative to one another and to the problem(s) that claim their attention?" "What moods are created?" "What feelings or themes are evoked?" The pastoral and therapeutic frame itself becomes a part of the premise system, and is involved in the evaluation of the messages or set of messages it contains.

When teaching the introductory course to pastoral care and

counseling or to deviance or the seminar on the family, I usually select a number of color art slides which feature the themes of family life: such as those of Giovanni Bellini (1430-1516), *The Madonna of the Meadow* (ca. 1505; National Gallery, London); Jan Steen (1625-79), *A Peasant Family At Meal-Time* (National Gallery, London); or Frans Hals (1580-1666), *A Family Group in a Landscape* (late 1640s?; National Gallery, London). For themes of death and dying, I choose slides like Titian's (1480-1576), *The Death of Actaeon* (ca. 1560; National Gallery, London); and of the application of certain sanctions, Paul Delaroche's (1795-1856), *The Execution of Lady Jane Grey* (1833; National Gallery, London), or Rembrandt van Rijn's (1606-69) *Belshazzar's Feast* (1636; National Gallery, London).

The students must spend time looking at each slide, recording what they see and what relationships, themes, feelings, or emotions are evoked. Then the students are asked to share their perceptions with the class. The student's comments are written on a blackboard so that the variety of ways of seeing a single art slide are visible to all present. A painting is made up of a multiplicity of styles, attitudes, impressions, and perspectives which represent different things to different people. This means there is no single or perfect way to view a painting. In order to capture the reality of a painting one needs a multi-image approach, one that takes into account the many contrasting ways the observer can approach the painting simultaneously. A painting, then, is a metaphor for reality in that reality is made up of a multiplicity of perspectives, To paraphrase William James, there is not one, but many different levels of experienced reality and many different frames of reference or ways of seeing.[8] The large variation in ways of seeing and interpretation adds further to the diversity of reality for any given individual. In fact, the diversity of experienced and interpreted reality may be due to people's manifold social participations and the frames of reference offered them by their socioeconomic situations, and ethnic and gender roles. Frames of reference influence our perception; yet we can vary the frame of reference and discover still different aspects of the actuality before us.[9]

This exercise helps students to appreciate that their own unique ways of seeing plays an important role in how reality is being described within a frame. Any attempt to study a particular slice of reality will inevitably lead to limited understandings, since the boundaries of any unit of observation are always drawn by an observer. However, when perceptions of a work of art are shared in the classroom the boundaries of understanding are enlarged; and students may come to see that there are innumerable ways of interpreting what goes on inside each particular frame. This exercise leads to an in-depth discussion of the ways of seeing the topics under consideration, and the importance of the conceptual or theoretical grids that purport to "explain" or "define" a given slice of reality. Again, the frame around a picture or slice of reality serves to order or to organize the perception of the viewer and the participants. Students may also learn to appreciate how the reality under consideration is limited by the picture frame or by psychological frames. The painting or the activity of what is going on inside the picture frame may stimulate a denotative story about the underlying narrative that gave rise to the painting. The painting assists us in seeing how the story is framed and also serves as a metaphor for the narrative.

Classical paintings and their implicit narratives may serve as metaphors for students who are learning to be pastoral family therapists or counselors. Classical paintings as metaphors for real life situations can be particularly valuable in dealing with issues involving family groups or individuals and the wider social, economic, and political environment, when the stories contained in the paintings are made isomorphic with the real life situation of people during the course of therapy.[10] Narratives, when captured in a classical painting, can be used to suggest solutions, promote insight, reframe situations, or even to deliver paradoxical directives.[11] As Philip Baker has pointed out, "artistic metaphors are useful when one wants to reframe a subject's expressions in another sensory modality."[12]

To illustrate how this principle of a frame works, I want to discuss an art slide and then a family therapy session.

In the classroom I begin with a slide of Titian's interpretation of the Greek myth, *The Hounds of Actaeon*. After showing the slide and encouraging the class to share their observations, I briefly sketch some relevant aspects of the story. Actaeon was out in the mountains hunting with his companions and about fifty well-trained hunting dogs. At the end of a full day of hunting, they de-

23. Titian, *The Death of Actaeon* (ca. 1560; The National Gallery, London).

cided to take a rest. Needing some space for himself, Actaeon decides to walk alone in the forest. He inadvertantly intruded on Artemis's bathing place, saw her naked, and lacked the good sense to know that gawking at a naked goddess was a capital offense. She was so angry that she flung water at him. Where the water struck him on the head and lower body, he grew horns and was transformed into a stag. Actaeon ran away. He passed a clear stream, noticed his own reflection, and saw that he had been transformed into a stag. Actaeon's own dogs caught the scent of a stag and attacked, tearing him to pieces.

Titian, an Italian Renaissance painter, captures this story in his painting, *The Death of Actaeon* (fig. 23). Titian has not completely metamorphized Actaeon in the painting. But in the story Actaeon is completely changed into a stag. Titian gives Actaeon human form to add to the shock and reality of the story. The element of shock is that Actaeon is still human, and his own dogs should have recognized him. In the myth Actaeon becomes a stag and his identity is disguised. In Titian's painting Actaeon is still partly human, and his dogs should have recognized his humanity. In the myth Artemis is not present when Actaeon is being attacked by his hounds. But in Titian's painting Artemis is present although it is Actaeon's own dogs who destroy him. The theme of unprovoked death, or "you cannot completely control your life or destiny" emerges from Titian's visual interpretation of this Greek myth. It is this theme of unprovoked death that has captured Titian's imagination.

Inside the frame of the painting, the figure of the huntress goddess, Artemis, is more than twice the size of Actaeon. There is a great uniformity of movement from the left to the right of the painting. As Artemis and the trees move from left to right, they help to convey the idea that Actaeon is falling backwards when he is attacked by his hounds. Titian's contrasting use of reds, browns, yellows, and flesh tones brings the landscape to life and creates a somber mood.

In this discussion I attempt to convey the idea that the art slide delimits as it depicts a very special moment within the narrative. The art slide is an instruction to the viewer to think of the story from the artist's vantage point. Within this frame the viewer's perception of the story is organized in a special way as her or his attention is directed to certain details of the story, while ignoring other features of the same narrative. The implicit message is that the essence of the whole story can be found in the details inside the frame.

Entering into a painting is analogous to the process of entering into a situation in pastoral care and/or family counseling. An example from family counseling clarifies the similarity: the students are shown a still frame from a video of a family therapy session and asked to identify what they see inside this still frame. To illustrate, I have chosen a family of five (the "G. family") which consisted of a father, mother, and three children, two daughters and a son. The students are asked to note who is in the picture; who is sitting next to whom; what relationships or set of relationships are visible; how the children are positioned; what expressions are on people's faces; who is in the center of the picture; what moods are created; and what feelings and/or themes are evoked by this still frame. The students are asked to share their observations. At this point I share some additional information.

Prior to the family's arrival, the therapist had received a letter from the referring physician indicating that she was the medical doctor for the wife and three children, but the father was under the care of another physician. The referring physician also indicated that the husband had been hospitalized for a "nervous breakdown" and is currently under the care of a psychiatrist. According to the psychiatrist, the father is a regular participant in group therapy and cannot talk to his wife, let alone with the rest of his family in a group. The physician further indicated that the wife and three children were under "tremendous stress" at home due to constant arguing and fighting in the family. The physician was referring the G. family for therapy.

The G. family arrived at the pastoral family therapist's office for the first time. When everyone was seated, the father leaned forward and said, "Dr. S., let me begin by bringing you into the picture about us all . . . just so that you don't come in completely cold." Several family members sighed. The pastoral family therapist responded to the father's offer, "I would like to hear from you, but first I want to check in with other members of your family."

The father turned to the mother and asked, "Is that alright with you?" The mother responded, "Yes, sure!" The father then said to the therapist, "Alright." Beginning with the eldest sibling, each family member made a brief statement and shared a vignette or episode about the events that brought him or her to seek help at this time. Later in the session, the father was able to bring the pastoral family therapist out of the cold and into the picture, by telling a longer story about his family, as he saw it.

After sharing this additional information, I ask the class to compare this new information with the information derived from their own shared observations of the still frame. In this way students can learn to use their visual information as a resource alongside the information given by others.

The letter from the referring physician had framed the family as one with a sick or mentally ill adult male who could not talk in front of his own family. Other family members were described as being under tremendous stress from constant arguments and fighting. During the first family group therapy session, the father presented himself, with the cooperation of family members, as a father in charge. Initially, the family framed their own reality as they saw it and their framing differed from that of the psychiatrist in the letter and from the referring physician. Each family member's shared vignette contained the fragments of experience which made up the family's story, the story of their lives.

Given this description of the family's situation, the class is then invited by the instructor to consider the best ways to evolve a frame for pastoral family intervention. The process of pastoral family therapy is a framed interaction between the referring parties, the pastoral therapist(s), and the family members. Their many ways of perceiving the family's difficulty constitutes the therapeutic context. Perhaps a single meaningful enactment of the family's problem gives the clue for therapeutic change. As a special case of pastoral care, pastoral family therapy is an attempt to reframe the family's ways of perceiving and behaving so that family members can enhance one another's spiritual and emotional development.

Learning to enter into a classical art painting through a slide may be seen as an analogy to the frame-setting situation of families who seek help from their pastor(s) or therapist(s). To talk or enact the family's quandry within the social psychological frame of therapy is to give the pastoral therapist material for reframing and therefore for therapeutic change.

This essay has suggested that paintings or slides of classical paintings may be used effectively in teaching students how to use visual perception to enter into situations of pastoral care and family counseling. The principle that framework is crucial to effective pastoral care and family counseling has been emphasized. To paraphrase Gregory Bateson, the picture frame is an instruction to the viewer that he or she should not extend the premises which obtain between the figures within the picture to the wallpaper behind it.

The art slide may serve as an analogy for teaching students how to enter into a complex situation and to observe how the bits and pieces of a pastoral and/or therapeutic situation are woven into a narrative. By learning to enter into one medium (i.e., a painting), students may learn to enter into another medium (i.e., pastoral care or counseling situations), when art and pastoral care are related in the classroom. The resemblance between entering into a painting and entering into a situation of pastoral counseling or care is striking. Both occur within a delimited psychological frame, that is to say, a spacial and temporal bounding of a set of interactive messages; and both are separated from a wider all-encompassing narrative.[13]

NOTES

1. Gregory Bateson, "A Theory of Play and Fantasy," *Steps to an Ecology of Mind* (London: Paladin, Granada Publishing Co., 1973), p. 187.

2. Gill Gorell Barnes, *Working With Families* (London: MacMillan Education Ltd., 1984) p. 105.

3. Erving Goffman, *Frame Analysis: An Essay on the Organization of Experience* (New York: Harper Colophon Books, 1974) p. 11.

4. Richard Bandler and John Ginder, *Reframing: Neuro-Linguistic Programming and the Transformation of Meaning* (Moab, UT: Real People Press, 1982), p. 2.

5. Gill Gorell Barnes, "Family Bits and Pieces: framing a workable reality," in Sue Walround-Skinner, ed., *Developments In Family Therapy* (London: Routledge and Kegan Paul, 1981), pp. 302–4.

6. E. H. Gombrich, Julian Hockberg, and Mac Black, *Art, Perception, and Reality* (Baltimore: Johns Hopkins University Press, 1970), p. 16.

7. Barnes, "Family Bits and Pieces," p. 309.

8. William James, *The Principles of Psychology* (New York: Encyclopedia Britannica Co., 1952), p. 641.

9. Burkhart Holzner, *Reality Construction in Society* (Cambridge, MA: Schenkman Publishing Co., Inc., 1968), pp. 1–19.

10. Philip Barker, *Using Metaphors in Psychotherapy* (New York: Brunner/Mazel, Publishers, 1985), p. 149.

11. Ibid., p. 142.

12. Ibid., p. 62.

13. Bateson, "A Theory of Play and Fantasy," p. 164.

13

Informing Religious Studies with Contemporary and Earlier Visual Arts Portraying the Human Body: A Kinesthetic Teaching Method

DOUG ADAMS

The human form emerges with increasing frequency in painting and sculpture during the past twenty-five years as artists such as Stephen DeStaebler (b. 1933) and George Segal (b. 1924) create works that affirm the human body as the medium through which ambiguity and transcendence are experienced and expressed.[1] This essay demonstrates a kinesthetic method to inform religious studies with visual arts that portray the human body by focusing on two of Stephen De Staebler's sculptures and George Segal's The Holocaust *(1984; Legion of Honor Museum, San Francisco) which resonate with several subjects in Hebrew and Christian Scriptures. For religious studies to be engaged by contemporary art works, this kinesthetic method is useful; but the method also informs religious studies of earlier periods as exemplified with two frescoes by Michelangelo Buonarroti (1475–1564).*

In my course "Spirituality in Twentieth-Century American Art," this kinesthetic method is presented in a session preparing students to spend an hour with a different work of art as primary research for their weekly essays. The course description follows:

Twentieth-century artists in America offer a wide variety of spiritual experiences for those who learn to look. With many class sessions in area museums, we learn to sense finitude and infinity and control and chance in creation from Pollock, Rothko, Newman, Gottlieb, Still, and Reinhardt (Thomas Merton's close friend); return to earth and pilgrimage from Smithson, de Maria, Christo, and Noguchi; feminist sacramental perceptions from O'Keeffe to Chicago and Nevelson; post-critical ironic reaffirmations of world from Duchamp to Johns and Rauschenberg; transforming light from Irwin, Turrell, Bell, and Lippold; and reaffirmation of the human body as an expression of the transcendent from DeKooning to DeStaebler and Segal.

The abstract expressionists eliminated the overt human form along with subject matter in the art of the 1940s and 1950s, and argued that abstraction was the way to experience and express the transcendent. Jane Dillenberger and Lawrence Alloway have independently shown that there are residual references to the human form through the verticality, human dimensions, and other dynamics in some abstract expressionist art.[2] But Segal and DeStaebler have reasserted that the spiritual comes through articulation of the human body in art. Sam Hunter and Don Hawthorne summarize Segal's commitment:

> Segal was particularly resentful of the dualistic dictum that linked abstraction to transcendence. Spirit, he was convinced, was not to be achieved at the expense of the body: both his Jewish heritage and sensual temperament dictated that universal emotion and psychic or sacred ideals could only be conveyed through "the reality of what I could sense, touch, see."[3]

During a postdoctoral Smithsonian fellowship at the National Museum of American Art, I learned teaching methods that helped students to see and integrate details that newly inform them, and to remember forms they have previously experienced. This kinesthetic method of replicating the body positions of the human figures in a painting or sculpture makes students aware of the ambiguities expressed in the art and helps them both remember and transcend interpretations associated with their earlier experience of a particular subject matter. This method reveals dynamics often missed in viewing such familiar works as two frescoes by Michelangelo as well as the new art of Segal and DeStaebler.

The Kinesthetic Method and
Michelangelo's Frescoes

When looking at a slide of Michelangelo's familiar *Fall of Adam and Eve* (1508–12; Sistine Ceiling, Vatican City), many classroom viewers report that the figures are in repose. Such an observation reflects the viewers' own relaxed seated body positions or what they have previously sensed in other representations of Venus and Adonis whom Michelangelo's Eve and Adam resemble in some respects. Easily missed by the sedentary viewers are the tensions and ambiguous intentions expressed through Michelangelo's representation. To become newly informed, students assume the positions of Adam and then Eve.

To assume the position of Adam, one stands and keeps one's knees somewhat bent with the right foot stepping straight forward toward the surface of the fresco; but the right knee is turned in somewhat toward the left. For the upper left thigh to appear as it does behind Eve's head and for the phallus to be as visible as it is, the hidden left foot must be placed substantially to the left but not too far into the background. The upper torso is turned sharply to the left so that most of the back is exposed. Both arms are extended at head level with the left hand clutching the tree limb in the background and the right hand pointing toward the serpent in the foreground. The head faces the direction of the right hand. In this position, a body experiences a tremendous tension. There is substantial ambiguity as to which direction this body is going: it is on the brink of falling. Such kinesthetic insights add to the students' understanding of whether this Adam knows what he is doing and sees that he is choosing between two or more directions.

To assume the position of Eve, one sits with knees bent sharply and feet drawn up just below the buttocks. But the upper torso turns somewhat to the left with the left arm extended high above the head and to the left toward the serpent. The head turns sharply to face the left hand. In a sexually suggestive shape, the right hand is close to the right rib cage and pelvic area. And as Leo Steinberg and John Phillips have observed, she would be in oral intercourse with Adam if she were to turn her head back to the right where it would be in line with her lower body. These kinesthetic insights help students understand the artist's conception of what Eve knew. Through the kinesthetic method, tensions and intentions increase our knowledge of the *Fall of Adam and Eve*.

A kinesthetic interpretation of the Christ figure in Michelangelo's *Last Judgment* (1534–41, Sistine Chapel, Vatican City) complicates students' previous understanding of the work as damning many persons. Ambiguities become evident as to whether the Christ is sitting or rising; and the hands may be blessing or threatening. His head faces toward neither hand but off to the lower left. Some priests who took this position in class reported a remembrance of celebrating Mass with hands in those positions at moments of consecration or benediction, when the priest often looks off to the side to read the appropriate texts. The position of Christ's legs reminded many of them of rising from a kneeling position at the consecration of the Mass. And they had not yet read of the painting's original title (*Resurrection*) or Leo Steinberg's interpretation of the hands as blessing.[4] Ambiguous understandings are appropriate for a fresco that stands before the altar of a Mass that invites viewers to partake of the Eucharist for their blessing or damning, depending on how they approach it. Expectations strongly affect what the viewer experiences.

The Kinesthetic Method and Segal's *The Holocaust*

With sculpture, a kinesthetic method of teaching is essential. The possibilities for interpretive ambiguity are increased as one must move around the sculpture to see more than one part of it; and one may see only a part at any one time. When the sculpture contains more than one human figure, the potential for a kinesthetic method and for ambiguities are greater. Consider George Segal's *The Holocaust*—ten life-size white bronze bodies lying on the ground and one standing at a barbed wire fence. Eleven students reassemble the sculpture, each assuming the position of a different one of the figures. Such an assemblage allows each student to experience not only one figure's internal sense but also that figure's external awareness of others in the total work.

The site of the art further increases the possibilities for ambiguity. Some proposals would have placed the work conspicuously in the center of the Legion of Honor's front parking lot where a large fountain stands. But the sculpture is placed to the north, below the level of the parking lot; and so the visitor may walk from the parking lot toward the museum without seeing *The Holocaust*. If one does approach the area of the sculpture, one will view it from above (see fig. 24); and then one has a choice of turning away or going down to the sculpture by one of two routes (a stairway to the left or a ramp to the right). One has two paths to enter into the sculpture: from the steps at the far left, at a pile of four emaciated bodies most reminiscent of photographs from concentration camps; or from the foot of the ramp at the near right, at the feet of a Venus-like young woman who lies perpendicular to an Adonis-like young man with her head resting on his right side.

While standing above the sculpture before coming down the stairs or ramp, its nearest parts are this full-bodied young couple at one's right and the figure of a heavy-set man and boy at one's left. When the students assume the positions in the sculpture, they become aware of details they might not otherwise notice in such a complex work. The young woman reports that her head and shoulders rest on his right rib cage and make her aware of his breathing; and she discovers a partially eaten apple in her left hand. And while she senses no one else in the sculpture, his left arm rests on the abdomen of the central figure; and the young man is quite aware of the central figure's breathing, although he sees only that central figure's right hand. Although they begin to consider relations of Adam and Eve to *The Holocaust* and see the central figure as God, students are cautioned to await other reports before developing a full interpretation.

Those taking the positions of the older man and the young boy report that they see only each other. The boy's vision of the older man's action is obscured by the man's left hand placed over the right side of the boy's face; and the boy's hands are tightly drawn up behind his back as if they are bound. At first, the students report that the man seems to be protecting the boy or shielding him from seeing anything troubling. But as the man more fully embodies the sculpture, he realizes that his right hand is a fist that is separated from the boy's head by the central figure's intervening left arm. That arm is all he knows of the central figure. From this kinesthetic experience, students see the central figure as God's angel and begin associating Abraham's intended sacrifice of Isaac

24. George Segal, *The Holocaust* (1984; Legion of Honor Museum, San Francisco).

with *The Holocaust*. Only later do they read Jane Dillenberger's "George Segal's *Abraham and Isaac*: Some Iconographic Reflections,"[5] where she discusses his earlier representations of this theme: *In Memory of May 4, 1970, Kent State: Abraham and Isaac* (1978; Princeton University Chapel, Princeton); and *Abraham's Sacrifice* (1973; Mann Auditorium, Tel Aviv).

How are students to understand these familiar biblical subjects in this new configuration entitled *The Holocaust*? One student remembers that the word *holocaust* is associated with the word *sacrifice* in the Hebrew Scriptures. The students who embody the central figure and one of those in the heap of figures find themselves in cruciform positions. And the figure at the right foot of the central figure remembers similar positions in Crucifixion or deposition scenes. And those who look at the sculpture from above, or from the other side of the fence, observe that the whole work is in cruciform shape with the long vertical line composed of Abraham/Isaac, the central figure, the figure at the central figure's right leg, and the figure standing at the fence. The horizontal line is composed of the heap of bodies, the central figure, and Eve.

Urged to consider alternative interpretations, other students note that the whole work forms a star of David. And some remember that many well-fed persons were gassed on arrival at concentration camps before they would have become emaciated; so all of the bodies could be included in a death-camp scenario. And one may interpret this holocaust through the idea of sacrifice as presented in the Abraham and Isaac story. Or the central figure who can be interpreted as a crucified Christ could also be seen as nature itself, as I suggested by a comparison to *The Scream* (1893; National Gallery, Oslo) by Edvard Munch (1863–1944). Munch noted, "I listened to the Great Infinite Cry of Nature." But then as students hold their mouths in the central figure's position, they observe that the mouth of Munch's howling figure is in a vertical shape while the mouth of Segal's figure is in a horizontal shape more like the mouth seen on carvings of mourning humans from the New College bell tower, Oxford.

The central body's flaccid phallus is the most prominent display of genitals in the sculpture; for many of the other figures' genitals are not visible. And that display could support an interpretation of the central figure as a genesis of life or an embodiment of nature.

(Only two women are evident in the sculpture; Eve and an emaciated woman in the heap of bodies. Although not exposed, Eve's genital area is prominent.)

The student standing at the barbed wire fence with his back to all the others says that he feels lonely and more dead than alive. But Segal maintained an ambiguity about this figure's attitude by keeping his hand a little distance above the wire. In the original conception, Segal had planned to have the man's hand touch a wire;[6] but not wanting to imply suicide by that gesture on wires that were electrified in the camps, he kept a short distance between that hand and the wire in the final installation. He is the only isolated figure in the sculpture; for all the rest touch or are touched by at least one other person.

When compared to his isolation, the figures on the ground appear more interactive. Their interrelation defies the horror of the holocaust. On the ground, all of the figures' heads point inward toward the central figure, and so establish a strong sense of total relationship that diminishes if all the bodies turn around in the opposite direction with their heads far away from the central figure. (And a sense of exposure and vulnerability increases in that reversed position.)

The student embodying Eve feels very alive; and her sensuality contributes to the sense of lively survival as Segal acknowledges:

> She is an ample, earthly figure, suggesting nature's abundance even in death, a Persephone image of renewal. "I became as interested in Eve's sensuality as anything else," Segal stated in an interview. "It has to do with survival."[7]

In the heap of bodies, the student embodying the cruciform figure senses that he is being propelled upward; and on top of the heap, another student senses his body could thrust upward as in a dive. As the students assume the positions of figures in the sculpture, the central figure reports that he feels an increasing responsibility.

When they first come to *The Holocaust*, many students see only the horror of death. However, after embodying some of the figures, they see many more details and sense some relationships that witness to life. Life or death may be seen as predominating. Multiple interpretations of *The Holocaust* are possible as one may begin with Abraham and Isaac or Adam and Eve. Christian Scriptures are evoked as well as Hebrew Scriptures; and one may see a cruciform or star of David in the overall composition. The central figure may be interpreted in many ways: as God, as God's angel, as Christ, or as an embodiment of nature.

The Kinesthetic Method and DeStaebler's Sculpture

The kinesthetic method reveals religious dimensions in works of art without explicit religious subject matter. Stephen DeStaebler's sculptures rarely deal with biblical characters. One exception is his *Crucifix* (1968; Newman Center Chapel, Berkeley). But his works resonate with the biblical faiths' concerns for the individual human body. He says,

> These religious concerns are not what make me a figurative artist, but they do help me to rationalize the validity of dealing with figurative forms.[8]

He has long maintained a tension between separateness and fusion, and very recently likened those categories to my discussion of communitive and unitive art forms that correlate to different theologies.[9] His works avoid an idealization of a whole human form and instead affirm a transcendence through fragmented bodies. Such assemblage of fragments asserts that the human being is "not a whole or a unity but an idiosyncratic bundle of contradictions."[10]

When students sit in his stoneware clay chairs entitled *Seating Environment* (1970; Lower Lobby of University Art Museum, Berkeley), each finds one chair that best fits his or her own body. These seats are highly individuated places and not as similar as they first appear. The students report that their own different body shapes feel affirmed by the experience of finding a fitting chair. That affirmation is appreciated by those students whose bodies would not win them awards in our body-conscious culture.

DeStaebler's sculptures of the human body have similar effects. As the sculptures are made up of fragments (without fully articulated limbs), the kinesthetic method concentrates on taking the posture of a form that is seated. Looking at *Seated Woman with Oval Head* (1981; Private Collection; fig. 25), students sit on the edge of

25. Stephen DeStaebler, *Seated Woman with Oval Head*
(1981; Private collection).

desk tops or counters so that the lower legs hang straight down from the upper legs that are slanted down at a forty-five-degree angle. Their feet are flexed with toes pointing toward the ground; and the left foot appears in front. They hold their torsos and heads erect facing straight forward. This frontal presentation evokes a sense of transcendence and reminds the viewer of similar senses of seeing and being seen by the Pantocrator Christ figure (fig. 1) or others in Byzantine churches.[11]

This is not an easy position to maintain as students become aware of a precarious balance. (One ballet dancer reported that her upper torso, head, and feet felt like she was on pointe, although her legs defied that feeling.) If they lean forward, they feel as if they will fall. The figure is as far forward as is possible without falling. In that position, students feel a dignity that comes from several factors: the erect upper body and head, the balance of the body, and the sensation of being on pointe or at least being as far forward as possible. This kinesthetic knowledge was in contrast to what students initially thought about the sculpted figure which had appeared relaxed or hopelessly shattered on first viewing. The lack of arms added to the sense of dignity and historic worth as the work resonated with their memory of much surviving classical art; but DeStaebler's work is different from such classical sculpture as two students observed.

These two permanently disabled students reported that they felt affirmed by DeStaebler's sculpture with its fragmented legs, no arms, and fragile balance. For them, this work of art expresses the condition of bodily brokenness, not to decry the human condition (as many artists use brokenness) but to affirm deeply this condition. In contrast, their experience of classical sculpture had made them feel hopelessly inadequate; for they said their bodies could never measure up to those classical shapes. In viewing DeStaebler's work, most students integrate the fragments into what they assume are two legs; but one of the disabled students perceives more complexity in what could be other legs or additional supports, and helps others see more than two fragmented legs.

Summary

This kinesthetic method helps many students see in painting or sculpture the details they miss when just looking. This method helps the viewers remember similar body shapes and gestures they have experienced in other works of art as well as in daily life. It helps them also become newly informed by a work of art as they discover how the body shapes differ both from what they have previously seen in other art and what they initially think they see in the work of art under examination. Using this method with an entire class reveals how the work of art's ambiguities generate multiple interpretations.

The kinesthetic method informs religious studies with visual works of art that feature the human body. As the human figure is increasingly prominent in the art of the past twenty-five years, this method is helpful for religious studies engaged by contemporary art but can also aid in the incorporation of earlier art such as Michelangelo's. The method aids in the study of art with religious subject matter, as well as art with religious dimensions expressed through forms rather than through explicit religious subjects.

NOTES

1. Also during these past twenty-five years, one senses more often the human voice in music, first-person speech in poetry, and story in novels.

2. Jane Dillenberger, "The Stations of the Cross by Barnett Newman," *Secular Art with Sacred Themes* (Nashville: Abingdon Press, 1969); and Lawrence Alloway, "Residual Sign Systems in Abstract Expressionism," *Artforum* 12 (November 1973): 36–42.

3. Sam Hunter and Don Hawthorne, *George Segal* (New York: Rizzoli, 1984), p. 14.

4. Leo Steinberg, "Michelangelo's 'Last Judgment' as Merciful Heresy," *Art in America*, November–December 1975, pp. 49–63.

5. Jane Dillenberger, "George Segal's *Abraham and Isaac*: Some Iconographic Reflections," in *Art, Creativity, and the Sacred: An Anthology in Religion and Art*, ed. Diane Apostolos-Cappadona (New York: Crossroad Publishing Co., 1984), pp. 105–24.

6. The original maquette with the figure's hand on the wire is shown by Phyllis Tuchman, *George Segal* (New York: Abbeville Press, 1983), p. 104. At the Legion of Honor site, one often discovers that someone has pushed a wire down under the man's hand.

7. Hunter and Hawthorne, *George Segal*, p. 122.

8. Stephen DeStaebler and Diane Apostolos-Cappadona, "Reflections on Art and the Spirit: A Conversation," in *Art, Creativity, and the Sacred*, p. 30.

9. Doug Adams, "Theological Expressions Through Visual Art Forms," *Art, Creativity, and the Sacred*, pp. 311–18.

10. Ted Lindberg, *Stephen DeStaebler* (Vancouver and San Francisco: Emily Carr College of Art and Design and the Art Museum Association of America, 1983), p. 8.

11. Several months after students had made these observations, Stephen De Staebler spoke to the Pacific School of Religion summer session and explicitly confirmed that the frontal presentation of his works was intended to evoke a sense of transcendence as the Pantocrator and other Byzantine works of art do.

14

Images and Values: Television as Religious Communication

GREGOR GOETHALS

Like the flux of experience, television images rush past us quickly eluding our prolonged contemplation and critical analysis. This course is an opportunity to recapture, distill, and interpret those electronic images which create an environment of symbols as "real" as reality itself. The goal of this course is the development of a theological critique of the television medium by analyzing its implicit and explicit ideology.

Class involves a detailed visual analysis informed by the critical tools of theology and the sociology of religion. Beyond the required reading assignments, students present weekly reviews of particular television programs. Lectures and discussions are illustrated with off-the-air photographs from television shows and events. These slides permit the viewer to "stop" the flow of the medium in order to consider the complexity of the images that otherwise move so quickly.

The course structure is derived from the use of traditional forms of religious communication as models or analogues, with a particular emphasis upon their roles mediating societal meaning and value. The course's underlying question is: "To what degree have television images appropriated the role of traditional forms of religious communication in a secular and technological society?" After a consideration of television's transformation of ritual, icon, and evangelism, the iconoclastic aspects of the medium are analyzed. The thesis of these lectures is that television is a mediator of faith and values in American society. Therefore, audio-visual texts from television become significant materials for the teaching of religious studies.

American television is compared and contrasted to more traditional forms of religious symbolization. While there are profound differences, there are also basic connections. As in traditional art forms, television images shape and express a world view and embody values. While television often trivializes experience and presents an ornate emptiness, it is simultaneously a vehicle for constituting symbols of order. Television has become a way that many Americans, consciously and unconsciously, come to identify meaning and value. Where traditional institutions and high art have failed to provide meaningful public symbols, television images have filled the void.

The course entails a double view of television: first, the specific functions of television (the news informs, commercials sell products, and sit-coms and sports entertain); and second, all television images (news, comedy, commercials, soap operas) furnish the American public with fundamental symbols. Contemporary concepts of the "good life," the roles of men and women, technology, and the changing patterns of family and political life emerge from television images. This emphasis on television as a mode of symbolizing world views and societal values identifies this as a religious studies course, rather than a communication course.

Preliminary assignments and discussions center on the meanings of "religion" and "religious art." The interpretations of commercial television images as religious communication depend upon an understanding of a broad sociological definition of religion. Initial required readings include selected materials from classical sociologists of religion such as Emile Durkheim and Max Weber; and suggested readings by Victor Turner, Clifford Geertz, and Mary Douglas. At the onset of the course, students become conversant with sociological and theological concepts for understanding religion in its broadest and narrowest contexts. As the semester progresses, students are required to read Robert Bellah, *Habits of the Heart* (Berkeley: University of California Press, 1985); H. R. Niebuhr, *Radical Monotheism and Western Culture* (New York: Harper & Row, 1962); and John Wilson, *Public Religion in American Culture* (Philadelphia: Temple University Press, 1979).

The religious import of television can be best understood

through the Niebuhrian concept of faith as a human phenomenon which can "manifest itself almost as directly in science, politics, and other cultural activities as it does in religion." The readings from Bellah and Wilson analyze what has been variously characterized as American "civil" or "public" religion. This form of religion is less concerned with "salvation" than with "reality" and "values." These critical questions establish the foundation for an understanding of television images as the sacramental forms for the embodiment of religious value and meaning in a secular society.

Religious Art: Traditional and Contemporary

After a sustained discussion of these concepts of religion, the class begins a discussion of the varieties of meanings associated with the term *religious art* by viewing a sequence of seemingly unrelated slides: stained-glass windows from the south transept of Chartres Cathedral (twelfth century); television shots of the *700 Club*; Lionel Richie's Pepsi Cola commercial; Vincent van Gogh's *The Starry Night* (1889; Museum of Modern Art, New York); television shots of John F. Kennedy's funeral; a Super Bowl telecast; and an Eastern Orthodox icon.

Beyond their disparities, these are all images: some are obviously religious, while others perform ritualistic functions in a secular society. They are all visual symbols that mediate faith and values, and express popular sentiment. In a sense, they are all examples of religious art.

The most convenient categorization of religious art is that based on the identification of subjects from the Scriptures and/or their placement in liturgical settings. From this perspective, religious art suggests the enhancement of worship space through paintings, sculptures, glass, or tapestries that depict scriptural heroes or narratives. The style, materials, and craftsmanship of these images varies. The religious art seen in medieval cathedrals is unlike that in late Italian Renaissance churches. Certainly, it is different from the highly abstract and/or nonrepresentational art found in modern churches. If content is a major criterion of religious art, then the illustrations that appear in printed form, from the color reproductions in Bibles to Sunday School materials and church bulletins to those popular posters and bumper stickers with pious captions, might be included in this category. Of course the works of "old masters" might also qualify. Ironically, this would include religious subjects painted by Rembrandt van Rijn (1606–69) which were not executed primarily for a liturgical setting and are today found in art museums. Altarpieces, reliquaries, crucifixes, and other liturgical objects removed from a religious context, are viewed as "art" in a gallery or museum.

Museums also house works of art identified by some critics as religious art, for example, abstract expressionist canvases by Barnett Newman (1905–70) and Mark Rothko (1903–70). These artists indicated through the titles of the paintings or in conversations with critics their interest in spirituality or mysticism. Contemporary artists have drawn our attention to moral issues: for example, Leon Golub (b. 1922) has presented us with large, excruciating paintings that direct our attention to death and destruction. An afternoon at a major art museum indicates the various ways that religious experience is communicated through religious art.

Television as Transformation:
Ritual, Icon, and Iconoclasm

In this course, the analyses are dependent upon the use of traditional forms of communication as models. Religious rituals and icons are studied as analogical examples. The course's presupposition is that even in a secular and pluralistic society images are venerated and events perform ritual functions. The goal of this course is to understand the degree to which American television embodies our belief system and symbols.

Being so accustomed to ever-present television images, we often fail to see them as symbolic constructs. However, if viewed as symbolic artifacts of a technological society, comparisons may be drawn between their images and those artifacts historians study. Television shares with older, traditional forms the evocative power to attune individuals to a society's way of life. In analyzing how images functioned in premodern cultures, the student discovers that "art" was not an autonomous phenomenon. Rather, it performed the important role of legitimating central societal symbols.

Ritual is a primary model used to interpret certain aspects of contemporary television when it is defined as an audio-visual mode through which values are communicated and individuals are attuned to the larger symbolic order. Traditional ritual action provided a sense of knowing and of being in simple as well as complex groups. For example, ritual action was an indispensable part of the life of the Australian Aborigines, providing for the assimilation and nurture of individuals into a society and for the continuity of its basic symbols and world views. In a highly technological society, ritual is important for community identity. For contemporary Roman Catholics, the ritual of the Mass provides indispensable forms of communication, nurture, and renewal. Contemporary Protestants have similar identifiable liturgical forms of regeneration.

For example, in the Roman Catholic model, ritual is a sacred event reenacted within carefully measured boundaries of time and space. There are at least four traditional components to this understanding of ritual: first, a sense of sacred space as distinct from ordinary space; second, a frame of sacred time with carefully orchestrated rhythms; third, the enactment of an event significant to the community; and fourth, a patterned participation of believers.

Whereas in the Protestant Evangelical model, the emphasis of ritual is placed first upon charismatic leadership which brings about a special dependency in communication on the one who, in Max Weber's words, is endowed with "special gifts of body and spirit"; second, upon a ready adaptation of technology to enhance persuasive power; and third, upon the importance of the conversion experience.

Live television coverage of significant events has resulted in a radical extension of traditional ritual participation by the proxy-ritual-participation of television viewers. In order to understand this phenomenon, slides of traditional religious rituals are compared to slides of televised events. Television has ritualized a variety of ceremonies and activities in our democratic culture: for example, political events such as national conventions, election night coverage, presidential inaugurations, and presidential press conferences; the nightly news; sports events; and a variety of religious services including the video evangelists.

Icon is understood as a model for interpretive structure. Traditionally, a religious icon functioned as a form of attunement to the system of meaning and value in a society. Although derived from a more unified society than the contemporary one, this model served as a typology of the visual form which enables individuals to envision abstract values and to communicate a sense of belonging to a larger whole.

In American culture the predominately Protestant ethos of the nineteenth century limited institutional support for traditional religious images (fig. 26). However, American artists in the nineteenth and twentieth centuries have appropriated three visual metaphors as American icons which communicate participation in the larger symbolic order: the family, the machine, and nature.

Our sense of who we are as individuals comes, in part, from knowing what kinds of human groups we belong to. We are all complex individuals because we belong not just to one but to many groups: family, neighborhood, city, state, nation, and a working group. Frequently imaged by American artists, the family is a special kind of image as it communicates something about those larger and more abstract groups to which we belong. Fictionalized families on television are popular contexts for storytelling and for the visualization of human relationships. The different kinds of family groups seen on commercial television reflect and shape our changing ideas about individuals and groups in American society. A variety of different types of families have been presented on commercial television from the early series, *Father Knows Best*, to the current series, *The Cosby Show* (fig. 27) and *Kate and Allie*.

Our sense of self is not based entirely on membership in human communities. The ways in which we perceive ourselves are related to other groups of which we are a part. In our highly industrialized society, ideas about selfhood are shaped by society and technology. Self-images and images of the universe are closely related to the machines that move out of the earth's orbit into the universe. Also, we perceive ourselves as operators of machines, and fantasize about scientific and technological advances. We televise real events that seem like fantasies, including fantasies based on technological achievements as well as live coverage of space explorations. These televised images, like pieces of a puzzle, are combined to form our sense of what it means to know and to be a part of contemporary American culture.

In American society our sense of selfhood has always been related to the images of nature. Early American landscape painters provided the nation with an icon of the majestic natural order of which individual selves were a part. Whether through landscape painting, photographs, or television, images of the natural order to which we belong are collected in our mind's eye. This is another category which helps us understand our selfhood. Images taken from documentary specials on nature or fictional programs with a nature theme are one contemporary mode for analyzing the iconic nature of commercial television.

A third model or analogue for interpreting television images is iconoclasm which is a negation of imagery because of the power attributed to the image. In its strictest sense, iconoclasm as the destruction of images was simultaneously the destruction of that power inherent within the image. Paradoxically, in the modern world it is possible to speak of certain images as "iconoclastic images." These are images which, deliberately or inadvertently, seek to devalue or destroy power by exhorting and/or persuading the viewer that institutions or political persons need to be revalued.

This model of iconoclastic images can identify those television images that cause the viewer to question societal mores or values from the beginnings of the documentary tradition in American commercial television, produced by Edward R. Murrow and Fred Friendly, to contemporary programs like *60 Minutes*. There are also what might be called "inadvertent" iconoclastic images. Such images come from news broadcasts of the Vietnam War, the Watergate Senate Hearings, and current broadcasts regarding U.S. policies in Central America and the Middle East.

Television Commercials

Commercials punctuate television programming. They are studied initially in relation to specific shows. However, the separate analysis of commercials is an important and integral segment of this course. Drawing upon a wide range of iconic materials, commercials provide a fruitful and engaging study. The family and nature are frequently used commercial images, as is American fascination with machines. These motifs appear individually or in a series of complex relationships. Most importantly, commercials play a special role in our economic system.

26. Currier and Ives, *The Seasons of Life: Middle Age* (19th century; Traveler's Insurance, Hartford, Connecticut).

27. Scenes from *The Cosby Show* (1986).

Commercials are among the most challenging art forms in television. Those which are done well bring the most exquisite technology and artistry to commercial television. Many producers of commercials demonstrate an extraordinary sense of artistic perfection, even ecstasy, usually associated with so-called fine artists. These individuals love what they are doing and like to engage people in a mind-set. For them, persuasion is both an exciting business and an art form.

Successful television commercials bring together some combinations of those things venerated through American icons and values. For example, consider a series of frames from one commercial.

1. A boy and his dog are trouncing on a hillside: this is an evocative image of freedom and lightheartedness emphasizing an openness of land and sky.
2. The inclusion of sheep indicates that this is not simply a carefree romp in the countryside; the boy and his dog are working. The value of work is combined with that of play.
3. Another shot of the boy running includes a glimpse of trimmed trees and a picket fence. This environment suggests the domestication of American suburbia.
4. The face of an older youth is blended into the image. As sophisticated viewers, we know that the boy is daydreaming as he is running along, imagining himself grown-up.
5. In his daydream the youth is seen holding up his head in triumph to receive a medal.
6. The boy *is* clearly identified with the triumphant youth as he raises his head in triumph through his imagination.
7. As the boy reaches home, he bursts through the gate of a white picket fence. In this shot, the boy and his homeward leap are frozen into a small image. Imprinted above is the logo of McDonald's.
8. The final frame is a close-up shot of the Olympic Flame superimposed with McDonald's Golden Arches.

Taken together, these images create a value montage of play, work, countryside, farmland, competition, daydreams, ambition, discipline, hope, and triumph. This commercial was aired in connection with the Montreal Olympic Games.

The well-crafted commercial shapes and expresses much of our contemporary culture. Walter Mondale's turnaround in the 1984 presidential primaries could be associated with his appropriation of the then familiar phrase, "Where's the beef?" Another example of this merging of cultural interests with commercial messages is the inclusion of entertainment figures such as Lionel Richie and Michael Jackson in Pepsi Cola commercials. The sponsor and the producer draw upon well-established cultural symbols and personalities.

Beyond these symbolic aspects, the role that commercials play in the patronage of the communication system is studied. In commercial television, all types of programming—news, entertainment, sports, drama, gameshows, and documentaries—are sponsored by corporate advertising. Such sponsorship can affect the programs that are aired even to the shocking examples of advertisers' power to jeopardize programming. A dramatic example of this misuse of power was the advertisers' refusal to sponsor a CBS documentary, *The Guns of August,* which was critical of hunting. This advertising boycott and the furor over the documentary were so overwhelming that another CBS documentary hosted by Charles Collingwood analyzed the boycott and the controversial documentary.

In the American media system the power of patronage and the selection of symbolic content are too closely related. There is no Ministry of Truth such as George Orwell described in *1984.* However, a tacit Ministry of Commercials is the great webbing which holds together all commercial television programming. Commercials are so ingrained in American culture that it seems unpatriotic to consider an alternative. In fact, it is difficult to see how the vast marketing system in American society could operate without them.

Beyond this obvious economic factor, there is another significant cultural factor at the deepest levels of our commercial system: a residual religious motif that has been present in our Protestant Evangelical ethos. "Residual" connotes that there is nothing specifically religious in this motif. What is present in the internal structure and dynamics of the television commercial is the "evangelical" appeal to have a change of heart. All commercials depend upon the assumption of change: what *one* can become *if only* . . . you can become more beautiful, more successful, wealthier, smell better . . . *if only* you make the right decision about a product. Substitute the name of the product for the evangelical altar call and the strategy of the commercial becomes both a metaphor of *salvation*: one is saved from social horrors; and a metaphor of *desire*: viewers want to become or to possess something that appears to be beyond them. Just as the evangelists emphasize the importance of *choice*, so do television commercials. Choose this cold cream, motor oil, automobile, detergent, wax, toothpaste, dental cream, and/or antacid, and *you* will be saved from slow starts, headaches, ugliness, unpopularity, and bad breath. Salvation, desire, choice: these metaphors are deeply engrained in our religious ethos, and have been transfigured and assimilated into the structure of television commercials.

Having analyzed the functional similarities of television commercials and of icons, the analogical method also takes into account the differences: the *unlikeness* between those traditional religious forms and contemporary commercial television. The most striking and provocative difference is that the traditional iconic forms had an intimate acquaintance with suffering and death. In his book, *The Denial of Death* (New York: Free Press, 1973), Ernest Becker eloquently described the ways in which modern culture actually diverts our attention from our own finitude. Traditional forms of religious communication put the viewers in touch with the heroic transformations of defeat, suffering, and death that transcended cultural myths and values.

Since the terms *ritual* and *icon* have been so closely associated with traditional religion, these words are usually reserved for category descriptions of communication media that occurred within the context of institutionalized religion. Given that the modern techniques of communication are so technically sophisticated, there has been a reluctance to dislodge ritual and icon from their traditional contexts. However, if we dislodge these forms, we can better understand the symbols that bind isolated individuals together into a society. More importantly, we will discover that among competing rituals and icons, some provide a more profound orientation to life and death than others.

The power of commercial television is to indoctrinate us into a

public system of symbols. If we do *not* critically evaluate the symbols of American television, we constantly risk the danger of becoming prisoners of illusion. We will not realize that there is a
choice to be made. We will become the contemporary counterpart
to those prisoners in Plato's parable who named the shadows cast
on the wall of the cave and believed that they were naming themselves and all other realities.

PART IV

BIBLIOGRAPHIES

15

Sources for the Study of Judaism and the Arts

JOSEPH GUTMANN

Mention the words Jewish art and one is immediately confronted by a flood of negations. An often repeated scholarly opinion has it that Judaism has always denied the image: a rejection firmly rooted in Israel's formative period and solidly lodged in Israel's collective unconscious. Jewish participation in the arts, it is believed, was circumscribed by the anti-iconic biblical injunctions, in particular the so-called second commandment (Exod. 20:4–5). This prevailing attitude of scholars has largely prevented students of Jewish theology and religion from being exposed to the visual arts.

Yet in recent years the discipline of Jewish art history has made available a wealth of significant resources for the study of Jewish religion and theology, and has restored to Jewish scholarship, which was exclusively text oriented, a visual dimension heretofore ignored. It is now realized that the testimony of Jewish art can serve not only to augment but to modify and correct the vast Jewish literary tradition. For Jewish art frequently highlights, more accurately than the text tradition, the complex three-and-a-half-millennia involvement of Jews with multiple civilizations, cultures, and societies. Two major issues confront the student of Jewish art: the assumed taboo against images and the problem of how to define the apparently contradictory nature of Jewish art.

The source material in this bibliographic survey demonstrates how the visual arts and architecture relate to and participate in the long history of Judaism, both past and present. This list makes no pretense at being complete; it is simply a selected list of important publications available in English, and is intended primarily to serve as an introduction to the subject for students of theology and religion.

For a thorough discussion of the complex role that the second commandment and images play, not only in Judaism but also in the sister religions of Christianity and Islam, the interested reader is referred to the fine essays and the extensive up-to-date bibliography in the book edited by Joseph Gutmann, *The Image and the Word: Confrontations in Judaism, Christianity, and Islam* (Scholars Press, 1977). As Jewish art reveals no unique style, but generally refracts the Jewish involvement with multiple non-Jewish civilizations and cultures, it naturally bears the stylistic characteristics of these multicultural experiences. It also poses the perplexing problem of ascertaining the nature of Jewish art. The most important recent publication concerning the definitions of Jewish art are to be found in the collection of essays edited by Clare Moore, *The Visual Dimension: Aspects of Jewish Art* (Rowman and Allanheld, in press). A good general introduction to the entire subject of Jewish art, with excellent illustrations, can be found in the articles by leading scholars in *Jewish Art, An Illustrated History*, revised edition, edited by Cecil Roth (New York Graphic Society, 1971). *A History of Jewish Art* (reissued by Kennikat Press, 1973), a shorter book by the late pioneering scholar Franz Landsberger, although somewhat dated, is still the best survey on the subject. An excellent bibliographical source up to 1965 is Leo A. Mayer's *Bibliography of Jewish Art* (Magnes Press, 1967), edited by Otto Kurz.

Whether biblical archaeology is to be considered an intricate part of Jewish art is a debatable question. Of the many books published on this subject, the best and most readable introduction for the general reader is by Harry M. Orlinsky, *Understanding the Bible through History and Archaeology* (KTAV Publishing House, 1972). For the student desiring detailed information on the subject, the fine up-to-date collection of essays by leading scholars in *Biblical Archaeology Today*, edited by Avraham Biran (Israel Exploration Society, 1985), is recommended. The best summary for an understanding of Solomon's Temple within the biblical context, as well as the influence this temple exerted on later Jewish, Christian, and Islamic art and thought, is the collection of essays with up-to-date bibliographies gathered in the volume edited by Joseph Gutmann,

The Temple of Solomon: Archaeological Fact and Medieval Tradition in Christian, Islamic and Jewish Art (Scholars Press, 1976).

The most astounding discovery for the study of Jewish art is a synagogue, excavated in 1932, in the Roman military outpost of Dura-Europos, which is accurately dated A.D. 244/5. Its extensive cycle of figural paintings has necessitated reexamination of long cherished theories on the origins of Christian art, the attitude of Judaism toward images, and the types of Judaism practiced not only in the Syrian desert town but also in the larger Jewish centers of Palestine and Babylonia. Many books have been devoted to this amazing discovery. The magisterial and detailed study of Carl Kraeling, *The Synagogue* (KTAV Publishing House, 1979, augmented edition), has not been superceded. A summary of recent scholarship on the synagogue since Kraeling's final report was first published in 1956 is available in the articles of eminent scholars in the book *The Dura-Europos Synagogue: A Re-evaluation (1932–1972)* (Scholars Press, 1973), edited by Joseph Gutmann. The stimulating and elegant thirteen-volume opus, *Jewish Symbols in the Greco-Roman Period* (Bollingen Foundation, 1952–68), by Erwin R. Goodenough, devotes three volumes to the Dura synagogue (vols. 9–11). For an incisive, critical review of Goodenough's methodology, see Morton Smith's article, reprinted in *The Synagogue: Studies in Origins, Archaeology, and Architecture* (KTAV Publishing House, 1975), edited by Joseph Gutmann.

The origins and development of the synagogue are still matters of scholarly dispute. Many of the contradictory theories proposed by scholars are gathered in a series of articles in two books edited by Joseph Gutmann, *The Synagogue* (mentioned above) and *Ancient Synagogues: The State of Research* (Scholars Press, 1981). Extremely valuable also are the important articles by leading scholars in two recent books edited by Lee I. Levine, *Ancient Synagogues Revealed* (Israel Exploration Society, 1981) and *The Synagogue in Late Antiquity* (American Schools of Oriental Research, 1987). The latter publication deals with such topics as the art and architecture of the early synagogue, its inscriptions, and the relation of synagogue images to contemporary liturgy.

Decorative and figural mosaics in synagogues dating from the fourth to the sixth century A.D. have had several studies devoted to them. The excellent survey of these mosaics by Ernst Kitzinger, *Israeli Mosaics of the Byzantine Period* (New American Library, 1965), and the beautiful volume by Meyer Schapiro and Michael Avi-Yonah, *Israel, Ancient Mosaics* (New York Graphic Society, 1960), are strongly recommended. The recently discovered synagogue mosaics at Hammath-Tiberias are critically analyzed by Moshe Dothan in *Hammath-Tiberias* (Israel Exploration Society, 1983). Also noteworthy is the fine study by Bernard Goldman of the sixth-century Beth-Alpha synagogue mosaics, *The Sacred Portal, A Primary Symbol in Ancient Jewish Art* (Wayne State University Press, 1966).

During the Roman period, Jews followed the contemporary practice of burying their dead in catacombs. These catacombs sometimes have sculptural decoration on the walls and on the commissioned sarcophagi. Those of Rome, dating roughly from the third and fourth centuries, also have pictorial decoration. The aforementioned work by Goodenough contains a good survey of these catacombs. The book by Harry J. Leon, *The Jews of Ancient Rome* (Jewish Publication Society of America, 1960), concentrates mainly on the Roman catacomb inscriptions, but contains some good illustrations of the catacombs. An excellent book on Jewish sarcophagi is *Sarcophagi from the Jewish Catacombs of Ancient Rome* by Adia Konikoff (Franz Steiner, 1986). These important findings of the Beth-She'arim catacombs in Palestine have been diligently catalogued and described in the three-volume work *Beth She'arim* (Rutgers University Press, 1973–76) by Benjamin Mazar and Nahman Avigad.

The Jewish involvement in the medieval Islamic and Christian civilizations is manifest in surviving synagogues and in illustrated manuscripts. The synagogues reveal not only new liturgical needs, but the adaptation of new architectural forms. Carol Krinsky's *Synagogues of Europe* (Architectural History Foundation, 1985) and Rachel Wischnitzer's *The Architecture of the European Synagogue* (Jewish Publication Society of America, 1955) convincingly interpret the spiritual and architectural significance of European synagogue architecture. In addition, the Krinsky book has excellent plans and photographs of synagogues.

Some works on specific synagogues or synagogues of a certain period make major contributions to our knowledge of the development of synagogue architecture. Two books worth singling out are

the well-researched study by Otto Böcher of one of the oldest synagogues of Europe, the twelfth-century Worms synagogue, in *Fest-
schrift zur Wiedereinweihung der Alten Synagoge zu Worms*, edited by
Ernst Roth (Ner Tamid Verlag, 1961), and the work of Francisco
Cantera Burgos, *Synagogas españolas* (Instituto Arias Montana,
1955).

The only detailed study in English of the remarkable wooden
Polish synagogues is by Maria and Kazimierz Pietchotka, *Wooden
Synagogues* (Arkady, 1959). A model of research on nineteenth-
and twentieth-century German synagogues is by Harold Hammer-
Schenk, *Synagogen in Deutschland. Geschichte einer Baugattung im
19. und 20. Jahrhundert* (Hans Christian Verlag, 1981).

The best studies by outstanding scholars on the much debated
issue of the existence of illustrated Jewish manuscripts in classical
antiquity (which may have influenced Christian art) are gathered
in the book edited by Joseph Gutmann, *No Graven Images: Studies
in Art and the Hebrew Bible* (KTAV Publishing House, 1971).

Judaism, Christianity, and Islam are all essentially religions of
the book, and the sacred words of divinity are lavishly adorned in
all three religions. In the course of its involvement with many host
cultures, Judaism adapted the splendid abstract ornamentation
found in such Islamic texts as the *Qur'an*, and the Romanesque,
Gothic, and Renaissance styles found in Christian liturgical books.
The earliest Hebrew manuscript illumination comes from ninth-
century Islamic Palestine. In Europe, Hebrew manuscript illumination dates from the thirteenth to the fifteenth centuries. The
production of illuminated Hebrew Bibles, liturgical, medical, and
philosophic texts resulted in such masterpieces as the Spanish Hebrew Kennicott Bible and the German Darmstadt Haggadah, both
now available in magnificent facsimile editions. Good one-volume
studies that include beautiful color plates from outstanding medieval illuminated Hebrew manuscripts are Bezalel Narkiss's *Hebrew Illuminated Manuscripts* (Keter Publishing House, 1969) and
Joseph Gutmann's *Hebrew Manuscript Painting* (George Braziller,
1978).

Jewish Life in the Middle Ages (Alpine Fine Arts, 1982) by Thérèse
and Mendel Metzger utilizes illuminated Hebrew manuscripts
in order to give a vivid picture of secular and religious life in medieval Europe. *A History of Jewish Costume* (Peter Owen Lim-

ited, 1981) by Alfred Rubens widens our knowledge of the unexplored field of Jewish dress. Jewish coins and medals are discussed in two fine books by Daniel Friedenberg, *Jewish Minters and Medalists* (Jewish Publication Society of America, 1976) and *Jewish Medals from the Renaissance to the Fall of Napoleon (1503–1815)* (Clarkson N. Potter, 1970). A unique aspect of Jewish art is the practice of micrography: the utilization of Hebrew letters to form both figural and abstract designs. Leila Avrin's *Micrography as Art* (Israel Museum Jerusalem, 1981) traces the origin and development of this unique art form.

Some splendid examples of Jewish ceremonial art objects from Western Europe are extant today. Generally they were executed by master Christian smiths, as Jews were often denied the opportunity of joining Christian guilds or of forming their own guilds. From the sixteenth to the eighteenth centuries these objects reveal such Christian styles as the Baroque and the Rococo. A thorough discussion of the origin and development of Jewish customs and practices and the ceremonial objects linked with them can be found in the erudite essays gathered in *Beauty in Holiness: Studies in Jewish Customs and Ceremonial Art* (KTAV Publishing House, 1970), edited by Joseph Gutmann. For comprehensive studies with extensive bibliographies of the ceremonial objects used during the Jewish holidays and in the synagogue, the books, *The Jewish Year* (E. J. Brill, 1975) by Isaiah Shachar and *The Jewish Sanctuary* (E. J. Brill, 1983) by Joseph Gutmann, are recommended. The diverse objects employed during birth, marriage, and death are examined in Joseph Gutmann's *The Jewish Life Cycle* (E. J. Brill, 1987).

Some thoroughly researched catalogues of unique collections of Jewish ceremonial art in Judaica museums are worthy of consultation. Recommended are *The Feuchtwanger Collection of Judaica* by Isaiah Shachar (Israel Museum Jerusalem, 1981); *Jewish Treasures from Paris from the Collections of the Cluny Museum and Consistoire* by Victor Klagsbald (Israel Museum Jerusalem, 1982); *Danzig 1939: Treasures of a Destroyed Community* (Jewish Museum New York, 1980); *Catalogue of the Jewish Museum London* (New York Graphic Society, 1974), edited by Richard Barnett; *Jewish Ceremonial Art* by Stephen Kayser (Jewish Publication Society of America, 1959); *Treasures of The Jewish Museum* by Norman Kleebatt and Vivian Mann (Universe Books, 1986); and *The Pre-*

cious Legacy: Judaic Treasures from the Czechoslovak State Collections (Summit Books, 1983), edited by David Altshuler.

The development of lavishly illustrated Jewish marriage contracts, especially from seventeenth- and eighteenth-century Italy, are faithfully reproduced in sumptuous color in two volumes, *Italian Ketubbot. Illuminated Jewish Marriage Contracts* (Associazione Amici Università di Gerusalemme, 1984), edited by Liliana Grassi, and *The Ketuba: Jewish Marriage Contracts through the Ages* (Lewin Epstein, 1986) by David Davidowitch.

With the legal emancipation of the Jews in the Western world in the nineteenth century, the artist of Jewish birth was no longer tied to a legally organized self-governing medieval-type Jewish community, and no longer expressed the collective beliefs and symbols of that community. While artists might be Jewish by accident of birth or by affiliation with the Jewish religion, any manifestation of religious feeling was now personal and not communal. Their art came to reflect their national and international allegiances. Beginning with the late nineteenth century, Jewish subject matter generally does not appear in the works of artists of Jewish origin, for they often no longer worked for the Jewish community or for Jewish clients. Furthermore, with the separation of church and state in the nineteenth- and twentieth-century Western world, traditional religious definitions of art can no longer be employed.

During this period, both the church and the synagogue have had to content themselves with art styles emerging from the secular sphere. It is thus that the art of modern Israel reflects international styles with Jewish subject matter appearing only sporadically. Two books which explore current trends in Israeli art are *Artists of Israel: 1920–1980* (Jewish Museum New York, 1981), edited by Susan Goodman, and *Art in Israel* (W. H. Allen, 1966) by Benjamin Tammuz and Max Wykes-Joyce.

In the nineteenth century artists of Jewish origin were enabled to obtain training in art schools, which earlier had been generally closed to them. One of the first artists to emerge in the nineteenth century was Moritz Oppenheim, whose paintings of scenes of traditional Jewish life once hung in many Jewish homes. For a treatment of his work, see *Moritz Oppenheim: The First Jewish Painter* (Israel Museum Jerusalem, 1983), edited by Elisheva Cohen.

Since the end of the nineteenth century, many artists of Jewish birth have become internationally acclaimed masters; among them are Amedeo Modigliani, Jacques Lipchitz, and Chaim Soutine. Some of these masters, such as the American Max Weber (see *Max Weber* by Alfred Werner [Harry N. Abrams, 1975]) and, of course, Marc Chagall (see *Chagall* by Susan Compton [Philadelphia Museum of Art, 1985]), often devote paintings to Jewish subject matter. A tragic reminder of the indescribable horror of the twentieth century, the massacre of innocent European Jewry at the hands of the Nazi hordes, is sensitively explored in *Art of the Holocaust* by Janet Blatter and Sybil Milton (Rutledge Press, 1981).

The search for a meaningful symbolic form in contemporary synagogue architecture is beautifully elucidated in Avram Kampf's book, *Contemporary Synagogue Architecture* (Union of American Hebrew Congregations, 1966; see also Rachel Wischnitzer's book, *Synagogue Architecture in the United States* [Jewish Publication Society of America, 1955]). Equally insightful is Kampf's book, *Jewish Experience in the Art of the Twentieth Century* (Bergin and Garvey, 1984).

All of the books cited deal with the visual language of the three-thousand-five-hundred-year Jewish religious experience, a dimension frequently overlooked in Jewish religious studies. Though art is never a dominant factor in the Jewish religious tradition, as is the case in Christianity, its exploration can shed light on and deepen our comprehension of the complex history of Judaism.

16

Sources for the Study of Christianity and the Arts

JOHN W. COOK

The arts have always been an essential aspect of the language of the Christian tradition and today there is no corporate act of worship by any group of Christians that does not appropriate some aspect of the arts to enact its praise and prayer. A critical sense of what the Christian tradition has intended in its artistic expressions and what it intends today can serve the study of Christianity. While the arts involve many forms and media, I am concerned here with sources for the study of the visual arts.

Since students of theology and religion have had less experience studying art and architecture than the traditional theological disciplines, it may be helpful to make some suggestions concerning content and method. The discipline of art history has produced a wealth of valuable resources for religion and theology. The strength of the art-historical discipline for religion and theology lies in the methods and sources it has made available. With precision and scrutiny, art historians have for some time been delving into primary documents (visual and verbal) of the Christian faith.

The materials listed in this bibliographic survey illustrate how the visual media of art and architecture relate to and participate in the story of Christendom, past and present. This is an abbreviated

An earlier version of this essay appeared under the title "Theology and the Arts," in *Theology Today* 34 (April 1977): 45–51. This revised version first appeared in *Art, Creativity, and the Sacred: An Anthology in Religion and Art*, ed. Diane Apostolos-Cappadona (New York: Crossroad Publishing Co., 1984), pp. 321–29. It is reprinted here by permission.

list, an introduction to the range of insights available in the visual arts to students of religion and theology.

Our study of the world of the New Testament and the nature of the early church is enriched when we include the witness of early Christian art. An excellent introduction is available in André Grabar's *Early Christian Art* (Princeton University Press, 1980 [1968]), and a broader view is presented in the highly readable, if abbreviated, study by Edward Syndicus under the same title, *Early Christian Art* (Hawthorne Books, 1962). The best set of illustrations of the Christian witness in catacomb fresco painting is found in Pierre du Bourguet's *Early Christian Painting* (Viking Press, 1965). His introductory essay contributes to our appreciation of the liturgical background of these remarkable paintings.

The most valuable recent publication concerning the relationship of early Christian art to the late antique world is the collection edited by Kurt Weitzmann entitled *Age of Spirituality* (Metropolitan Museum of Art, 1979). This volume is the catalogue of the exhibition held at the Metropolitan Museum of Art in the winter of 1977–78 on late antique and early Christian art from the third to the seventh century. The articles and excellent illustrations contribute to our understanding of the visual arts of the early church in their historical and cultural setting, with contributions from many eminent scholars; the bibliography is the best and most up-to-date available in a single volume today. This volume, in combination with Frederik van der Meer's *Atlas of the Early Christian World* (Nelson, 1958)—in which illustrations from the art of the early church are presented with translations of relevant ancient texts—gives an insightful picture of the life of the early Christians.

Our understanding of the meeting places and practices of the early Christian house churches is informed by house-church (*tituli*) excavations in Rome and in the small town of Dura-Europos in Asia Minor. A summary of the findings concerning the meeting places of the young Christian communities in Rome is given in the opening chapters of the remarkable book by Richard Krautheimer, *Early Christian and Byzantine Architecture* (Penguin Books, 1965). The complete and meticulously detailed reports of the evidence from ancient Rome are available in the large folio volumes by the same author, *Corpus Basilicarum Christianarum Romae* (Pontif. Istituto di Arch. Cristiana, 1937 and following).

The earliest house church known today from physical evidence is a renovated private home that became a gathering place and center of worship in the first half of the third century at Dura-Europos. Its full story is beautifully told in Carl Kraeling's *The Christian Building* (J. J. Augustin, 1967). A more elaborate and sumptuous building at Dura-Europos, the Jewish synagogue, is interpreted in Carl Kraeling's *The Synagogue* (KTAV Publishing House, 1979). A summary of scholarship on the synagogue was published in a series of articles edited by Joseph Gutmann under the title *The Dura-Europos Synagogue: A Re-evaluation (1932–1972)* (American Academy of Religion, 1973). For a general introduction to the study of this town and its art, see Ann Perkins's *The Art of Dura-Europos* (Oxford University Press, 1973).

When the church emerged in its more public forms, after the Peace of the Church at the beginning of the fourth century, the monumental Christian basilica structures in centers like Rome, Constantinople, and Jerusalem, illustrate a dramatic shift in the ecclesial needs and self-understanding expressed in architecture. This astonishing story is reported in the above-mentioned works by Krautheimer. One of the most surprising parts of the story is about the buildings that Constantine's architects constructed in Jerusalem around the places accepted as the sites where Christ was crucified, buried, and resurrected. Kenneth Conant's "The Holy Sepulchre" (*Speculum*, vol. 31, pp. 1–48) is a good introduction. A more recent interpretation of the archaeological as well as literary evidence is Charles Coüasnon's *The Church of the Holy Sepulchre in Jerusalem* (Oxford University Press, 1974).

The mosaics, sculpture, and architecture in the splendidly preserved monuments of fifth- and sixth-century Ravenna, Italy, provide a spellbinding chapter in the artistically creative language of the Christian faith. The complexity and beauty of this art records an essential chapter and reflects a rich, faithful tradition. Get a glimpse of it in Otto von Simson's *The Sacred Fortress* (University of Chicago Press, 1948), Spiro Kostof's *The Orthodox Baptistery of Ravenna* (Yale University Press, 1965), Giuseppi Bovini's *Ravenna Mosaics* (New York Graphic Society, 1956), and the relevant sections of André Grabar's *The Golden Age of Justinian* (Odyssey Press, 1967).

The production of Bibles, liturgical books, and theological texts resulted in such masterpieces of Christendom as the Book of Kells, the Utrecht Psalter, numerous books of hours, and other amazing illuminated manuscripts. A good one-volume introduction to the history of illuminations is available in David Diringer's *The Illuminated Book* (Philosophical Library, 1958). An excellent commentary, beautiful color plates, and a bibliography are to be found in Kurt Weitzmann's *Late Antique and Early Christian Book Illumination* (George Braziller, 1977).

The history of illuminated manuscripts in the Christian tradition relates necessarily to the early monastic movements because the scriptoria of the monasteries were responsible for book production in the Middle Ages. The nature of medieval monastic life is reflected today in the remains of architectural monuments that embody so much of that legacy, and a few studies of that architectural history probe the significance of those forms and the faith they house. Wolfgang Braunfels's *Monasteries of Western Europe: The Architecture of the Orders* (Princeton University Press, 1972) enlightens our understanding in that it presents thorough scholarship, reproduces excellent plans and photographs, and translates original texts that help us to evaluate the monuments within the range of ideas that created them. In that regard, the soon to be published series of papers entitled *Monasticism and the Arts*, edited by Timothy Verson, John Dally, and myself, can serve as an excellent complement to Braunfels's study.

Three recent works on three different medieval monasteries make major contributions to the study of Christianity, and each illustrates in its own way how these works of art embodied a tradition. Kenneth Conant's many years of research on the monastic community at Cluny is published in *Cluny, les églises et la maison du chef de l'Ordre* (Medieval Academy Press, 1968). G. Forsyth's and Kurt Weitzmann's *The Monastery of Saint Catherine at Mount Sinai* (University of Michigan Press, 1973) is the only study in English that makes that remarkable place available through its art. Of course one of the great publishing events of the 1970s was Walter Horn's *The Plan of St. Gall* (University of California Press, 1980). This elegant three-volume study is the product of a life's work and shows how a rare medieval architectural plan can be a primary source concerning Carolingian religious sensibilities.

Too often, studies of religion generally, and of Christianity specifically, neglect the Byzantine world. The mysteries of Byzantium and Eastern Orthodoxy tend to intimidate rather than inspire. However, a wealth of new material is available, especially about the religious significance of Byzantine art and architecture. Thomas Mathews's *The Early Churches of Constantinople, Architecture and Liturgy* (Pennsylvania State University Press, 1971) is a model for seeing how archaeological evidence reveals a community's context for worship. Cyril Mango's *Sources and Documents of Byzantine Art* (Prentice-Hall, 1972) is actually a sourcebook in the history of doctrine. Our fascination with the Byzantine icon is substantially informed by the following studies: Gervase Mathew, *Byzantine Aesthetics* (John Murray, 1981 [1969]); Leonid Ouspensky and Vladimir Lossky, *The Meaning of Icons* (Mowbray Press, 1981 [1969]); Eugene N. Trubetskoi, *Icons: Theology in Color* (St. Vladimir's Seminary Press, 1980 [1973]); and Leonid Ouspensky, *Theology of the Icon* (St. Vladimir's Seminary Press, 1978).

The architecture of the Byzantine tradition is summarized in its earlier stages in Krautheimer's volume on early Christian and Byzantine architecture. See also Heinz Kähler's *Hagia Sophia* (Praeger, 1967), Cyril Mango's *Byzantine Architecture* (Abrams, 1976), and T. Mathews's *The Byzantine Churches of Istanbul* (Pennsylvania State University Press, 1976).

The richest development of religious art in Western civilization is represented by the Gothic cathedrals. Seldom have the arts carried so much of the religious mentality of an age, or sought to embody such spiritual significance. Otto von Simson's *The Gothic Cathedral* (Princeton University Press, 1974 [1956]) and Emile Mâle's *The Gothic Image* (Harper Torchbooks, 1958) convincingly interpret the sources. Two publications of translated documents of the time suggest the role of the arts in the church of the Gothic era: Erwin Panofsky's *Abbot Suger* (Princeton University Press, 1979 [1946]) and Paul Frankel's *The Gothic* (Princeton University Press, 1960). The flavor of the period is uniquely captured in Henry Adams's beautifully written *Mont-Saint-Michel and Chartres* (Princeton University Press, 1981 [1905]). Adams's breadth of sources and personal insight make the volume especially relevant to studies of the age of faith.

The strength of the Christian tradition in the Italian Renaissance has been neglected in light of the overwhelming emphasis on classical sources in Renaissance humanism. However, the Christian story is an essential aspect of the Renaissance: see Peter and Linda Murray's *The Art of the Renaissance* (Oxford University Press, 1963). Studies of the individual artists of this period are especially important. James H. Stubblebine's *Giotto: The Arena Chapel* (Norton, 1969) is a set of documents and essays about Giotto's great cycle at Padua of the life of Christ. Masaccio's work, and the influence of the reformer Savonarola on the work of Botticelli are fascinating illustrations of Christian responses in the arts. Especially poignant are studies of Donatello and Michelangelo. See, for instance, Frederich Hartt's *History of Italian Renaissance Art* (Abrams, 1969), Charles de Tolnay's *The Art and Thought of Michelangelo* (Pantheon Books, 1964), and Charles Seymour, Jr.'s *Michelangelo: The Sistine Chapel Ceiling* (Norton, 1972).

An excellent introduction to the Renaissance in the North is Otto Benesch's *The Art of the Renaissance in Northern Europe* (Harvard University Press, 1967 [1945]). Significant to the artistic and religious attitudes at the beginning of the Reformation is Wolfgang Steckow's *Northern Renaissance Art 1400–1600* (Prentice-Hall, 1966). The central figure of Albrecht Dürer comes alive in Erwin Panofsky's *Albrecht Dürer* (Princeton University Press, 1948). The story of one of Christianity's most important works of art is told in Georg Scheja's *The Isenheim Altarpiece* (Abrams, 1969), a beautifully illustrated and documented interpretation of Mathis Grünewald's masterpiece. The role of the arts in the Reformation is discussed in A. G. Dickens's *Reformation and Society in Sixteenth-Century Europe* (Harcourt, Brace, and World, 1966), and although a great deal remains to be clarified about Reformation iconography, a valuable study and model of scholarship is Charles Garside's *Zwingli and the Arts* (Yale University Press, 1966). The best study of the relationship between the arts and Reformation theology is Carl G. Christensen's *Art and the Reformation in Germany* (Wayne State University Press, 1979), a well-researched book with theological depth and an excellent bibliography.

The Counter-Reformation responded to the Reformers vigorously through the arts. The visual arts in the service of architecture and altars burst forth in the Counter-Reformation as if they were essential to the enterprise. Baroque art forms became a language for the intentions of the Roman Catholic church, and the church's patronage of the arts was at an all-time high. See Rudolph Wittkower's and Irma Jaffe's *Baroque Art: The Jesuit Contribution* (Fordham University Press, 1972), Rudolf Wittkower's *Art and Architecture in Italy, 1600–1750* (Penguin, 1958), Germain G. Bazin's *The Baroque* (Norton, 1978 [1968]), and the comparative study concerning Catholic piety and the arts in Robert T. Petersson's *The Art of Ecstasy: Teresa, Bernini and Crashaw* (Atheneum, 1970). One of the best studies of high Baroque art in the Christian context is John Rupert Martin's *Rubens: The Antwerp Altarpieces: The Raising of the Cross and the Descent from the Cross* (Norton, 1969).

Many sources for the study of Baroque art in the life of the church are readily available, and although this apparently opulent era is often out of favor today, it demonstrates a powerful use of decorative art forms born of a particular Christian point of view.

The story comes together and reaches new heights in Rembrandt. W. A. Visser't Hooft's *Rembrandt and the Gospel* (Meridian Books, 1960) gives the essential points, and Jakob Rosenberg's *Rembrandt, Life and Work* (Phaidon Press, 1968 [1948]) is the best one-volume introduction.

Studies of the subject matter of traditional Christian art (iconography) provide basic information for reading about content and symbolic function in narrative visual art. There are many encyclopedias of iconography, but the most recent and the best for Christian subject matter is found in the volumes by Gertrud Schiller, *Iconography of Christian Art* (New York Graphic Society, 1972 and following). A more general introductory study is available in one paperback volume, James Hall's *Dictionary of Subjects and Symbols in Art* (Harper & Row, 1979 [1974]). This book serves as a reliable handbook for viewing paintings from varied periods and styles.

If one is interested in the seventeenth and eighteenth centuries and in Christian attitudes reflected in American art and architecture, two good studies are Marian C. Donnelly's *The New England Meeting Houses of the Seventeenth Century* (Wesleyan University Press, 1968) and the first volume of Jules Prown's *American Painting* (Rizzoli, 1980). Especially helpful in this regard is the catalogue of an exhibition of American religious art from 1700 to 1900 by Jane Dillenberger and Joshua Taylor entitled *The Hand and the Spirit* (University Art Museum, Berkeley, 1972).

The story becomes complicated in the modern period because

traditional religious definitions and subject matter in the arts have broken down. It is fascinating to observe, however, that a religious dimension remains constant even in the midst of change. Simply put, the problem is how to discover the authentic religious consciousness in the arts of the late-nineteenth and twentieth centuries. One can begin with the visionary art of William Blake in Anthony Blunt's *The Art of William Blake* (Columbia University Press, 1959).

Some nineteenth-century art movements addressed specifically religious questions. For instance, A. W. N. Pugin's *The True Principles of Pointed or Christian Architecture* (St. Martin's Press, 1973 [1841]) and Vincent van Gogh's *Complete Letters*, 3 volumes (New York Graphic Society, 1958). Curious phases claiming religious motivation are seen in Edward Lucie-Smith's *Symbolist Art* (Oxford University Press, 1972), Robin Ironside's *Pre-Raphaelite Painting* (Phaidon, 1948), and Charles Chassé's *Les nabis et leur temps* (La Bibliotheque des arts, 1960).

For a glimpse at twentieth-century religious attitudes in modern art, see the anthology by Herschel B. Chipp, *Theories of Modern Art* (University of California Press, 1968), keeping in mind questions about the nature of the "religious" in these sources. Personal points of view are recorded in works like Wassily Kandinsky's *Concerning the Spiritual in Art* (Wittenborn, Shultz, 1947), Hans Jaffe's *De Stijl* (London, n.d.), and Pierre Courthion's *Georges Rouault* (Abrams, 1962). Jane Dillenberger has made some of the modern material available to religious studies in two different volumes and numerous articles; see her *Secular Art with Sacred Themes* (Abingdon, 1969), and the catalogue for the exhibition she and John Dillenberger organized, entitled *Perceptions of the Spirit in Twentieth-Century American Art* (Indianapolis Museum of Art, 1977).

The story reaches a peak in the works of Barnett Newman and Mark Rothko: by the 1970s they had produced an art that sought great religious and moral depth. See Lawrence Alloway's *Barnett Newman: The Stations of the Cross* (Solomon R. Guggenheim Museum of Art, 1966) and Diane Waldman's commentary in *Mark Rothko* (Solomon R. Guggenheim Museum of Art, 1978).

All of the texts cited here concern the visual language of the religious experience—a language that is too often neglected in modern religious studies and practice. Reclaiming this major facet of the Christian tradition, rediscovering the authentic language of the arts for the life of the church, and incorporating this material into religious studies can broaden and enrich our understanding of Christianity.

Special Topic Bibliographies

These special topic bibliographies have been prepared as introductions to the interdisciplinary study of religion and the visual arts in the Judeo-Christian traditions. None of these listings is comprehensive or complete. The materials selected for inclusion have been chosen for their availability and intelligibility for students beginning this type of inquiry. The section on Jewish art supplements Joseph Gutmann's bibliographic essay as the section on Christian art supplements John Cook's bibliographic essay. The editors wish to thank David and Linda Altshuler, Jane Dillenberger, John W. Dixon, and Joseph Gutmann for their assistance in the development of these special topic bibliographies. These listings have been updated and revised from their publication in *Art, Creativity, and the Sacred: An Anthology in Religion and Art*, edited by Diane Apostolos-Cappadona (Crossroad Publishing Co., 1984).

Sourcebooks in Religion and Art

Bernen, Robert and Satia. *Myth and Religion in European Painting, 1270–1700: The Stories as the Artists Knew Them.* New York: Constable, 1973.

Cirlot, J. E. *A Dictionary of Symbols.* New York: Philosophical Library, 1972.

Cooper, J. C. *An Illustrated Encyclopedia of Traditional Symbols.* London: Thames and Hudson, 1978.

Encyclopedia of World Art. 15 vols. New Jersey: McGraw-Hill Book Co., 1959–68.

Ferguson, George. *Signs and Symbols in Christian Art.* New York: Oxford University Press, 1954.

Moore, Albert C. *Iconography of World Religions: An Introduction.* Philadelphia: Fortress Press, 1977.

New Catholic Encyclopedia. 15 vols. New Jersey: McGraw-Hill Book Co., 1967.

Theories of Religion and Art

Apostolos-Cappadona, Diane, ed. *Art, Creativity, and the Sacred: An Anthology in Religion and Art.* New York: Crossroad Publishing Co., 1984.

Bowlam, David and Henderson, James L. *Art and Belief.* New York: Schocken Books, 1970.

Brandon, S. G. F. *Man and God in Art and Ritual; A Study of Iconography, Architecture and Ritual Action as Primary Evidence of Religious Belief and Practice.* New York: Charles Scribner's Sons, 1975.

Burckhardt, Titus. *Sacred Art in East and West.* London: Perennial, 1967.

Eliade, Mircea. *Symbolism, the Sacred, and the Arts.* Ed. Diane Apostolos-Cappadona. New York: Crossroad Publishing Co., 1985.

Hunter, Howard, ed. *Humanities, Religion and the Arts Tomorrow.* New York: Holt, Rhinehart, and Winston, 1972.

Laeuchli, Samuel. *Religion and Art in Conflict.* Philadelphia: Fortress Press, 1980.

Maritain, Jacques. *Creative Intuition in Art and Poetry.* Bollingen Series, no. 35. Princeton: Princeton University Press, 1978.

Martland, Thomas R. *Religion as Art, An Interpretation.* New York: SUNY Press, 1981.

van der Leeuw, G. *Sacred and Profane Beauty: The Holy in Art.* New York: Holt, Rhinehart, and Winston, 1953 (1932).

Weiss, Paul. *Religion and Art.* Milwaukee: Marquette University Press, 1963.

Jewish Art

Barnett, R. D. *Catalogue of the Permanent and Loan Collections of the Jewish Museum.* London: Harvey Miller, 1974.

Bialer, Yehuda L. and Fink, Estelle. *Jewish Life in Art and Tradition from the Collection of the Sir Isaac and Lady Edith Wolfson Museum.* Jerusalem: Heichal Schlomo, 1980.

Feldman, Arthur et al. *The Maurice Spertus Museum of Judaica: An Illustrated Catalog of Selected Objects.* Chicago: Spertus College of Judaica Press, 1974.

Gutmann, Joseph. *Jewish Ceremonial Art.* New York: Thomas Yoseloff, 1964.

Kanof, Abraham. *Jewish Ceremonial Art and Religious Observance.* New York: Harry N. Abrams, 1970.

Kirshenblatt-Gimblett, Barbara. *Fabric of Jewish Life.* New York: Jewish Museum, 1977.

Namenyi, Ernest. *The Essence of Jewish Art.* New York: Thomas Yoseloff, 1960.

Narkiss, Bezalel, ed. *Journal of Jewish Art.* Vols. 1–5. Chicago: Spertus College, 1974–78. Vol. 6–. (Jerusalem: Center for Jewish Art, Hebrew University, 1979–.

Yerushalmi, Yosef Hayim. *Haggadah and History: A Panorama in Facsimile of Five Centuries of the Printed Haggadah.* Philadelphia: Jewish Publication Society of America, 1975.

Christian Art

Davies, Horton and Hugh. *Sacred Art in the Secular Century.* Collegeville: Liturgical Press, 1980.

Dillenberger, Jane. *Style and Content in Christian Art.* New York: Crossroad Publishing Co., 1986 (1965).

_____, with Taylor, J. C., Murray, R., and Soria, R. *Perceptions and Evocations: The Art of Elihu Vedder.* Washington, DC: Smithsonian Institution Press, 1979.

Dillenberger, John. *A Theology of Artistic Sensibilities.* New York: Crossroad Publishing Co., 1986.

_____. *Benjamin West: The Context of His Life's Work.* San Antonio: Trinity University Press, 1977.

_____. *The Visual Arts and Christianity in America.* Chico: Scholars Press, 1984.

Dixon, John W. *Art and the Theological Imagination.* New York: Seabury Press, 1980.

____. *Nature and Grace in Art.* Chapel Hill: University of North Carolina Press, 1964.

Eversole, Finley, ed. *Christian Faith and the Contemporary Arts.* Nashville: Abingdon, 1962.

Harned, David B. *Theology and the Arts.* Philadelphia: Westminster Press, 1966.

Hazelton, Roger. *A Theological Approach to Art*. Nashville: Abingdon, 1967.
———. *Ascending Flame, Descending Dove*. Philadelphia: Westminster Press, 1976.
Heyer, George S. *Signs of Our Times: Theological Essays on Art in the Twentieth-Century*. Grand Rapids: William B. Eerdmanns, 1980.
Kung, Hans. *Art and the Question of Meaning*. New York: Crossroad Publishing Co., 1981.
Lowrie, Walter. *Art in the Early Church*. New York: Norton Classics, 1969 (1947).
Martin, David F. *Art and the Religious Experience: The "Language" of the Sacred*. Lewisburg: Bucknell University Press, 1972.
Miles, Margaret R. *Image as Insight: Visual Understanding in Western Christianity and Secular Culture*. Boston: Beacon Press, 1985.
Morey, Charles E. *Christian Art*. New York: Norton Classics, 1958.
Nichols, Aidan. *The Art of God Incarnate, Theology and Symbol from Genesis to the Twentieth-Century*. New York: Paulist Press, 1980.
Regamey, Pie-Raymond. *Religious Art in the Twentieth-Century*. New York: Herder and Herder, 1963 (1952).
Ross-Bryant, Lynn. *Imagination and the Life of the Spirit*. Chico: Polebridge Books, 1981.
Rubin, William S. *Modern Sacred Art and the Church of Assy*. New York: Columbia University Press, 1961.
Schwarz, Rudolf. *The Church Incarnate: The Sacred Function of Church Architecture*. Chicago: Henry Regnery, 1958.
Steinberg, Leo. *Michelangelo's Last Paintings; The Conversion of St. Paul and the Crucifixion of St. Peter in the Capella Paolina, Vatican Palace*. London: Phaidon, 1975.
———. *The Sexuality of Christ in Renaissance Art and in Modern Oblivion*. New York: Pantheon Books, 1984.
Wolterstorff, Nicholas. *Art in Action: Towards a Christian Aesthetic*. Grand Rapids: William B. Eerdmanns, 1980.

Photographic Credits

THE EDITORS AND THE PUBLISHER wish to thank the custodians of the works of art for supplying photographs and granting permission to use them.

1. Courtesy of the Byzantine Photograph Collection, ©1986 Dumbarton Oaks, Trustees of Harvard University, Washington, D.C.
2. The National Gallery of Art, Washington. Robert and Jane Meyeroff Collection.
3. Bildarchiv Foto Marburg/Art Resource, New York.
4. Bildarchiv Foto Marburg/Art Resource, New York.
5. The Institute of Archaeology, The Hebrew University of Jerusalem.
6. Yale University Art Gallery.
7. Photograph by Jo Milgrom.
8. Courtesy of The Pierpont Morgan Library.
9. Cliche des Musées Nationaux, Paris.
10. Cliche des Musées Nationaux, Paris.
11. The National Gallery of Art, Washington. The Widener Collection.
12. Österreichische Galerie, Vienna.
13. The National Gallery of Art, Washington. The Samuel H. Kress Collection.
14. The National Gallery of Art, Washington. The Samuel H. Kress Collection.
15. Alinari/Art Resource, New York.
16. Alinari/Art Resource, New York.
17. Photograph by John W. Cook.
18. Photograph by John W. Cook.
19. The Tate Gallery, London.
20. The Phillips Collection, Washington, D.C.
21. Alinari/Art Resource, New York.
22. Giraudon/Art Resource, New York.
23. The Trustees of The National Gallery, London.
24. Photograph by Doug Adams.
25. Courtesy of the artist.
26. Courtesy of The Travelers Insurance Company, Hartford.
27. © 1986 Carsey-Werner Company.

The works of Marc Chagall and Pablo Picasso © S.P.A.D.E.M., Paris/V.A.G.A., New York, 1986.

Contributors

DOUG ADAMS is Professor of Christianity and the Arts at Pacific School of Religion and is a member of the doctoral faculty in Theology and the Arts at the Graduate Theological Union. A former post-doctoral fellow in art history at the National Museum of American Art, Adams is the author of numerous articles on the relationship between religion and the visual arts.

DIANE APOSTOLOS-CAPPADONA is Professorial Lecturer in Religion and the Arts at Georgetown University. She is the editor of *Symbolism, the Sacred, and the Arts* by Mircea Eliade (Crossroad Publishing Company, 1985), *Art, Creativity, and the Sacred* (Crossroad Publishing Company, 1984), and *The Sacred Play of Children* (The Seabury Press, 1983).

JOHN W. COOK is Professor of Religion and the Arts and Director of the Institute of Sacred Music at Yale University. His graduate studies were at the University of Bonn, Germany, and Yale University.

JANE DILLENBERGER is Professor Emerita, the Graduate Theological Union, and Adjunct Faculty, Pacific School of Religion. The author of numerous articles on religion and the arts, her most recent book is *Style and Content in Christian Art* (Crossroad Publishing Company, 1986).

JAMES L. EMPEREUR, S. J., is Associate Professor of Liturgical and Systematic Theology at the Jesuit School of Theology, and is a member of the doctoral faculty in Theology and the Arts at the Graduate Theological Union. He was the first editor-in-chief of

Modern Liturgy and the founder of the Institute for Spirituality and Worship. His most recent book is *Prophetic Anointing: God's Call to the Sick, the Elderly, and the Dying* (Michael Glazier, 1982).

GREGOR GOETHALS is Professor of Art History and Director of Graduate Studies at the Rhode Island School of Design. Her most recent book is *The TV Ritual: Worship at the Video Altar* (Beacon Press, 1980).

JOSEPH GUTMANN is Professor of Art History at Wayne State University and Adjunct Curator at the Detroit Institute of the Arts. He is the author of numerous books and articles on Jewish art, including *Hebrew Manuscript Painting, Jewish Ceremonial Art*, and *The Image and the Word.*

WILLIAM HENDRICKS is Professor of Christian Theology and Director of the Center for Religion and the Arts at Southern Baptist Theological Seminary. He is the author of numerous articles on Christianity and the arts.

MARGARET R. MILES is Professor of Historical Theology at Harvard Divinity School. Her most recent book, *Image as Insight: Visual Understanding in Western Christianity* (Beacon Press, 1985) explores the use of visual images as historical evidence.

JO MILGROM is a member of the faculty at the Center for Judaic Studies of the Graduate Theological Union. She is the author of *The Binding of Isaac: A Primary Symbol in Jewish Thought and Art.*

JACOB NEUSNER is University Professor and Ungerleider Distinguished Scholar of Judaic Studies and Co-Director of the Program in Judaic Studies at Brown University. The author of numerous works on the history of Judaism in the talmudic period, he has recently edited an abridged version of E. R. Goodenough's *Jewish Symbols in the Greco-Roman Period* (Princeton University Press, 1986).

NICHOLAS PIEDISCALZI is Professor of Religion and Director of the Master of Humanities Degree Program at Wright State University. The author of numerous works on religion and contemporary society, his most recent book is *Three Worlds of Christian-Marxist Encounters* (Fortress Press, 1985).

STEPHEN BRECK REID is Associate Professor of Hebrew Scriptures at Pacific School of Religion and a member of the doctoral faculty in Biblical Thought at the Graduate Theological Union.

ARCHIE SMITH, JR., is Foster Professor of Pastoral Psychology and Counseling at Pacific School of Religion and is a member of the doctoral faculty at the Graduate Theological Union. His most recent book is *The Relational Self* (Abingdon Press, 1982).

Index